An Elderly
Eclectic Gentleman

JIM WARREN

Published by:

FriesenPress

Suite 300 – 852 Fort Street
Victoria, BC, Canada V8W 1H8

www.friesenpress.com

Distributed to the trade by The Ingram Book Company

Table of Contents

Thanks to my Pianist for her sharp pencil, ready wit and common sense, not to forget the time and effort necessary to streamline the manuscript!! Thanks to Anne, who got me started and with her drive stimulated me to start writing in the first place. Thanks to Ruth and Rob for their support and insistence that I trust my senses. They and my parents are the dramatis personae in the play of my life and my story!

Succession

The lichen grows on bare rock,

no earth, little sustenance,

a tenuous foothold to life.

It asks for sun and time,

and grows, defeated, grows again.

It rains, it grows, summer drought comes,

it dies, to grow again with rain,

and when it dies, it leaves a a little behind.

Soil? Or is it the merest memory of lichen

becoming soil?

So, mosses grow, a different plant,

thicker, greener, richer,

withstanding drought a little more,

because of the poor precursor

which took a foothold where no other could.

The Extraordinary Ordinary

When Esther Summerson ventured out after months of a completely confining illness from smallpox; a deadly disease before Edward Jenner's discovery, as it was then, she spoke for Dickens and for all of us about the realized world around us. As she looked from the carriage for the first time in months, she said, "I found every breath of air, and every scent and every flower and leaf and blade of grass, and every passing cloud, and everything in nature, more beautiful and wonderful to me than I had ever found it yet. This was my first gain from my illness." To emerge into the light from whatever dark night of the soul that you have been confined to, is a revelation that the ordinary is truly extraordinary. To merge your streams of consciousness and unconsciousness with the streams of Mother Nature, seen and unseen, heard and felt and smelled! The profound, once experienced, is enough! To expect it again is greedy. To have it always would render it powerless. The lasting gain is not in the exultation, but in the serenity. Go with the flow!

Pool

Growing up on the bald prairie, the poolroom was in the barbershop and the swimming pool was a local slough. You could skate on the slough in the winter, swim in it in the summer and raft on it in the spring thaw. It was fun and all your naked friends were there to swim. In the poolroom you could watch the local shark take quarters off all the visitors, playing snooker or eight ball, and drink a coke with your friends and play against the barber for nickels if he didn't have a haircut to do. There was always something going on. When we built a house much later in Lotus City, despite the pianist's misgivings I wanted to recapture the feeling with a pool table and a swimming pool. You can never go back! It had nothing to do with blue water and green felt! It had nothing to do with affluence or lack thereof. The children learned to play pool reasonably well but a parent is only so much fun. We eventually got rid of the underused pool table since it was attractive but bored! "Use me or lose me", I heard it say. The swimming pool was a somewhat different matter. For about three years it required a lot of work to keep it clean, since it was under trees, in migratory bird lanes, and enjoyed by all those water-loving algae. When we first moved in, on November 1970, I kept the boiler on to heat the pool through the Christmas season. I must have been mad; mistook myself for King Farouk; and caused all the fog on Ten Mile Point that winter! In 1974 I had heated the pool for the months of May through to July and observed that no one else had swum in it. I jumped in from time to time because I felt guilty that this pristine womb was so lacking in the pleasure of fecundity. "Use me or lose me ", I heard it say. I turned the boiler off. No one noticed the pool was cold for the rest of the summer because no one swam in it. At the end of September I announced that the pool heater had been off for three months. They were all mad at me. C'est la guerre! It was my fault in the first place. You may try to go back in time but you can't take the family with you.

Toilet trials

Occasionally over the number of years of joint usage of the toilet, difficult gender issues have arisen from time to time due to inadvertency on my part, never intent. Like Pavlov's dog, repetitive stimuli have to be applied over the years to establish consistency in behavior that is acceptable. There has never, to my knowledge, been electroshock treatment to condition my responses, though I cannot testify fully to that since shock treatment does alter memory. Senior moments notwithstanding, even I eventually learned to always restore the toilet seat to its place of repose after use. There temporarily ceased to be expostulations of rage emanating from the occasionally incautious! Having conquered that neglectful and disrespectful habit of leaving the toilet seat up, a second problem began to surface that again resulted in tensional moments. Positioning the seat at the point of repose after use still resulted from time to time, in wet drops on the seat. Since I was careful to lower the seat after life's "ever rolling stream" it was unclear to me that the source was mine. Since no other male was around, it was a mystery, surrounded by a conundrum! I was at least 'a person of interest' and guilty 'til proven innocent. Our lovely old blind Samoyed eventually proved to be the culprit. I discovered one day by accident she preferred to drink water from the toilet since unlike the water dish, it was always in the same place. With her hairy muzzle she would dribble a little on the seat. I think she was embarrassed about her habit, so she drank surreptitiously. She was completely blind from adolescence, so over the years she had learned her way around without benefit other than from distant hindsight. She was pretty careful and we loved her! Both dog and man were exonerated. For the pianist and me she was never to be Pavlov's dog.

Cost of Leisure

I read somewhere of a French gentleman, living on the beachfront in Normandy who required his children and grandchildren to bring back a sack of seaweed for his garden each time they went to the beach. No pleasure without accompanying industry. It was not declared in the article that he compelled his friends to do likewise! Had he done so, it is possible that he would end up having few friends as well as progressively indifferent issue. Over the years, I had taken a leaf from this man's book and endeavored where possible, never to take or do something to the right of me at point B, without doubling up by bringing something back or doing something to the left of me at point A. Work on the way down and work of a new nature on the way back; or leisure on the way down and leisure on the way back; or a combination of both! Trying to never waste a moment, either at play or work! Programming! Wasted moments and leisure may have much more in common than we realize. One of the things they have in common is that they are often both derided by those who have little of either! Work and play may have much more in common for the fortunate, who may not be able to differentiate between them. I wish I had composted the Frenchman's leaf in my earlier days rather than seen it as an opportunity. Now that I am older, walking into a room I even forget what the hell I am hereafter so that, A and B programme doesn't work for me any longer! Thank heavens! It's moot whether it is better in the mind's eye to have engaged in this sort of work cycle over a short working life, and then move to complete leisure for the balance, or to combine them through your lifetime! I can't judge but I suspect that a happy balance through one's life, a willingness not to impose your values on others, and strive to work at the things you love, is the fortunate choice. Live for the present, not the future. Reality says the future is nowhere! This balance applied now gives autonomy to you and everyone you love!

Exposure and anonymity

At a certain stage of life there is less and less time available "to have a kick at the cat". If one has something to do, then do it while there is still a guarantee of your faculties, or at least, as one believes they are still present! If you have something to say, or if you believe you have something to say, the Internet affords a medium that allows anonymity. There is a certain freedom in this as one can dip their toe in the water and test the temperature without jumping into the lake and finding it's too frosty to swim. If one is a cowardly lion or is fearful of being a tin man or a scarecrow, one may have to find an expert behind a screen who will give a green light to publish! If I come with a proposed book that is not a book but a compilation of anecdote, history, reverence, irreverence, garden-variety humour and recycled wisdom I know that most will say there is no coherence to this material! True! Incoherence is representative of the human condition. If you believe you are always coherent it is proof positive that you are not. We really never have a single theme if one is truly a holistic human being. If you write of your realities or your fantasies you are still writing your autobiography. All writing is revelatory! To put a name to your exposition is fraught with the danger of "going to jump in the lake". Fear of exposure is only present the first time you take your clothes off and go naked. After that it becomes easier as you realize there is less to lose than you thought. Years ago when my brother Ken got married I hosted a stag at our home with his friends. My brother was a schoolteacher and I did not know his friends. The stag turned out to sag quite badly by mid-party and was very boring. I needed an idea! We had a large swimming pool off our living room. I took a chance, discarded fear, and announced we would have a water ball contest with pickup teams. Thereupon, in the living room I took off all my clothes in front of these strangers to jump in the pool. To my relief so did my 13 year old son and my brothers, and then everyone did the same. The party no longer sagged. We had a hell of a good time. I took a gamble. The outcome could have been dreadful! I now shudder to think of it. If my life is sagging, despite risk of exposure, I want to take a chance!

Infradig

This was a word that Aunt Mabel used to declare "the unacceptability", of things, or matters, or people. Moreover no amount of opinion to the contrary, or the etymology of the word, was of any interest to Aunt Mabel. Whether it was dishes, other than china, or furniture not mahogany, or rhubarb, or Catholics, or Socialists, controversy mattered little to her! They were all infradig. Living in Small-town, Saskatchewan as she did, it seemed necessary to her to work at bringing some enlightenment to the bald prairie. Aunt Mabel was a highly intelligent and sensitive woman whose sweetheart was killed in the Great War and she, at that young age, never fully recovered from the stream of "What might have been". That disappointment or despair after a period of inanition may lead in time to a renewed period of decision-making and refueled energy to move on. Taking charge and firming up resolve led in her case to strong feelings and unwillingness to bend. It was her salvation. The dogmatic among us become most lonely of creatures because no one is willing to challenge them due to the futility of argument. No one is willing to listen with attention because they have heard it all before. All the interaction is lip service to avoid unpleasantness. No one is a winner because a wall creates a zone of separation with Aunt Mabel or others of similar persuasion. Infradig has nothing to do with stuff or ideas or people. It speaks nothing to the present reality. It is an old idea! Dignity never came because of the things valued by Aunt Mabel. Dignity comes from your acknowledgment of yourself! Once you do that, and you really know it, nothing you ever do will be below dignity!

The World, A condominium ocean liner

It must be a growth industry! The cruise ships get larger and longer and higher and the amenities proliferate like fruit flies! Now, ships like The World, whose time has apparently come, are floating condominiums with a permanent cliental that are citizens of the world at large! They live aboard all or part of the time; visiting and observing the sights of the world, by water. Wow! The World moored off our little, possibly exotic to some; certainly funky to many; island in the Salish Sea. There are no docking facilities for boats of cruise ship size on Lotus Island, so The World anchored out a mile and a half from the town in the harbour. We locals and yokels spent the weekend gawking at her! The ship's tender plied the water back and forth on an hourly basis with its condo cargo as they visited the town and the market all weekend, but the passenger-owners were here to simply absorb the bucolic atmosphere. They must have arrived for that reason, since no Club Med like ambience exists here. A battle anew about our role in the tourist industry is about to occur with the Nimbys and the Progressives on Lotus Island. The Progressives will prevail. Money, like water, flows to the lowest level. I am not self-righteous. I like money and water too, but ecotourism is what we have been largely all about. Our strong point! How much green rootedness to sacrifice for the right balance? Those of us who live here and have done so for a long time have deep roots. We are not exactly spectators. We are the inspected. I'm not really sure that a condominium on the ocean, with many ports of call, and a rootless existence is all that appealing. Schubert wrote of Der Wanderer. The song says, "Where are you my beloved land?" I can answer that because I am a 'stick in the mud'!

Leonard Cohen

For my 75th birthday my daughter gave me a 2-part disc of the essential songs of Leonard Cohen. He chose selections from his repertoire and though I am not sure why, he didn't include some of the favorites. I suppose he's entitled since he is my age and therefore taking the long view back, thinking elegiac thoughts and trying to add to his legacy. He is my favorite poet. He sings from the heart; he is not dishonest; he pronounces his words so you understand easily; and his music is exciting and novel. His books are a diary of his life and describe the changes that have been wrought as he has evolved into a Canadian Icon. Though some of his poetry is dirty and some opaque, there is a constant sense of openess and humanity; a sense of humility, uxoriousness, and at times despair with the world and him in it. Welcome to the world of candour, I say. That's why he speaks to so many! Who would have 'thunk' that success would be reinvented for him in this day and age with its love of virtual reality? Few, and him probably least of all! His modesty becomes him at the present time. The pianist makes fun of his voice and says his songs are for men. A man's songster! That may be the case, but Jennifer Warnes and kd Lang are acolytes as well. Man's songster may be thought to be the case by some, but the attendance at his concerts belies that opinion. Whatever he has, he has it in spades!

The Touchwood Hills

Though not as well known as the Cypress Hills, the Touchwood Hills in Saskatchewan are another height of land left by the glacier as it receded. The Touchwood Hills are the point of land at which Henry Kelsey, the great overland explorer, turned back east after his epic travel (1690-1692), a century before any other white man visited the area. There is a cairn to mark his furthest point of exploration. I grew up in the Touchwood Hills. Our little town became sequestered from the Muskowekwan Reserve when the Grand Trunk Railway was built and a depot was needed. The original land treaty was signed by the Cree Chief Muscowequan in 1874 at Fort Qu'Appelle with the other Chiefs of Little and Big Touchwood Hills! My friend and I, both of us from town, played midget hockey with the Indian team from the Oblate Fathers Mission School. The Cree Nation boys from the Muskowekwan reserve welcomed the two of us and we felt part of things! We never felt white when we were there. There is nothing like sport to unite young men. We were a good team, but we only had two forward lines and two defensemen. We must have been in good shape. The outdoor rink we practised on was at the Mission and the roads were not good in the winter. A local batchelor farmer, who liked to watch hockey, took the two of us from town out to the practise on the back of his tractor in October and November. He went to "the coast" after November for the winter. He told us it didn't snow in Burnaby. I remember thinking about Burnaby as we bucked through the drifts. As we stood behind him on the tractor, wind with driving snow whistled by our cheeks. We held onto the tractor seat for dear life. "One day", I said to myself, " I will go to Burnaby! "

Pelagic Buses for Scholars

About 100 high school students on weekdays, make a journey of an hour or so each way to and from the high school back to their island homes by water. We are island people and water is our highway. We live in a Southern Gulf Island area with four outer islands and the larger Lotus Island with the high school, serving the entire area. These Gulf Islands lie, or more properly, bask, in what is now called The Salish Sea. Every day the pianist and I watch the two large water buses, The Scholar and the Graduate, transporting their precious cargo to and fro, passing our harbour side window leaving for the outer islands at 6: 45 am, returning at 8:15 am and transporting the students home later in the afternoon. The commitment of society on these islands to education and scholarship is enormous. The commitment of the youth is exemplified by the sacrifice of time due to the travel required. The winter in the northern waters, while largely inshore waters, is still periodically rough and cold and dark at the times of coming and going! If you are prepared to put that much time and effort into getting an education, it follows that you take yourself seriously. You have the right to be taken seriously by everyone else as well. The curious thing about it all is the trip through the islands is one of the country's, nay, one of the world's major beauty spots, even from time to time in the winter, but the students so take it for granted that it's old hat. As they get older and depart the islands they will come to realize I am sure, the incredible nature of their school journeys. In the meantime they have fun, talk a lot, text a lot, do their homework and never bother to look out the window.

CawCawphony

My neighbor has a large stand of West Coast Maples and Cottonwoods near our property. In addition I have Holly and Hawthorns near the property line. These thornbearing trees are safe repositories for nesting crows. The nests are well hidden from marauders. I have an orchard with cherries and small fruits, amongst others. The crow's bedrooms, nursery, and living room appear to be largely on the interproperty area. The kitchen, dining room and toilet are on the pianist's and my property in Western Red Cedar trees overlooking our deck. This seems to be fledgling time and the constant cacophony is frightful. There seems to be a crisis of ownership between the humans and the crows. The crow's kitchen also doubles as the toilet. When eating a cherry, or a small red plum, the crow, after picking a juicy one in the garden brings the cherry to the kitchen. The kitchen is a branch where some food preparation goes on, positioning the cherry or the plum between the toes on the branch, tenderizing the skin, pitting, and finally swallowing. The crow's gastrocolic reflex is triggered by the meal. They appear to have a highly sensitive trigger prompting the gastrocolic event, possibly due to the shorter distance from the stomach to the rectum than your's or mine. Since the favorite place to eat is the kitchen/toilet overlooking our painted deck, we are greeted with abundant guano that seems to have remarkable adherent properties. This gastrocolic event is accompanied, dare I say, by enthusiastic crowing. Maybe even derisive! Each time I leave the house to toil in the soil the watch bird announces my progress. If I bring my pressure washer to remove hardened and adherent guano I am greeted with a chorus of insults. They don't seem to care! The variety of vocalizations they have is remarkable. It's just they are so darned intrusive, or maybe it's me that is intrusive.

Rationality

I no longer am irritated over the exclusionary principle of rational people, promoting exclusively rational things, to other exclusively rational people. With the "rational" there seems to be something smugly self satisfying, about something not very satisfying! Particularly troublesome is the attitude of dismissiveness toward anything that cannot be accounted for by a mechanistic view of life. What about the big questions of life? The how; the why; the wherefore of existence! Rationality never provides certainty therein. There is always the next, yet to be explained phenomenon. Religion is never certain, because despite faith many things are inexplicable and undermining. We all live by the seat of our pants, and faith is omnipresent in the big questions, religious or irreligious. Rationality is a step in the twilight, with things undiscovered but faith that they will be; religion is a step in the dark with things yet undiscovered but faith that they will be. No one has a choke hold on truth. Most have given up abstract thought or existential reasoning as too opaque and too troubling. "Leave it to the experts, the philosophers", they say. Why leave the most important aspects of our time to "experts" and seek diversions that buffer your reality? Truth, from whatever feeble standpoint, only exists for those with a candle, and candlepower is only so bright. It is however, bright enough to let some walk a path, but where they are going is at best, only glimpsed. There is no place for dogma on either side of the big questions of life. We have to deal with uncertainty as a matter of humanness. It encourages us to explore, think and grow. Better to know what you don't know, than think you know what you can't know. Pity the person who has concluded they have arrived at the full knowledge of the God filled or Godless universe. A portion of humility and a capacity to listen to the world, your neighbor, or the

Ground of all Being may serve you in good stead. I have found that each step of insight seems to raise more questions than more knowledge. I suppose it's better to know what questions you'd like answered, than not knowing what questions there are to ask.

Shrinking and expanding

If you ever watched a time-lapse cartoon of the ageing process you would know what I am going to say! I have weighed and taken the height of hundreds of patients over the years. They always think they are taller than they are, and weigh less than they do. It's not a cheerful job. We have considerably more than a baker's dozen intervertebral disks in our back contributing to spinal length and a bunch of vertebral bodies as well. Over time, these plump and resilient disks dehydrate and narrow. This loss of height is a result of a natural degenerative process. The vertebrae flatten as well, as we age, and so we lose several millimeters of height from each disk and also from each vertebral body. In addition, because vertebrae flatten more in the front of the vertebrae than the back, the spine bends a bit forward, further contributing to the loss of height, from the shoulders to the pelvis. That's why my mother's head eventually sank below the top of the car seat when she was driving, and my mother-in-law ended up eating at the table with her chin near her place mat. They lived much longer than their husbands and so displayed the natural changes fully. The limbs, on the other hand, do not vertically shrink, so that the shortening, when sitting is the more dramatic, and the foreshortened, when standing, can reach their knees without bending forward. Since for me, I'm now in that group, the loss of several centimeters in the shoulder- pelvic interval decreases the vertical volume available in the abdomen for our guts, so the belly expands sideways. Egad! Ergo, I've become more potbellied. Couple that partly facile excuse, with the substitution of muscle bulk by fibrous tissue, and one's legs become skinnier and skinnier. Man becomes a globular stick man. A nurse friend watching me walk down the hall in a patient hospital gown one day said, " You know, my father would have said you look like a fat man being carried by a chicken." If there is anything more revealing, less concealing, than a patient's hospital gown, I don't know what it is.

Standing in the wind

Over the years I have served in responsible positions, and other roles in various organizations. I was basically a chairperson or committeeman only because I found it hard to say no. If you serve long enough and don't make too many mistakes you will eventually become top dog 'til they realize you aren't. I'm inherently lazy and therefore developed early on, a penchant for delegation and an honorable reluctance to take credit for another's good work. This was not altruistic, but in fact a continuation of my self interest in doing less, by encouraging others to do more. I confess I've felt guilty in the past for some of this lassitude since others of a more skeptical bent have seen through my subterfuge. The one redeeming factor was however, my ability to stand in the wind, however stiff. Someone needs to do it. At least that's what I tell myself. It isn't thick skin because often suffering arises and bruises are inflicted. Hopefully if you do the right thing for the wrong reasons, or the wrong thing for the right reasons, you can at least keep your balance in the wind. If you do the wrong thing for the wrong reasons, you are toast and deserve what you will eventually get, which is blown away. I can remember my father saying to me once, if he said it a hundred times, " Jim, you have an excuse for everything, all of the time". I know that about myself. I was a dreamy boy growing up who was always optimistic about himself and everyone else. If you always think things will work out in the end and you haven't absorbed the fact that they don't, then the wind is not a problem to you at the time. I picture this feeble minded guy standing in a hurricane, smiling and saying, "At least it's not a tornado." Blows your mind!

Ashes

The pianist and I took our daughter the other day to see our plot where we will eventually be planted! I lay down in the section that we have chosen and it felt comfortable; a grassy knoll next to the Celtic cross in acreage of rolling hills with a blue sky and scudding clouds above. My daughter took a nice picture of me in repose on my spot. I had asked the pianist earlier if she would consider sharing the same urn with me so our ashes could be mixed since I am such a codependent! She was adamantly opposed to that idea and stamped her foot. "I want to rest in peace." she said, "I have lived with you for 54 years and shared the same bed but I want privacy for my ashes. My vow extended to have and to hold as long as we both shall live!" Well that was pretty clear. "What's more," she said, "Your ashes are likely to jump and turn repeatedly and snore a lot and that's not going to be a restful peace for me! I'll finally get to have a good sleep! " I rethought the matter and it is probably not practical anyway as the timing is everything in these matters. I'll have to be a big boy!

Bee Bumbling

Wild bees had made a nest in the Styrofoam float under the seat of my rowboat. The hollowed out home in the Styrofoam was not accessible to sprays since it was hidden from view and they were never pleased to see a face near their home. The boat sits on a ramp down to the beach. I elected to drown them because I knew no other safe way to get rid of them. Lack of ready access prevented spraying and I didn't want to burn my boat seat if I tried to set the nest on fire. I hate doing this to bees. It's so contrary to Mother Nature's grand design. My son-in-law and I manoeuvred the boat gingerly at intervals onto the beach. We pulled it down a foot or two and then ran away when the angry bees looked around for the enemy. Pulling and scattering eventually got the boat off the ramp and on to the beach and relatively level so it could be filled completely with water. We then filled the boat to above the bee's nest with water from the hose. The tide came in but thankfully it was calm. I went down in the evening to see the results. All the daytime foragers were back, and were angry and hanging around the ramp. I couldn't ramp up the boat up since it was full of water and the bees wouldn't let me near it. In securing it for a further tide I was stung and fell over on the beach trying to evade the bees. No problem! The following morning I was going to work and searched high and low for my cell phone. I phoned myself in various locations. No luck. I finally went down to the beach where I fell. There it was, lying on a pile of seaweed. It had rained that night. It was perched on a seaweed line indicating the high tide margin. I was sure it was trash. Then it rang. The pianist was calling me. This whole epistle sounds like an episode with the Keystone Cops at work. They always seemed to get their man the hard way! I needed to get to Lotus City quickly to do something easy like surgery!

Syphilis

Received wisdom has always said that the New World provided Europe with potatoes, tomatoes, tobacco and syphilis. I wrote a treatise on syphilis as part of a graduate studies programme at UBC refuting the idea that syphilis originated in the New World. At the time I was taking an Archeology minor on the way to an Anatomy degree. Ancient Corinth, a coastal city, was from the evidence of excavations at the time, the major Mediterranean port into the heart of Europe. From excavations of the healing Temples of Asklepius, some of the more interesting findings were the votive offerings. These were pottery replica of the anatomical part of the patient that the priests of Asklepius had healed. They were accompanied by patient testimonials that hung on the walls of the temple. The votives could be purchased off the shelf at an adjacent Stoa and given to the priests by the grateful, or if you were rich you could commission a custom made part by an artisan. Curiously enough, many of these replicas were male genitalia. Problematic for the student in these matters was that the nature of the disease was not displayed in the replica, so the pathology was unclear. The Asklepiads it seems, insisted that only "disease cured" pottery specimens were to be hung on the sacred walls. My treatise advanced the idea that the prevalence of genitalia was evidence of syphilis in the Old World since the natural progress of the primary chancre ordinarily disappears in a short time and secondary syphilis, that appears much later, would not seem connected. Since archeologists don't know anything about syphilis, this treatise was accepted. That was 1960 and I was 26. As wisdom gradually seeped in, I have for some time, realized it was impotence that the priests were curing! Adjacent to the healing temple was the Temple of Aphrodite. Aphrodite was the Goddess of Love and the patroness of prostitutes. The goddess and her minions doubtless assisted with aphrodesiac gifts! It was unlikely they gifted spirochetes! Teamwork counted!

It's no wonder St. Paul was so exercized about morality in Corinth!

Eagle Trial

This morning, looking out in the harbour, at some distance, I watched two monster wings flapping with what appeared to be desperation. At first it looked like a seal. On close inspection it was a mature eagle in the water trying to take off to no avail. The pianist and I watched for about 10 minutes as it intermittently flapped and struggled and got nowhere. I couldn't bear to watch any longer as I thought it was exhausting itself and soon would drown. The pianist said the same thing as we were going out to the car to leave the house. Suddenly she said, " Look, it took off!" I looked back and it was gone. Then it hove into view in a tight circle just in front of us, close to the water, flying easily with what looked like a big bird in its talons. Not a Bufflehead or a little duck, but probably a Merganser since there are a lot of them out there right now. The prey was almost too heavy for the eagle to lift off since they are impaired because of the half wing swing they have at the water surface. If the eagle can't lift off, it can drown, as it is hard for it to detach from the prey due to claw locking. Makes you think doesn't it, how easy it is to bite off more than you can chew? Can't move on, can't let go, nearly going under, seduced by the big prize. Little and often; little and often!

"A Trip to the Farm"

Second year University French was mandatory in the pre-med class at Manitoba. I entered second year Science with a background of one previous high school year of French. It soon became apparent that I was out of my depth and destined for disaster! Most of the class were from St. Boniface and taking the course to refine their own working language and to belong to the French Club that met regularly. I was sitting with a senior student in the cafeteria and must have had a doleful look as I ate my bag lunch. I shared my dilemma with him as my cause seemed hopeless at that stage. I saw no way out. He listened to my tale of woe, my putative career gradually eroding away and failure looming large. "Hey listen", he said, "If you get out the old final exams in French for the last ten years you will see that there is always 50% of the mark for an essay in French. They give you a choice of topics and if you write an essay on a trip to the farm, it'll apply to most of the topic choices." I received a glimmer of hope from my rescuer, but I'm sure I looked dubious. However, what that sage said was true! The topic choices in the old exam papers I reviewed included, An Exciting Experience, (a trip to the farm), What You Did Last Summer, (a trip to the farm), An Enjoyable Journey, (a trip to the farm). This was a straw I was willing to grasp. Before the examination I carefully crafted a French essay, letter perfect, accent perfect, on "a trip to the farm". Sure enough, the angel I met at lunch over my bologna sandwich was right! My essay fitted three out of the ten current topic choices. I scraped through French with little to spare. I learned a lot though; that you don't always need talent to succeed if you have a will and a way out. P.P.D., (Persistence Pays Dividends).

Anthropomorphizing

We certainly speak to our animals, and see them as responding fellow creatures! It is well known that gardeners who are successful, speak to their plants as they nurture them, seeing the response as evidence of a mutual understanding. Findhorn became the modern Mecca of this movement. From the time of the early Greeks however, the interchangeable nature of man into both the animal and vegetable kingdoms was an undisputed fact; the assumption of the anthropomorphic interchange of man and his fellow kingdoms. What about the minerals? I find myself speaking regularly to our freezer, rototiller, and our cars amongst the other minerals we live with. I speak to them lovingly as creatures that might have a glimmering of understanding! Now of course, this is to most a piece of arrant foolishness such as could be expected from an elderly eccentric gentleman, but I often see people talking to minerals such as I've described. Their lips are moving with the same obvious intensity as mine. Sometimes they appear to be cursing their mineral. That mineral is unlikely to respond to that kind of treatment. We have names that the pianist gave to our minerals that we drive. The Nissan Axess is called Blue Bottle and the Rav4 is called Green Dragon. We have clearly not really humanized them, so this is limited anthropomorphizing. After all, we are all composed of similar molecules in constant agitation so what's wrong with being a member of the animal, vegetable and mineral kingdom and seeing only a few degrees of separation. The biggest drawback I can see to this idea is the possible unwillingness of the mineral, vegetable and animal kingdoms to be anthropomorphized since Homo sapiens is continuing to mess things up.

Summer camp

Kemo kymo dera wah, mahee mahoe marumpside pom-madiddle, soupfat periwinkle, niptom nipcat, singsong city won't you kymeoh? When I was 12 years old I was sent to Camp Waconda. I remember almost nothing of the two-week experience of the camp, but I do remember that I hated camp. I think we were still in the mindset of Lord Baden-Powell and the Boy's Own Annual. I can't even remember if my little brother Ken was there or not, but he probably was. The only recollection I have of the camp was the nonsense verse that I learned and has been with me for a lifetime. So far! What a curious thing is the mind! That one should have committed such blather to one's soft wear for life, but blanked out the memory of the unhappy period entirely. I have a vague memory of "pledging myself to thee", (Camp Waconda), but I'm sure my fingers were crossed. This is not a criticism of the camp. How can you criticize what you can't remember? Some of us are not adaptable to camp life. I'm sure that I was a homeboy and was accustomed to a life without much regulation. My parents allowed a great deal of freedom to us in those days and regimentation would have been anathema to us. I'm sure my mother thought camp would be good for me. It's not always possible to determine what is good for someone else, even as loving parents. All my children however benefited from my camp experience insofar as they all have full knowledge of, and can recite, Kemo kymo at the drop of the hat.

Dr. Flower

My mum and dad in retirement lived in a high-rise rental unit in Lotus City for a number of years. There were a large number of units rented almost exclusively by elderly people. My dad, in his heyday had grown an abundant number of dahlia and gladiolus and missed the prospect of cut flowers always being available for their home. He spent half of his horticultural lifetime as well, giving away flowers to all and sundry. It was his shtick! Since I am a chip off the old block I have grown dahlias for a number of years in some volume here on Lotus Island. I grew gladioli for a while as well but eventually quit because the deer eat the florets. They don't eat the leaves, but what is a glad without flowers? The deer here may browse a little on some of the dahlias, but not much, and then only the leaves. If they are too persistent I give the plant a spray of Plantskyyd. I started taking dahlias to my parents at Lotus City once a week. They had a few friends they asked me to bring some for as well. My donations were well received and soon most of the other renters also waited for me outside as I showed up in the parking lot at the same time every Wednesday. My "customer" base grew like wild fire. They called me Dr. Flower. I'm not sure that I liked the name. It sounds like Dr. Dolittle, or Mr. Rogers, not an image I necessarily coveted. However, the name stuck so I had to wear it. In point of fact I loved the idea of dahlias spread throughout the apartment block. No doubt there was some ego fulfillment for me. Nothing is fully clean. The love of color and beauty by older people in a concrete apartment made the gift giving a continuation of my dad's generosity. It was a boon to me as well because a few days later, the dahlia would have needed deadheading so it was really little additional trouble. My dad died, my mother moved to a nursing home, my truck expired, and I ended my flower toting activity!

Mother's boy

In 1951 I started university in Winnipeg. It was a big sacrifice for my parents at that time inasmuch as I could not earn enough during the summer to meet all the expenses necessary. My dad was a railway stationmaster in a small town and his income was about 350 dollars a month. Not a bad salary in those days. From January on, he sent me 125 dollars a month to tide me over 'til May when I started work again. One third of his monthly gross income! It boggles the mind! I never thanked him enough in his lifetime. I think in retrospect I was a very callow youth. But I was a mother's boy. My interim university marks the first Christmas were abysmal. I failed everything! I put it down to culture shock. I promised my parents at Christmas holidays that I would work harder at my studies. The first week back in Winnipeg I took a new girl to a dance cabaret, Jack's Place, a roadhouse on Pembina highway. We were dancing on the dance floor when along came the Roving Reporter. The radio station was playing the music from Jack's Place and the reporter was interviewing the patrons. Of course we had our "mickey " under the table and bought our mix from "Jack". It was a lot of fun and I had set aside my parents concerns. My mum and dad were sitting in the living room in the small town station at that time, listening to the music from "Jack's Place". The reporter said, "Here's a handsome fellow who looks like he's enjoying himself with a lovely girl. Let's talk to him." My mother said, at that moment, to my dad, "I bet that's Jim!" Now how in the world could a woman, 400 miles from Winnipeg, in a little prairie town, know that in a city of 500,000 people, that it was her son referred to on the radio who must be the "handsome one". I confirmed her intuition by speaking to the reporter, pleased to be the center of attention. I loved my mummy and she loved me. Connectedness is a wonderful mystery!

The Scion

Grafting a shoot of a fine plant specimen on a hardy rootstock to propagate it widely, or create a more hardy plant, altered shape or size, makes sense. It's been done for years and horticulture, as we know it, could not exist without grafting. Down deep however, it still seems to me a manipulation of Mother Nature. It's a bit hypocritical on my part to say this since my garden, like everyone else's, is full of grafted specimens. The nomenclature of the shoot as a "scion" must come from a particular past, when the promising offspring was "grafted" or lifted to a new setting. A successful take of such a graft in the case of a plant would depend on accurate matching of the cambium layers, secure fixation for a period of time and avoidance of contamination. This careful attention to detail was not practised by those charged with the grafting and transplanting of people in the 17th and 18th century, dispersing excess populations to this shore. It was a higgledy-piggledly mix and included both the pianist's and my families of origin. There were no "scions" there! Some survived, some didn't. There was no matching of people to their cambium layer. There was no consideration of the right season to graft. There was no tight wrapping and waxing for fixation and protection from movement. There were no measures taken to avoid contamination. "Luck and pluck" were the governing principles of that transplantation and grafting. We tend to forget how much we owe our forebears. They are a national treasure, warts and all. Someone hopefully will emerge as the family librarian in each generation to retain history or herstory! Then we will augment the knowledge of from whom we are come, from where we came, and by what means we were grafted.

The Antimacassar

I was once, years ago, invited to the Lieutenant Governor's for a state dinner with the president of Vorarlberg. I had never been to the Lieutenant Governor's before, nor since, but at the time the pianist and I felt a little special, as if we had been singled out as "comers". In point of fact, when the truth came out, the dinner was a cast of one hundred and the content was a sprinkling of a middling mix of business, professional, political and artistic without anyone particularly grand. We had a lot of fun. I had worried myself silly before we went that I wasn't up on etiquette sufficiently to carry off this venture into society. I therefore purchased Amy Vanderbilt's "Complete book of Etiquette" to teach myself a crash course on how to behave in heady company. I read the book from cover to cover assiduously! The book was written in 1952. It stated that a man should bathe at least once a week, and must apply hair oil regularly to groom himself well. The oil may have been macassar oil. Hence of course, the need for an antimacassar! I think the penny dropped with me that even in the 1970's Amy's book was dated. I skipped her advice. The pianist found my panic station somewhat amusing. My mother had antimacassars she inherited from my nanny and she used them because in those days we applied Brylcream to our heads from time to time, only a little dab I believe, but enough to stain the back of the good chair or divan without an antimacassar. There seems to be something elegant about a patterned crochet lace. We used to have some as I recall, but the pianist ditched them when no one any longer had an oily head. We still use lace doilies on the drink tray. The pianist is more practical and less affected than I am. Oh well! I have to look in the mirror and ask myself, "What kind of a man is interested in doilies?"

American prosody

An interesting contrast with our American friends is the ostensible passion they bestow upon their city-states in song! Celebrating themselves in their cities with metrical dreaming! I can't imagine a Canadian rhapsodizing about Edmonton, Winnipeg, or Ottawa! What is it about us, in that we love our country, but tend to praise with a faint damn, rather than some corny, evocative, efflorescence? Maybe it's us at fault, not Americans. We sometimes, I think, wear our national heart off our sleeve, except for hockey. If it's Down in New Orleans, or Meeting in St. Louis, or Dreaming of Galveston it seems to me Americans all want to be somewhere they aren't. If it's Vagabond shoes in New York or Flowers in the hair in San Francisco, it seems to me they are looking for a change in life style. They are not sure where they are going but they want to know the Way to San Jose, without it seems, much idea what they will do if they find the right direction and get there. Having said all that, we as Canadians may be a charmless bunch without the finer feelings the Americans seem to display about their homeland cities. Certainly the Irish and the Scots are also full of musical blather about their bays and islands and their songs are incredibly evocative and passionate. I think we, as Canadians, are far too prosaic about our country. I don't include Newfoundlanders! I envy the passion of the songsters even if it is a bit of blarney! Would that we would let our hair down a little more, and push out our chest, stand a little straighter, and be proud of peace, order and good government and God keeping our land, even if it is a little colourless.

A neighbor from Hell

One of our colleagues, Dr Z, had a puckish sense of humor. He had a neighbor from hell, also one of our medical colleagues. The neighbor from hell was a man who brooked no opinions or actions that deviated from his own self-adulating point of view. When I first moved to Lotus City and appeared exhausted after a successful and difficult case, the neighbor from hell asked me if I thought I would ever, "amount to anything"! You get the idea! Thank God he was Dr Z's neighbor and not mine. The neighbor from hell, whose name, let us say, was Andrew, had a very short trigger. He could supply ire at will, in a nanosecond! As a result, the bolder amongst some of us, those with a mean streak, would play Andrew like a trout after a dry fly, as he would always rise to the occasion. It was hardly mature and seasoned behavior on anyone's part really, but understandable. Dr Z, at some point acquired a dog, a German shepherd. The dog was enormously friendly and liked to wander over and stand on its hind legs, leaning with its paws on Andrew's fence, looking at him and wagging his tail. Andrew loathed Dr Z's dog, not without good reason! Dr Z, not one to be restrained, or let the opportunity for ironic humor escape him, named his dog Andy. He would of course call the dog repeatedly for all manner of reasons, at all times of the day and late in the evening saying, "Here Andy, good boy! Good doggy Andy, bury doggy do do!" and so on! Of course Andrew would act with fury, but impotent fury. It is not clear to me now, who was the neighbor from hell! Probably it was both of them; maybe all of us; the tantalized, and the tantalizer; the obvious and the inobvious. It's easy and wrong to be more sympathetic to the cool and funny bully, than the overt, pejorative, crank!

Women's movement

The demise of Sadie Hawkins Day was one of the watershed moments in the evolving feminist revolution. There is no longer any need or interest in Sadie Hawkins! It is a quaint piece of history that no modern woman would give any thought to. And yet, in 1952 when I was in university it was a big deal. People forget! When I started medical school in 1953 there were no women in my class of 65 students. Other medical classes had maybe 1 or 2 women! Now, at UBC the women outnumber the men in the medical school classes. There is a lot of talk in the past few years about breaking the glass ceiling. Now it's happening and is inevitable.

The question to ask here is not is it fair, because it is obviously fair. The real question is: is there an advantage to mankind that this is happening? The answer to this is yes! I remember a few years ago a feature article in the Globe and Mail referring to the first woman CEO in Canada working for a major Toronto hospital. The author must have had almost no capacity to think outside the box! I spent a lifetime working in hospitals from 1957 on in which the CEO was a woman. Many Salvation Army hospitals like the Grace hospital in Winnipeg had a female Brigadier. That is a CEO in name and in fact. There was no question about who was boss. The Catholic run hospitals in Canada had a Mother Superior. That is a CEO in name, as in fact. There was no question about who was boss. When governments bought these hospitals from the religious orders for a dollar, the glass ceiling was instituted! Now it will start to crack again! What goes around is coming around in the hospital bureaucracy. So what's the advantage for mankind? The feminine mind may be generally willing where conflict exists, to spend more time getting to consensus if it is remotely possible! The male mind I believe, is less inclined to spend the same effort for consensus, but will easily go to "majority rules". They say, "We're not going to waste any more time with this." There is a need for both approaches! I wonder when will the churches wake up and acknowledge the feminine strength that can be brought by leadership? It's certainly happened in spades in medicine in the last quarter century. It's just that the church, the government and the bureaucracies are slow. The churches originated the hospitals in this country and began with that ethic of female leadership. Since female leadership works in the healing field, why not also in the salvation field? Why not any field?

Pride

The year I was in grade 12 my mother wrote to her father and her twin sister. It wouldn't have been easy for her to write those letters. She told them both that my marks were good and that I would do well as a student at university. She asked them for financial help as she and my dad did not have the ability to provide enough of the necessary means. My mother was willing to risk her esteem for my sake! My grandfather and my aunt responded with enough money to augment my summer earnings and the amount my family could provide. After the first three years, I was able to finish paying for my medical degree costs more or less on my own. Later, the year my mother wrote the letter, I met my aunt in Winnipeg at a family gathering. She was a family doctor who practiced medicine in Connecticut and was married to a wealthy husband. I was glad to see her and take the opportunity to thank both her and my grandfather. At that age the ambivalence I felt; gratitude mixed with a sense of embarrassment for my family, was extraordinary at the time despite the graciousness and support they had provided. There is certain vulnerability when one asks for help and I had grieved for my mother. I had always had pride in my family and myself. Pride can blind you from the gift that others give to lift you on your way. Pride can lead you to believe that you are self- made! My marks were good because of my wonderful teacher who stimulated his four students in the grade 12 class! When one lives as we did in a small town and your dad is the stationmaster, he may not make much money, but you still are a family that rates in the pecking order. As my friend Ian says, "When we were growing up we didn't have much, but we didn't know there was much!" The interview with my benefactors was a heavy trip for me. I was sixteen and I wanted to be powerful. I needed in my mind to protect my family! I felt poor and weakened for the first time in my life. We may have struggled, but in the society that was ours, we were never poor. Poverty is often relative!

Bugs

Today I took my garbage bags out of the garbage cans and double bagged them to take to the garbage depot on Lotus Island! It's a good service and the cost is four dollars a large bag! After I emptied my cans, I noticed one of them had a collection of six black beetles about one and one half centimeters long. Since I go to the depot every week the beetles are obviously newcomers. They are clearly adults. There was a time when I was knowledgeable about entomology. I spent my third year in Science at the University of Manitoba studying invertebrate zoology as a prerequisite to admission to Medical School. I aced the course! The professor was R.K. Rankin-Hay. If you pronounce it with feeling, and drag the name out, it makes a euphonious couplet! He knew his stuff. I loved entomology, as it was one of those courses where the harder you worked the more you absorbed. I was like a blotter that year. Since we still called our bald prairie home "The Bread Basket of the World", there was a large Agricultural Faculty at Manitoba providing degrees and also diplomas to many farm boys we called "Aggie Dips"! They had an insect museum in the Aggie building that was to die for and those of us trying to get into medicine haunted the rooms, learning about the Class, Insecta, probably the most important part of the invertebrate world and certainly the most complex. Most of the invertebrates as far as I could tell were only interested in eating and procreating. This was of some interest to imaginative 19 year olds. The invertebrate's habits on the whole were simple, but the insects; their habits were legion! The Aggies concentrated on the sections of Insecta that were significant in agriculture, but those of us who were in Science faculties could study the panorama of insects whose ubiquitous dwelling places and complex habits were of compelling interest. Still, complex aside, the ornamentation is ultimately geared toward eating and procreating. It always gets down to this, doesn't it? I just dumped out my six beetles on the ground since I don't identify with them now. They can procreate somewhere else.

The Handkerchief

In the olden days most civilized men pulled out a large linen handkerchief for nose blowing, and women a smaller and more elegant hanky. In this day and age it seems a less sanitary act to expel a big honk into a handkerchief taken from your trouser pocket and then stuffed back to use again. On the other hand, when the pianist and I were in Prince George years ago she was intrigued by the consummate skill of a man who displayed finger nose dexterity with a big honk deposited directly on the sidewalk without a trace left on the face or finger. I remember my grandfather and great granddad with monster, wrinkled handkerchiefs blowing, wiping and stuffing without a qualm. The linen hanky was a favorite in days of yore as a Christmas present from the thrifty. It may have been embossed, if given to a woman, or had a flower stitched on. If it was initialed at least it stayed in the same hands. No one traded hankies! Thank goodness for tissues now. My great grandfather also kept on his person in readiness, a gold toothpick that had an ear spoon on the other end. We children waited in breathless anticipation to see the ear spoon used. We used to laugh that the "snot rag was common but the ear spoon was a sight to behold!" No kid used a hanky! He either sniffed all the time; "Go blow your nose!"; or hawked, had a runny nose or a dangle-booger. The tailor always put a little breast pocket on the suit for the dress up handkerchief, but latterly it became no longer de rigueur so the pocket remained empty. Occasionally, when stepping out, a tiny fabric peak sewn on a chunk of cardboard was inserted in the breast pocket to give the gentleman "style". Even though it was a fake, it was not a sorry, soggy, snot ridden specimen!

The Thicket

The Thicket; even better the Briar Patch, are sanctuary for small feathered and furry friends; the denser the thicket the better! If in the well-ordered and cultivated garden there are periodic small thickets, especially near your windows, you will enjoy an abundance of creatures and also provide a measure of safety for them! Your abundance will increase since these thickets will be home and partial larder for the broody! It's unfortunate that urban dwellers may have more difficulty establishing the thicket since they are necessarily untidy, the briar patch even more so-- and often an affront to scrupulous neighbors. Here in the rural garden on Lotus Island, Mother Nature's display of thickets blend with the efforts of the elderly eclectic gentleman. Mother Nature gardens in her own inestimable way and I in my trial and error fashion. The bird feeder and the birdhouse, while of some value, do not supplant the thicket or briar patch in meeting the needs of the creatures. In fact they may foster a culture of dependency that is counter productive to the wellbeing of the vulnerable. Well meaning activity on the part of animal lovers toward the wild, may expose them to more predation and disease and interfere with survival skills in an uncertain world. This applies to our children and the fellow creatures as well as us. We hominems also need a thicket sanctuary where we can return after we venture out. We all live in an uncertain world and need to learn survival skills rather than provided handouts if we are innately capable. Blessed assurance however is that our thicket may still be there. Kindness is: come as close to Mother Nature as you dare!

Boat coffee

When you are seriously salmon fishing and trolling three lines, you are busy. The herring strip has to have the right action and be checked repeatedly for weed if the water is littered. The herring strip bait has to be changed regularly. The treble hooks have to be sharpened to hold a strike and the depth of your bait requires repeated adjusting in order to locate the level the salmon are at. Also, with the timing of the tide change, and the Solunar Tables for bite times, these critical events dictate a further frenzy of activity to get the location right and boat positioned for an effective and straight run. All of the other boats are vying for what seems to be the best position. We scan the horizon, trying to see who is catching fish, and where. We watch for flocking gulls over a herring or bait ball being pushed to the surface by underlying fish. When we steer through tide whirlpools, and miss sudden depth changes, it can lead to line tangles, loss of gear on the bottom, and loss of precious fishing time. How then, given this intense activity, is it possible to dovetail time for coffee? Boat coffee is the answer. In our family it was famous. Made with a kettle on the propane stove in the midst of this frenzy; water not necessarily quite boiled, poured into a plastic cup with instant coffee dashed in, sugar dashed in, and the white powdered peril added. It's usually stirred with whatever is rapidly at hand; a screwdriver or pencil. The boat is always damp, so the coffee, the whitener and the sugar were always caked a bit, so had to be levered out of the jars with the screwdriver or the fish knife. You may find this hard to believe, but in the great scheme of things, boat coffee is delicious. The alternative was Chicken in a Mug. It's not really chicken and we didn't have a mug. The water was always just warm enough to mix the powder. It was a salty concoction of dubious chemical composition and due to the damp was equally caked to a semi-hard concrete consistency in the jar. Its relationship to a chicken may be suspect. Nevertheless it was good on a cold winter morning on the bounding main and gave one a feeling of satisfaction and satiation. It just goes to show that it's not what you drink, but where you drink it, and with whom you drink, that really matters.

I wish I'd said

Yesterday, I was sitting on the bench in front of the grocery store reading a book of poetry while waiting for the pianist. She was shopping and I don't relish tagging along while decisions are being made for which I have little expertise. As I sat in the sun, a young fellow came to the bench and began to stuff the groceries he bought into his backpack. He noted my book and asked, "Do you have any wisdom for me?" I am always taken aback at questions out of the blue like this, but I probably shouldn't be. An old fellow sitting on a bench in the sun probably looks harmless and is a good subject for a gentle kidding. I said something in reply that was completely banal and that was the end of it. We both smiled. I have since thought of what I could have said since every encounter we have, may or may not be ordained. If you believe there is even a chance of this, you might take it seriously. I could have joined the repartee in kind and said something like, " A wet bird never flies at night", or, "Don't shoot an albatross on the way to the tropics or the wind will die and so will all your crew!" Stuff like that is chatter however, and has no lasting power. Maybe I'm too serious, but the best alternative is to answer a question with a question. You may say it's silly to answer a question with a question but I say, "What's wrong with a question?" Something simple! "Welcome to Lotus Island. How are you enjoying it? Are you going to grace us with a stay for a few days?" A churlish question I could have made in reply would be," What do you think I am, a fortune cookie?" It's easy for me to be a smart aleck but even if someone seems a bit patronizing, gentleness and interest will lead you down the right path. You never know who you are talking to, or if you are sent!

Evergreen Magnolia

Smack-dab. right in the middle of our view of Lotus Island harbor is our large Evergreen Magnolia (Magnolia grandiflora). It has been a fertile source of family interaction for years as to it's origin, utility, morphology, and status. Since it is a short, squat, wide monster, it looms large in the ensuing debates. It was bought as a pot plant for our former house, to sleep on a poolside deck. There is argument as to who bought it. My elder daughter and I think it was bought from K-Mart by her boyfriend to ingratiate himself in 1973. My brother thinks he bought it for me as a present for my birthday the same year! It lasted on the pool deck 'til 1980 when we moved it to Lotus Island and planted it as a little tree in front of the cottage. There it grew like Topsy to a beautiful specimen, eventually 20 feet high, but was starting to interfere with the sea view. Moreover, Lotus Island is not South Carolina and the tree's summer blooms are sparse. Beautiful and fragrant, but sparse! Here, these are prized plants for the large glossy leaves. I remember clearly one winter day remarking to the pianist that we had the best specimen of Magnolia on Lotus Island. That night we had a heavy snowfall and the tree broke in half with the snow load. I was punished for my prideful remark! Broad-leaved evergreens are a risk in snow load areas! There was serendipity however in this calamity as the view returned, much to the pleasure of the pianist. Since then I have trimmed, or had it trimmed, to maintain the view and it has become progressively more portly. The current controversy is; it is taking over the yard; it produces few flowers, and it requires arduous trimming to maintain its height. Moreover, it is now said to be a tree that is not a tree but rather a monster shrub. Despite this, I am adamant that it stays, since I have become even more attached to it and can claim to have the fattest Magnolia on Lotus Island.

The Bathtub

Lying stretched out in the bathtub with the jets in full bore, the water piping hot, and sinking into the bubbling streams is heaven to one who grew up with the galvanized tub on Saturday night! The pink midriff, where the hot water draws a line is submerged in the foam of the soap. Having the luxury of time allows one to soak 'til the water becomes cool and the finger skin goes white and wrinkled. One can lift his feet above the water line and watch his toes wiggle at his command. Slowly the thickened nails will soften in the long soak and allow the clippers to ease their way through the nails without effort. Lying in one's own water with the surrounding desquamate that you shed along with whatever dirt and sweat you provide is a small price to pay for the luxury of whole body immersion and whole body jiggling. Undoubtedly true! Someone else may say, "I'm going to have a fast shower." That person is a person on the go. It's no nonsense cleansing. With showering, all the dirt and desquamate immediately go down the drain! It's almost too pristine. I don't judge those who shower, harshly in any fashion, but it does not have the same cachet as the long and voluptuous bath. Their fingers will not be white and wrinkly; their toenails will be hard; and their muscles will not be relaxed and softened. They won't have a rubber duck to watch float alongside and they can't make big bubbles. At the end of a long bath when you have nowhere to rush to, there is a sense of serenity as you look in the mirror at your shiny face. If this typecasts me as a voluptuary, at my stage in life I do not care. It's a simple form of indulgence!

A So-called Lawn

Pojar and Mackinnon, in their book, Plants of Coastal British Columbia, describe 200 different grasses in coastal B.C., Washington and Alaska most of which are indigenous to the area. Today I cut my so-called lawn, composed of a variety of these grasses, for the second time this year. When we moved here in August 1979, the pianist and I inherited a meadow amongst other contributions of Mother Nature. The meadow grasses were three to five feet tall and mighty impressive. Over the years I have mowed our meadow regularly, turning it into what has become a passable lawn, though not of the same nature as it's more civilized brethren from the seed store or turf farm. The multiplicity of grass varieties in the so-called lawn remind me a little of the grade 8 class at school. Some short, some tall, some plump, some skinny and pimply but all quite beautiful and growing at different rates. Because of that characteristic, to give it a semblance of lawn it must be cut regularly or it looks dreadfully thatchy. By close mowing over time there is a population shift to the finer blade varieties. I have also, over time, planted store bought seeds in some areas that I converted to lawn. It of course grows evenly and looks well even if one misses the occasional cut. In time however, the sown lawn and the so-called lawn do begin to resemble one another, much like two people such as the pianist and I who have lived together for eons of time and are a product of the same living and ageing co-habits. I suppose if our lawns were in Lotus City I might feel a bit out of place, but here in the boondocks no one sees the lawn except those whom we choose to invite. I guess, in addition to putting your own stamp on a piece of ground, it's good to try to retain as much as possible of the gift that Mother Nature has freely given.

Jigging for Herring

Jigging for herring with my children on the Tillicum Bridge and the Bay Street Bridge in Lotus City was an easy and productive activity in the 70's. The herring spawn in the spring was up the narrow ocean inlet called The Gorge. The Gorge narrowed at the Tillicum Bridge causing crowding of the herring on the way to spawn as they headed into the Gorge Lagoon. A lovely spring afternoon with the jig dropped into the tidal current and teased up and down was simple and effective. Little yellow and red flies beautified the tiny hooks. The line was weighted by a small round lead weight at the end to counteract the current and 5 to 7 tiny hooks spaced up the line. We were after bait for our salmon fishing activities. We cut herring strips from the whole herring, froze them, and then used the strips as baitfish. The strips were cut in the prescribed fashion to resemble a crippled herring when trolling. Apparently the salmon thought this an easy prey, though I confess, I was never privy to their thoughts. We were often crowded together on the bridge with the Nordic bunch, mostly "old boys" who were jigging for herring to pickle, make roll mops and eat fresh. They were even keener than we were. Now there seem to be fewer herring around. I don't know if anybody jigs any longer on the Gorge bridges. It may be a thing of the past. The main use for herring these days seems to be obtaining roe from the spawning herring. The huge numbers caught by seine netting include all the males of course. It may be economically sound but it seems an awful waste of a species that is an integral part of the food chain. Moreover, it also reduces a food source for people of a certain custom that made good use of the entire fish, male and female. Now they are just rendered after the roe is extracted from the females. Oh well, progress I guess! The processing chain and the food chain are not the same: one is a creation of man; the other a creation of Mother Nature!

Dahlia time

I pulled all the dahlias out from under the straw where they have been sleeping all winter. Even though it is warm enough on Lotus Island to winter them in the ground, our dirt is too wet in the winter since we are below the Hundred Hills and they will rot. They have done so in the past when I was lazy one year and failed to lift them. Why we always learn the hard way I never know. They came through with less than 3 percent rotted this year, which is pretty good for me. I used to wash and dust them before storage but now just shove them, dirt and all, under copious amounts of straw beneath a tarp. The bulbs are particularly nice and plump this year. Now I have to split them as they are compounded and multiply compounded. Quite the job! I also have to haul and compost the straw. I find it quite interesting that some named varieties of dahlia have dramatic propagation potential and some, chiefly the larger flowering types are much more feeble about compound bulb production. If I were a commercial grower I would care about that. Where else can you get 5 or 10 bulbs for 1 per annum with some varieties? I'd be a millionaire if I could do that with money. I like dahlias better than most flowering plants since they are user friendly, propagate like stink, and bloom all summer. The deer may browse the plants a little but they do trifling damage to them. The slugs are voracious with dahlias but a few early morning rounds and tallying the count that you achieve cutting the slugs in half will make them soon disappear. It's still pretty cold out, but I have some drier areas, and will take a chance on planting the ones that have sprouted. The sprouting bulbs have an innate intelligence. Normally, it's best to plant them when the oak leaves are the size of squirrel's ears. I have no oak trees to check, though I have squirrels. They say we are to have a very warm April so I wish it would hurry up and come. A watched kettle never boils.

Houseplant Jungle.

I once grew a Monstera deliciosa that became, over time, so big that the aerial roots grew into our green shag rug and broached the floorboards. It leached out all the dye from the rug where it rooted. This was in the olden days when shag rugs were de riguere. Needless to say I was not popular with the pianist. The children and I had lugged this plant from the greenhouse to the living room annually in the spring for years on a toboggan after I repotted it into progressively larger and larger pots. Eventually it became so heavy we had to hammer two by fours into the pot for 4 people to carry it. I must have been mad. I eventually was forced to give it to the Crystal Gardens in Lotus City, then a Civic Arboretum. At least they sent a truck to pick it up, along with my obscenely large Bird of Paradise that I had also been "over the top" with. My failing is I cannot easily get rid of plants that I have harboured for years but have outgrown their space. I have not learned my lesson and now struggle with a 30-year-old Rubber Tree (Fiscus elastica) that is 20 feet tall and has started to become unruly and leaf burned on top due to its proximity to a skylight. If I prune it, it leaks white rubber sap in great gushes and then develops a wild and crazy growth habit. When we were in Israel years ago at the Church of the Beatitudes on the site of the Sermon on the Mount, north of the Sea of Galilee, there was a Fiscus elastica planted by Mussolini in 1934, the year I was born. He planted it in order to be blessed for his conquering of Abyssinia. The tree was about 80 feet high, and was a beautiful tree despite the grotesque gesture of Mussolini. Imagine planting a tree in the spot where Jesus preached "blessed be the peacemakers", in order to celebrate killing and conquering your neighbor. My house tree is long, lank, and a victim of my own botanical hubris. It is not the plant's fault! The pianist is into African violets and Streptocarpus. That makes more sense for little old people.

"What, Me Worry?"

In 1943 and 1944 my mother would take my brother Ken and me on the Goose Line from Kindersley to Saskatoon, and then put us, by ourselves, on the Transcontinental to Uno, Manitoba, about 400 miles away. My uncle would drive up from Isabella, driving about 20 miles north in the model A and pick us up at about 1 am. I was 9 years old and Ken was 5. I was always worried, since I was in charge, that the train would not stop; I would sleep through Uno; and Ken and I would get lost. We never did. I don't think Ken ever worried. The Transcontinental stopped for us at Uno; the conductor was always prompt to appear in the day coach at the time; I never lost our tickets; and my uncle never failed to arrive. Ken and I spent two happy summers on the farm. When I was 3 years old I got on a streetcar in Winnipeg ahead of my mother who was temporarily diverted and I traveled the crowded streetcar a few blocks alone. I was worried! I remember it as if it was yesterday, seeing her racing along the sidewalk but unable to catch the streetcar. It reminds me of the scene where Dr. Zhivago sees Lara on the sidewalk and races off the streetcar but cannot find her. I got off the streetcar to catch my mother but like him, she was lost to me in the crowd. I cried on the street until a policeman came by and took me to the station. He bought me an ice cream cone. He chided me because I didn't at that age know how to tell the police where I was staying. Eventually my mother collected me. When I saw her I bawled again. I am afflicted with travel anxiety. I am also afflicted by time anxiety! My mother never worried about our traveling and she was rarely on time! Silly me!

A Change of Culture

The General Hospital in "Olympic City" was a teaching hospital. One A, was a medical ward where I was one of the two Junior Interns responsible for the day to day medical care of the patients. My colleague and I were on the floor for the entire month of May 1958 and became close to the nursing and other ward staff. The Senior Resident Staff and the Consultants came and went as necessary! The Professor of Medicine made rounds twice a week on preselected patients. He came with a retinue of Chief Resident and various medical students on what was a teaching round. The Professor was a kind and quiet man who accepted the due deference he was given with certain ease. He never played the martinet that was affected by some of his surgical colleagues. My junior colleague and I were sitting on the ward, doing charts early on the morning the Professor was due to appear! The air with the nurses was electric! There was a buzz! Something was up! Hitherto, they had all stood up when the Professor appeared, and remained standing while he had his charts gathered by the Chief Resident, and when he made preliminary observations. When the Professor came to the ward station that morning my colleague and I stood up but the nurses all remained seated and appeared busy, except the head nurse who remained seated, smiled at him and said, " Good morning Dr. Your charts are ready for you in the alcove and the patients are prepared, so I hope you find everything in order." She then ignored him and proceeded to do her job. I felt sorry for the Professor. He was totally nonplussed. The rug was pulled out from under him. He had received the first gust of a new wind that would eventually deconstruct the hierarchical structure. All change occurs gradually, in little increments, in peaceable kingdoms like ours, hopefully. It has to always be initiated however by someone else. "You can't pull the rug out from under you if you remain standing on it", says my friend Katherine. It may be true that this episode, self evident, will only be understood fully by old nurses!

Plato and Aristotle

Plato was a deductive thinker! He absorbed the style of Socrates and refined it. Aristotle was an inductive thinker! He was taught by Plato among others, and then rejected some of the deductive processes of Plato. Plato started from a premise and deduced by applying logic and interior argument leading to reasoning. He said to his students, " Go figure! " and they did. Aristotle on the other hand, broke with his teacher Plato and set up his own school. He said to his students, "Go observe!" and they did. Inductive thinking is reasoning, first based on experimental observation. Solutions follow, or fail to follow as the case may be, but thereby they are evidence based! Both processes still go on today. Both camps are useful. Aristotle was a physician among other things, so I guess he was one of the first bio-researchers. It's probably why I like him better. So Plato was a top down thinker and Aristotle was a bottom up thinker. Plato's school was the Academy and he sat, to teach and think as did Socrates. Aristotle's school was the Lyceum and it was called the "peripatetic school "because he walked "around the portico" when he thought and talked. One student could say, "I go to the sitting down school." Another could say, "I go to the walking around the veranda school." As an aside, we used to say that the top third of the medical school class, the Aristotles, made the best researchers; the middle third made the best doctors; the lower third made the most money! I suppose if you owned an Academy or a Lyceum, you could also earn a fair bundle thinking and teaching!

Heather and Heath

Walking on the Pentland Hills this spring with my son, a midlife eclectic gentleman, we observed the patches of Scottish heather on the hillsides burned by Rangers in a planned and programmed manner for renewal! Traveling a few years earlier in the fall with the pianist through Sutherland and Caithness, the hills were alive with the purple heather and the yellowing fern. The heather belongs! It seems indestructible. The Heather is blooming today in my patch on Lotus Island. It is unruly, grey green with dusty purple bloom and greatly favored by all manner of visiting little flying travelers, most of which I cannot identify. Entomology has been lost to me now. I don't prune my heather and I can't burn my patch to renew it. It's cousin, the white heather, is also unruly and somewhat larger. It is so nice to have the muted colors of the fall bloom. Mixed in with the heathers is the heath. They of course are mostly spring blooming so are presently at rest. Heath in most of the wet coast gardens is pruned rather tightly so the bloom is abundant and very showy. I don't think mine has ever had a haircut. Some of the heath in the patch is fuzzy, tall, shrub heath with small white bells in the spring. My patch all told, looks like a population of adolescents. They seed themselves, so some new plants come along, and new plants also take root from low branches, so they are a crowd ranging in size and age and flowering! "Bless'em all, bless'em all, the young and the short and the tall!" Aside from water they need aught else! They are user friendly!

Eating Crow

If you rise to the first level of your incompetence you will learn to eat crow or not survive! The Peter Principal is easily the most obvious phenomenon in the career of the rising star! When training in medicine in the olden days, humility was learned early and often. As one gained experience and knowledge in what was really a rigorous apprenticeship, there was a further step upward in the programme to new levels of applied skill and knowledge. Having skill and knowledge was never enough! The phrase used was not "having", but " bringing skill and knowledge to the practice of medicine". Each step up was accompanied by stumbles and more meals of crow. With time, crow becomes more palatable and more easily digested. You don't have to lie, or protect your ego, or remember what you said earlier to protect your tangled web! You just put on your bib and settle down to a new meal of crow. People knew that you would tell the truth because you had a cast iron stomach and could survive the vicissitudes of your marginally incompetent role. Over the crow eating meals, your "food for thought" imparts new skills. You will become more competent and stumble less as a result of crow flesh. You can enter the practice of medicine with the proper humility and knowledge that you are, and will be, an imperfect creature and that's OK! Enjoy your meal!

Rototill Your Compost Pile

After a hot, dry midsummer, the rain came for a few days and I rototilled my compost pile! It's a great way to mix the working material, but a cautionary tale is; avoid the front tined tiller. The rear tine tiller gives much more control in mixing, and you are less likely to fall off the compost heap. The compost I have consists of shredded hedge cuttings with lots of leaf, and old straw bales used earlier for dahlia bulb storage. These take time to digest! I throw some balanced fertilizer on it to speed up the working, and some of my nephew's Happy Farmer Bokashi (tm), with SCD Efficient Microbes! These latter two things are less important than the adequate mixing of the materials, and even more crucial still, the tiller brings up from below, the thin residual layer of compost I always leave behind when spreading the top material on the garden the previous fall. The layer of compost left behind is like the sour dough starter yeast that the bread makers prized and perpetuated for years. How could an old sourdough manage to live and prospect without his cache of yeast to sustain him? Last year's retained compost layer is also like the residual tea left as the cha-damari of the Japanese tea ceremony's raku bowl. A ceremonial tea statement that "We never take all from the world!" We return the compost to the land from whence it came, but leave a little behind as a starter for the next year's compost. This is practical. We also leave a little compost remaining behind because we do not take all from the earth. Like the raku, which also comes from the earth, we leave a little tea in the raku bowl, like water in a rock pool. What is left behind is a spiritual reminder that we always owe a debt to life for renewal!

Learning from Bad Examples

Pity the poor student that in life had only superb teaching and exemplary teachers. I learned much from my own failures and from those whose failures surrounded me. Periodic teaching from bad examples provides one with the zeal and stimulus to do better and emulate the best teachers you have encountered. The realization that you can do much better than that which has been offered will lead to renewed efforts on the part of the student. The stream of consciousness will be stimulated not only by good ideas, but also in the right hands, often by ideas that are barren. There is not much in life that is absolute. Received wisdom has ebbed and flooded over time and often given way to new and further wisdom. We are hammered these days with polarized disputes on almost every subject imaginable. You have been given five senses that allow you to come to your own conclusions. A sixth sense, intuition, which can be awakened, is buried deep within everyone. The seventh sense is crucial to the scientist. That is, common sense! Observe the world around you on your own terms. Smell the scents that waft in your air! Touch and feel the rough and the smooth. Listen to the sounds of the natural world. Taste the abundance you have been freely given. Wait and listen for the spirit to awaken you to fresh beginnings. Ask yourself "Does this make ordinary sense?" Know that all experiences are teaching tools, good and bad. Accept that with grace. That's what molds the collagen in character!

The Importance of Being Silly

Humor and cultural differences may often collide. The humor in Canadian culture, as frequently elsewhere, is often associated with self-effacing speech and action, general silliness, and irony. The nature of my writing often includes such an attitude. Being silly is serious stuff since it reveals and conceals, mocks with a gentle poke, and allows the author to remain attached to an unidentifiable point of view. I have noticed that off and on, my humor is treated with earnestness it does not deserve. Some of the more cultivated among us may not be given to knee slapping, belly laughing, frantic foot stomping, aisle rolling, juice depleting responses to humor. Silliness may be seen as outlandish! What about irony? Is that seen as deceptive or sarcastic, rather than appreciated for it's own humorous parody? Is self-effacement in humor considered degrading? Is there a cultural gulf in the way humor is expressed? I am still sufficiently infantile to enjoy slapstick, the more absurd the better. Physical humor is an art form that reaches all ages and stages. It is universal, but you have to let your hair down. You should know that an elderly eclectic gentleman brought up on material such as The Three Stooges, Laurel and Hardy, Bud Abbott and Lou Costello, Beyond the Fringe, and Monty Python, would not be confined to writing exclusively in earnest! For clever and funny repartee, The Importance of Being Earnest is still an example of the importance of being silly, but you can keep your hair up, you have to listen carefully, think, and chuckle without any need to be physical.

Hedge trimmer

UBS Hedge Trimmer Holder

As an elderly eclectic gentleman I am too feeble to manage trimming a large hedge and control a heavy long handled gas hedge trimmer without some creative inventiveness! My Rube Goldberg apparatus was a simple structure that employed a crutch secured to a boat engine mount, both apparatus readily available in every household of decrepits living by the beach. When it was trialed it was somewhat awkward and only moderately effective. The hedge I have inherited was planted by Mother Nature and consists of, among other things, hurtful, thorny, 'Rosa vulgaris', blackberry vines and hawthorns. The object of my invention allows the gas hedge cutter to perch on the handhold of the crutch, which takes the weight of the 7-foot trimmer. The engine mount base can be moved every 4 feet along the hedge and the hedge trimmed in a horizontal arc-like fashion. The hedge height achieved is consistent, due to the constancy of the purchase on the crutch handhold, which obviates the need for string or eyeball. I thought it was a good idea, but then my son-in law came along and just cut the hedge without my Rube Goldberg creation since he is an energetic eclectic gentleman. Since my hedge is 6 or 7 feet deep and trimmed to 4 feet high at the lawn and 12 feet at the water side; and is 200 feet long, it is a daunting task! I was blessed with his help. I did the mop up work and shredded the clippings the following day. Thank goodness for my son-in-law. If my family and friends abandon me, I may have to revert to my invention. I want to avoid being a laughing stock! It's getting harder!

Community vegetable garden

Lotus City provided parcels of vacant land for people who wished to grow their own vegetables and didn't have access to any appropriate land. These parcels provided were individual plots that were each 20 by 50 feet adjacent to one another. There was piped in water and an atmosphere of camaraderie and competition throughout the growing year. The plots became highly individualistic and reflected the personalities of those that toil in the soil. The plot the pianist and I had one year was in a community garden that was surrounded by a newly developed subdivision of houses. In an effort to improve my plot I answered an ad for manure. The man who answered said he could provide good pig manure. I asked him if it was mature and well composted. He assured me that it was, so I ordered a full truckload. When he arrived with his truck I came to meet him and show him my plot. When he backed up to my plot and raised the truck box, the product began to slide out, and I mean slide! It was immediately apparent that "dump" truck was the apt description of the vehicle. The pig manure was of recent origin. Shortly after the dump, I could see the windows of my proximate neighbors open and then quickly close. The smell was evil! I raced home and engaged my son to bring his gumboots and to dig in the manure before we were cited for olfactory offense. He did a good job. I confess the cauliflower and broccoli that year were of winning quality. The offence was never repeated.

The AHA Experience

The first time I saw Edinburgh was when I was convalescing from putting my hand in a running lawnmower. Scotland was the culmination of several months off for me, recovering from my mangled hand. The hour I put my hand in a running lawnmower, the family was in the living room watching Nadia Comaneci doing gymnastics on the balance bar in the 1976 Olympics. I had been agitated and rushing around, repairing our boat with caulk, anticipating being late for rounds on 17 hospitalized patients, my son had not cut the lawn as promised, and I was quitting smoking for the umpteenth time. The grass was moist and the mower became plugged. It was a hard mower to restart. I was in a hurry and it seemed like the mower outlet just needed a little quick clearing. You may not know this, but if you have a major injury, in the first few minutes there is no pain and things can be reduced or set on the field, but time is of the essence. Similarly with the lawnmower, I felt no pain but I could hear my fingers rattling against the rotating blades. When I went to the hospital, Ralph, the orderly in the OR told me later, it took him half an hour to wash my hand and clean off the blood, the boat caulk, the dog shit and the grass mash. Things did work out well. My fingers ended up a bit shorter and a trifle twisted, but functional. I couldn't do any surgery 'til the healing was complete! The point of all this is the months I had off were an "AHA!" experience for me, since hitherto, I had never imagined a life in which one did not live in a hurry up and fragmented fashion. The end of my convalesence was the trip to Edinburgh. It is a beautiful and ancient city and has a deep association with medicine. The pianist and I were there for the Festival and for a meeting of the English speaking Orthopedic Association. My son, the only male issue, who lives with his family near Edinburgh, said to me very much later how mellow I became and how he would have loved to have experienced that earlier! Too soon old, too late smart!

UBS

Ugly But Satisfactory was what my golf mentor described as my usual shot! Particularly so, if I hit a tree, bounced on the rough, and ended up in the middle of the fairway. The pianist described the pies I make as this! She says they taste as good as hers, but she carefully makes her pastry of even thickness and scallops the edges with precise evenness which I, of course, do not do. I had an old Toyota truck that rusted out because I hauled seaweed in it from the beach, augmenting my compost pile. One day I went to the dump with a bunch of garbage and as I was backing up, the corner of my front bumper caught the front-end loader that was parked on the dump road. It bent the end of my bumper forward about 70 degrees. It wasn't that big a deal for me because my truck over the years had become a "beater". It fitted in with a lot of the vehicles on Lotus Island. It gave me a sense of belonging! I ignored the appearance but the pianist was after me to fix my UBS bumper. We, at that time did not have an auto body shop on the island that I knew about, so I pulled in to the service station and asked the mechanic if there was a local place to take it. He looked at the bumper and then at me and said abruptly, "Get out"! I felt somewhat cowed, as he seemed stern. I got out with alacrity. I didn't want him to be mad at me. He got in the truck and drove it a short distance to a telephone pole, positioned the bent bumper against the pole and gunned the truck. My bumper was bent back almost perfectly! " There you are!" he said with a smirk, "No charge!"

The Boarding House

What ever happened to the boarding house? In the 50's all the out of town students I knew stayed in boarding houses. The boarding houses in Winnipeg usually had a variety of single working people and students. No student I knew rented an apartment with a friend or friends. I don't see how a student can combine the work of study and maintain a household to the same advantage! It also has to be furnished, usually with "early attic". The boarding house was often more comfortable, but there was a sacrifice of privacy for the benefits. Boarding houses certainly varied in quality. Women could make a living running a boarding house. The house I finally found as a student was a Godsend. My landlady supported her two daughters from the income she gained running a ten bedroom boarding house consisting of a mix of students and white-collar workers. We had two good meals a day, clean surroundings and quiet living. It was hugely conducive to study and other than keeping your little room tidy there was no other task to do. It did however require a regimented life style with respect for meal times and the needs of others. Unlike an apartment, there was no lease to sign and no damage deposit. It was relatively cheap for its day and housekeeping was always at a minimum for the boarder. If you worked at a regular job and took the bus, you could save money. If you were a student and close to the school you had a lot more study time. If it was a big boarding house you had company at meal times. My grandchildren are students and they all rent apartments with friends to share the cost, but at an increase in student loans. It works for them. I guess it's true that the past really is a foreign country.

Bowel movement

When your mother finally persuaded, cajoled or bribed you, to produce a poop in the potty, this seminal event meant for you, a showering of approval, a sense of providing great pleasure for your parent, and a newly found esteem. It is no wonder that in the recesses of our adult mind the appearance of the bowel movement gives a certain guilty pleasure to the assessment of length and breadth and color. Our cranial software retains that old imprint of wonder at that childhood event and the pleasure principle reappears. Growing up on the bald prairie as a youth, I was often denied this pleasure since the two holer outhouse was dark and dank. Inspection was difficult. The scatological merriment that often appears when matters such as these are considered is, in the pianist's opinion, confined to males only. And pointedly, some males! I guess this is so. There was a time in early medical history when detailed inspection of the lowly poop was serious business and one of the few diagnostic tools available. Appearance, color, consistency, odor; all entered the diagnostic armamentarium of the good physician in those early days. It became the 'ne plus ultra' tool. Now with diagnostic techniques augmented by imaging and fiber optic colonoscopy, poopology is confined to the laboratory! The lowly but interesting poop however, may at least, still be a fertile source for psychological inquiry.

It ain't about Deservin'

When Little Bill was lying on the floor and said to William Munny, "I don't deserve this!" William said, as I recall, "It ain't about deservin'!" Then William blew Little Bill away! In point of fact, Little Bill deserved everything that he got! Which makes me think about deservin' and entitlement and what happens if we are "good", or have the right genes, or the right stuff, or the right deep pockets. People, and I include me, take entitlement for granted. My prayers for example, though rarely formatted, are prayers of request rather than thankfulness. None of us has entitlement or deservin' as a given. I don't know whether there is a master plan the Almighty has for me, or I am simply to exist in the wonderful world He has created, to love, survive joyfully and endure. Whatever comes will test you and your will to do the right thing. There is no entitlement or deservin' here. William, to be charitable, despite his chequered career, did a bad thing for a noble purpose and I like to fantasize that it was redemptive. Perhaps William Munny was not one of the " Unforgiven".

The Fraser River Delta

When you leave the islands of the Salish Sea and drive through the Fraser River delta to Olympic City in October, you will see that the fields off the highway in the river delta are spectacularly red. These are cranberry and blueberry fields turning to their fall colors. You see very little if you stick to the highway; your eye on the ferry traffic ahead, but if you take a few minutes and wander a back road or two you are in for an enormous treat. There is nothing more attractive than miles of orange, red and brown for the short magical period Mother Nature and the berry farmer provide. Both berries grow best in the peaty, boggy, delta soil supplied over the centuries by the flooding of the Fraser River and the rotting vegetation! The sight of the fields is thrilling and at the same time sobering, knowing that the Fraser undergoes a major flood every 50 years. I remember feeling the same thrill with the colorful magnificence of miles of heather and fern massed in the hills of Caithness and Perthshire. The capacity of Mother Nature to provide the vegetation that will thrive in these difficult. particular soil types, allowing a uniformity of design from a duo-culture, whether planned by man or Mother Nature, is an interesting departure from the multiple mixed vegetation we usually see in B.C. Seems there are plants for every location! Darwin would be interested with the adaptation. So would Mendel. So should we!

The Golden Apple; Quince

Here find a reference: Euripides, Greek, 484-406 BC, " I would fly to the coast of apples of which many tales are told, the far Hesperian shore where the mighty Lord of ocean forbids all further voyaging and marks the sacred limits of heaven, which Atlas holds. There the immortal streams flow fresh by the couch of God where he lies with his lovely ones---and earth, the mother of life, yields up blessings of harvest to enrich a bliss that never ends."

Quince, the fruiting tree, not the flowering shrub, was of Mediterranean origin. It grew best there, but worked its way north-ward over the centuries and also grows on the islands in the Salish Sea. Here it ripens in November and is golden.

Undoubtedly the "apple" the Greeks and those of the Levant referred to, was the quince, since apples as we know them would find that climate unacceptable. The pianist's and my greeting and thank you card, courtesy of Euripides, is a reflection of the fact that here, both the apple and quince and for that matter, the medlar, strangely, all flourish on this small collection of islands in the Salish Sea of which it is said, has a Mediterranean climate. Can you blame me for liking it here? A bliss from the mother of life!

Humble Access

It's Sunday and it's church time this morning. It reminds me of the little bedtime prayer our mother taught us years ago and the one my brothers and I were required to say. It went, "Now I lay me down to sleep, I pray the Lord my soul to keep, and if I die before I wake, I pray the Lord my soul to take." The pianist says it is a frightening prayer for children and should be banned, but you know, when you think about that prayer, it requests about everything that you really need for yourself globally. To be kept and accepted! Harboured and taken! It's narcissistic but fits in well with the ego development of most children, and me also, if I am honest! The only other addition is the quick postscript, "God bless", to cover the parents and siblings and any other support staff! When I was 14 and my brothers 10 and 6, we all slept in the same room, but went to bed at different times. Our mother made sure Philip, the 6 year old knelt at the bed in an attitude of humble access, like the good Anglicans we were. He had to say the prayer out loud. Ken, who at 10, went to bed a little later, was permitted to say his prayers on his knees without supervision. I, at 14, said my prayers silently, and instead of kneeling in an attitude of humble access, I confess, I lay in bed and made a feeble concession to access by putting one foot on the floor. God is good. He didn't hold it against me, SO FAR! He knew I was just a kid. By the time my brother David was born I was 18 and had left home. My mother would not have let him escape praying, but he probably was a more contemporary prayer! There is much more to all this than just piety!

The Propylaea, a gateway like no other

When I took a course in the archaeology of the Athenian Acropolis at UBC in the late 50's, the professor told us that some architrave blocks on the original Propylaea were hollowed out on the sides like an I-beam. That piqued my interest since both ortho-pedic surgeons and Mother Nature are interested in structure and how it accommodates force and strain. When the pianist and I were in Greece, we walked through the Propylaea under newly restored beams onto the Acropolis. In the olden days the Greeks would have walked under the original stone architrave blocks; beams supported by large columns and supporting in turn, heavy superstructure. These beams were subject to strong bending moment! The Propylaea had the first, or as was believed, the first known loadbearing beam developed where the architect understood the I-beam principle, where with load bearing there is distraction force on the lower surface of the beam and compression force on the top surface of the beam. It followed then, that in the centre of the beam there must be little or no bending force, and therefore no need for heavy material to resist bend. Picture the 60 odd slaves trying to haul up with rudimentary winches, a solid block, vis-a- vis an I-beam block. Of course our long bones are hollow for the same functional reasons as the I-beam. Wolff's Law, a part of Mother Nature's gift to us, describes the growth of bone in response to the stimulus of stress demands. It's the same principle for us as the Propylea, except our Architect is always with us, working as a struc-tural engineer, shoring us up here and there as the need arises. If our long bones were solid we would all weigh 600 pounds. We build with I-beams these days. The Propylaea was the lamp that led the way. The architect in the 5th century BC was a genius. He may have twigged to the idea by thinking about the bending moment of his own femur.

The four elements

I was watering and turning my compost the other day and thinking of Empedocles. He, according to Will Durant, lived 500 to 430 BC. You may know, that he was the first to describe the four elements, of which the world is composed. It's still true, and my compost tells me that is so. The four elements are fire, water, earth, and air. This understanding was foundational to the classical philosophers that followed Empedocles. As I attended my compost, which was mostly straw and green vegetable matter, I added water and the pile in time became very hot. Deep down it was breaking up and becoming soil, warm, richly brown, and particulate. I piled it loosely, as it needs to breathe in order to work. It is true that the four elements are extraordinarily complex in their developed state, but the compost is the great leveler. All complexities are reduced to earth by means of air, heat and water. Even you and I, in all our complexity, will be returned to dust, and if we are burned in the undertakers compost bin, the heat will be much faster and hotter than my compost. So the compost pile, through air and water and heat, becomes earth, as does all else. Ironically, Empedocles died after the fashion of his philosophy. He became convinced that he was a god and could fly, so hurled himself into the mouth of a volcano. He couldn't fly; and so hurtled through the air and heat of the volcano, and undoubtedly returned to dust.

Prairie Grain Elevator

My first summer job when I was 15 was cleaning out the grain dust in the bottom of the bins in the Pool elevator for Bob, the operator! We lived in the railway station across the tracks from the Pool elevator, which also had an attached annex. My brother Ken used to sit in front of the railway office and shoot rats around the annex with his "22 "when our dad wasn't around. One day he aimed too low and the bullet hit the track and ricocheted through a window. That ended his rat-hunting career! The prairie elevators we knew are now an iconic reminder of a special past and a way of life when industrial farming was nonexistent. The elevators announced each town in large letters to those who passed through; a statement of importance to us. The elevator had a grated weigh scale where the grain truck was weighed full and then empty. Grain was dumped through the grate; samples were taken by the elevator operator for grading during the dumping stream, and then the grain was carried by the elevating buckets to the top of one of the 16, 80-foot high bins and poured out. During the fall and winter when the grain was loaded into boxcars it was not taken from the bottom of the bin. As a consequence, the detritus, rat droppings, chaff and dust settled to the bottom of each bin over the winter and spring to about three to four feet high. It was a dusty job cleaning the bins out; getting them ready for the fall harvest. The material got in your clothes, hair and nostrils. I was happy with my first paying job but I understand why Bob didn't want to do it. I was strong and never got sick. We didn't have running water so it was hard to keep clean every day since our water had to be hauled from the town pump and heated on the stovetop. My bath water in the galvanized tub looked like porridge at the end of each bath. I have a slightly jaded view of the romantic nature of the iconic prairie elevator.

Birdbrain

This apparently disparaging comment about the forgetful or the thoughtless requires some reexamination! For the past two months the robins at our plot on Lotus Island were notable for their complete absence. They were abundant during the early fall. Nothing had changed that would have occasioned their departure. The worms and bugs remained in plentiful numbers. One thing however is noted and that is the holly berries were not quite ripe during that period. The robins of course are omnivorous. They don't exist on protein alone. They must have, if not an internal clock, an internal calendar, or alternatively a readily available Dayrunner. The holly berries are now ripened! The robins are not " birdbrains"; they appeared in spades about 4 days ago. They started in the orchard by turning up the leaves in the windrows that I haven't been able to drag to the compost yet. Tossing their heads they threw leaves helter skelter, seeking the cringing bug or worm. Once I saw them I knew what they were really after. The appetizer may have been bugs and worms, but the entree consisted of my holly berries. The assault on the holly tree can start about the 5th of December and despite it being a loaded 50-foot tree they clean it up in 4 to 5 days! This year the tree was a bit late in ripening like everything else! How they knew? That kind of timing doesn't suggest a birdbrain is forgetful or thoughtless. They may not be able to spell well, but they are not stupid. Neither am I because I cut all the holly we needed three days ago, preempting their action. They can go to it all they want now! The only drawback to this feeding frenzy is the distributed seedlings I have to weed next year from the droppings. Nevertheless, L'Chaim!

The Motley Crew

As I march through the commercial nursery greenhouses from time to time I feel a touch of envy over the pristine, row on row of abundantly flowering or verdant houseplants for sale. They smack of the beauty of the young, but are often bought, treasured, and turfed when they are no longer so beautiful. If you see perennials as furnishing, to stage your house for beauty, you will see no sense in any alternative value to them. However if you anthropomorphize your houseplants, you will, as we have over many years, create a Confederation of a Motley Crew. The pianist has said, from time to time that we should get rid of some of these plants since they are too big, some are ugly, and they are taking over the house and greenhouse. I don't disagree with her observations about ugly and large, but have so far avoided implementing some of these suggestions. A good marriage seeks compromise. I also have a bottom line and have euthanized and buried the worst of them to the compost. Such an act is love in action since they will rise again in a new form. The survivors are old friends. They can be primped up to be at least acceptable, but it does become more and more of a struggle. They provide memories of the olden days when they were young and beautiful. I am not a callow person. I am loyal. The old plants can rely on us to give geriatric care; to water regularly; to avoid rich food; to amputate at times to stave off death. We are still more a happy home for the elderly rather than a hospice. We share their joy. There is a Cymbidium in bloom today that we have had for years. Some years it blooms, some years it doesn't! I have two others that have not yet favored us this year. I accept that. They have a mind of their own. I can always wait 'til Mother Nature chooses to reward us!

My Pro Career

In 1953 I was recruited to go to Wynyard, Saskatchewan as a baseball pitcher for their ball team! Since it was my summer job I needed the money for school in the fall. The team had the desire to be a winning team, but they had neither the money, nor a pitcher! A philanthropic business man in Wynyard who owned a service station, came to their rescue and paid me 250 dollars a month to pump gas and be a part time go-fer in his business, so that I could be at the beck and call of the ball team. 250 dollars a month was too much for the job I did for the business owner, but it was a generous expenditure made in the interest of his town's ball team. I, of course, was flattered that they wanted me. My pro career, since I was the only pitcher ,included pitching 3 days a week at local sports days around the area, and usually, since we often won, generally pitched three short games a day. My job on the field included carrying the equipment, bags and bats, to our next diamond since I was the only "paid " player. The team felt that was a reasonable request since I was only 19 and therefore couldn't go with them to the beer parlor in between games; a real source of discontent for me. Predictably, half way through the season, pitching without respite and having no brains to pace myself, I developed a severe rotator cuff tendonitis in my pitching arm! It was so bad I had trouble lifting the bag of jelly doughnuts I brought to the garage mechanics for coffee break twice a day when I was working the go-fer shift! The black day came when the ball team manager took me aside and told me the team was not making enough money to pay me anything further. I of course, couldn't pitch for them because of my arm but never thought to question why I was fired since my service station employer was paying me, not the ball team. I was of no further use. Used up! I did see the local doctor but he was a quack and gave me some talcum powder to rub on my shoulder! My pro career ended and I went back to the track at the CNR for the remainder of the summer! Oh, brief fling of greatness dashed!

Utterances

When my dad retired from the railway in Lotus City, and when he could no longer garden; but before he was anchored to the apartment by an oxygen hose, he did volunteer driving for the housebound! He was getting "on" however, and found driving in the city a bit tense. He would drive elderly or disabled people to the doctor or dentist, or to the hospitals, wait for them, and drive them back. He had not much else to do so he was content to wait for them. My dad was not a reader but he enjoyed engaging others in the waiting room in conversation since he was never shy! He was given to frequent exclamations in his conversation generally. These were never scatological or sacramentally incorrect but were provided with some passion nevertheless. His routine passionate epithet, prefacing remarks was "By Dad!" Certainly beyond criticism! One day in my office an elderly woman with a hip problem consulted me. At the end of our consultation she volunteered that she knew my dad and that he was often her volunteer driver. She said, "He's quite a character!" I agreed. Then she observed that when he drove her to an appointment he was frustrated with other drivers passing him and bumper hugging. She said he would mutter, or sometimes yell "You jackass" during the trip. I said, "I know that. He drives so slowly that people pass him abruptly and he is nervous. It's his word! We know it well." "Well ", she said, "I like your dad a lot, but one day I was very late leaving the apartment and he was waiting for me a long time. I just knew when I got to his car he was going to call me a jackass." "He would never do that!" I said. "You're right", she said, "He just smiled and said he hoped I was feeling well." I can see my dad now in my mind's eye, trying to remain useful; tense with driving, but enjoying the company of fellow strangers; staving off the eventual time of relative immobility; fighting the feeling!

The Pansy

The pansy, or for that matter the shrinking violet: what misnomers for timid or shy people! They are tough little plants! The pansies are anything but "pansies" and the violets may be modest in size but they are mighty! We had minus 6 centigrade here on Lotus Island last week. The foundation box chrysanthemums turned black but the pansies didn't turn a hair. How could anyone have taken these plants as a metaphor for timidity? The pansy was always the favorite flower of the pianist. As a little girl she saw the flower as a face! I can see that!

Anthropomorphizing again! Particularly for me as well, the yellow and brown petal arrangement is about as close to a little face as any flower I can think of. They not only are tough; they are not in your face. Never mistake modesty, shyness or timidity for weakness, in man or plant! I am long enough in the tooth to know that with other people or plants, what you see is not always what you get! On the island, the pansy winters over beautifully, waiting for that first soft warm breath in February to flourish when under planted with the daffodils in the foundation boxes. The reflected heat from the house allows them to spring forward. Being greeted by these harbingers of spring, as we leave the house, puts the spring in your step as well as in your heart.

End of life as we knew it

Doing Christmas cards this year reminds us once again that old friends and relatives are dropping off, one by one. When your cousins and friends are in the 70s, the attrition rate starts to undergo a modified geometric progression. This year my younger cousin's husband died of bladder cancer and a cousin of my vintage, 75 years, experienced her husband die of heart failure. There is nothing that can be said that is an easy emollient to the grief that comes with these partings. In a card you could say, as Percy Bysshe Shelley did, "When winter comes, can spring be far behind?" Time does heal, and spring does arrive again. Moreover, so many of our friends now are developing chronic and debilitating illness. Though many complain, need a sounding board, or compare joints and joint replacements, in time there is an acceptance of where you are. Accepting things is what it is all about. Living with your disability and adapting your life to fit can be a model for those who follow. Not everything can be fixed or altered. It is not helpful as Dylan Thomas wrote, " Do not go gentle into that good night, rage, rage against the dying of the light." There is so much stress in attempting to modify the aging process that we have lost the reality of the nature of life, illness, and death, seeing it as a battle to be fought. It's not giving up in defeat, it's giving in to the flow of life. If you think this is pablum, continue to rage, but it'll do you no good!

Deer Damage Prevention

On Lotus Island the deer have free "reign". They are medium sized mule deer and are no more skittish than cows in a pasture. There are virtually no predators other than cars, except for a few hunters in the fall; but there are no trophy bucks here. The odd hunter claims to be after meat. Whatever! One of the reasons the deer are bold is that dogs do not run free on Lotus Island. There are many sheep farmers and they shoot any dog that harasses their sheep. Often any pretext will do! Dog lovers contain their animals. The garden damage the deer do is confined to a few plant species, so most of us have avoided planting the vulnerable. In my garden I have not followed my own advice. At risk are Japanese Laurel (Aucuba japonica), Camellia, the Cedar variety(Smaragd), Azalea, and small leaf Rhododendrons. Also vulnerable are most spring bulbs other than Daffodils. Deer also eat Bergenia and some Sedum. Deer occasionally chew Dahlia. Since they browse and are alert, they seldom stay more than a few minutes in any one place. Their pattern of trail walking is absolutely consistent and predictable in time and space. I use smelly deer repellant, Plantskydd, on the deer vulnerable plants. If I spray on sunnier days it lasts one or two months. Once they've tasted a sprayed leaf, they change their pattern of browsing. If I leave the Plantskyddd container open it becomes even more foul and effective. Care must be taken because it stains the house siding. The stink around the house lasts for a day so I don't do it before a party. The presence of the deer on our lot, within proximity, is a delight we can only enjoy if they aren't fenced out. Aside from Rhubarb and Globe Artichokes, vegetables either need a fence or better still, plan to buy your vegetables from an organic marketer! I always think a home vegetable gardener spends a hundred dollars of effort and seed to grow ten dollars worth of produce.

My Mentors

I my lifetime I had two men who were truly my mentors-- and both of them were teachers. Years ago, I went on a men's retreat to a local church camp. There were about thirty men for a weekend and we had teaching sessions. The leader asked us to consider someone, other than a parent, who had been a mentor in our life, and why. Virtually all the men chose a teacher who had served such a role in their lives. I often wonder if teachers really know the power for good they have. I don't believe a parent can be a complete mentor. I loved my dad unconditionally and did not love my mentors, but the avuncular role they served, and the interest they took in me, made me want to emulate them. The pianist said to me once that I even started to walk like my Consultant chief for whom I was Registrar. He was an Australian bachelor in Plymouth who was more English than the English. My other mentor was my small town high school teacher in Grade ten, eleven, and twelve. He had dignity and treated us with the same dignity and respect and never raised his voice because he didn't have to. I'm sure the seriousness he felt towards us was key to my desire to succeed. My son had a mentor when he first started his career as a young Anglican priest in Montreal. I am grateful to that man as I never questioned my son's love for me, but valued the mentor's role and his sincerity. The son must move away from the father. Mentorship is a symbiotic role. The mentor benefits as well as those that are mentored. Mentorship is not just an art; it comes from the heart!

My father betrayed

My mother loved roast lamb and my father had a strong aversion to it! He was "unable" to eat mutton or lamb of any sort due to his experience when farming as a young man during the great depression. Most of his sheep sickened and were infested with maggots. He was scarred forever from this experience. When the pianist first met my mother, before our marriage, she was told that we "had veal" from time to time that was really lamb and it was to be called veal because of my father's sensitivity! The trouble was the poor benighted gentleman was unaware of this charade. It was not the case that he simply went along with the game of denial. He thought that the "veal " she prepared from time to time was awfully good. He had a simple and uncompromising faith in my mother's veracity. The pianist was simply appraised of the fact that my father's children, nudge, nudge, wink, wink, remained part of that deception over the years and she became part of the pact. My mother operated on the basis of, "what you don't know, won't hurt you." She provided her children with the love of lamb for all time and a somewhat tarnished sense of ethics. I am still a little guilty of my part in the duplicity. I don't think he ever found out!

Homeless in Paradise

This season on Lotus Island there are about forty homeless; almost all men. They flee the cold part of the country to survive outside on Lotus Island. We have had inclement weather lately; particularly cold and wet weather. Here we are in one of the world's most wealthy countries, and the best part of that country, but we have this disconnect! The Community Services provides shelter for six or seven persons if the temperature is below 0 degrees Centigrade. Otherwise they are on their own. Funding is always the problem. We have a food bank, a soup kitchen and the Copper Kettle, a feeding and counseling programme, but the nights are cold and wet and there is no room at the Inn. In our Anglican church we have a deck with a life sized Crèche of the Holy Family at the Stable. The figures are mounted on straw bales that act as a windbreak. Three or so homeless persons sleep at night behind or around the Creche. We worry about cigarette butts, the "piddling pail" and the bedclothes they leave for the next night. Our janitor has a problem with maintenance of the area but it is no accident that there is consent about allowing some shelter around the Bethlehem scene. We just have to live with the ambivalence and hope the bales don't catch on fire and that our insurability doesn't go up in smoke. It's little enough that we can do. One didn't have to worry about cigarettes in the days of Caesar Augustus. The Creche is a form of comfort, figurative and actual, however meagre, both now and as it was historically, to the dispossessed!

Time

When I was working hard in a career that spanned fifty odd years, time was always in short supply. The demands of work, family, income, debt and frantic fun took up most of the day and there was little room for that state of mind that leads to discovery. Now that I am seventy-five I have the time since most of the demands have disappeared. I'm not too old to make a new start. Ego concerns are not as problematic as it becomes less and less important to "amount to something". There is less drive to play to the crowd. I probably had an hour a day of "out of the box thinking time" when I worked. That meant, for over fifty years of working life, I had 18,250 hours of discovery time. If at seventy-five, I am blessed with six hours a day of thinking time; over eight years that gives me 17,520 hours. All I'm saying to myself is, "There is still time to get serious about yourself if you want to." Things don't go on forever. " Time, like an ever rolling stream, bears all its sons away: they fly, forgotten as a dream dies at the opening day". Perhaps I expect too much, hoping that dementia will hold off for eight years. The pianist and I sit every morning and guzzle coffee and look out the east window as the sun rises over the Salish Sea. Busyness begins in the sky and on the water. We are not a part of that "going somewhere" any longer. For us it is a seemingly slow and serene beginning but it is a necessary daily renewal! Time stands still for that hour or two!

Snow load

The bane of a gardener's life can be a wet snow load followed by a sharp frost. The evergreens here on the wet coast; Rhododendrons, evergreen Magnolia, Sweet Bay and tree Heath undergo breakage if the snow load is on brittle branches. Trying to brush the snow off in the cold snap adds to the breakage. Best is to pray! Over the last several years I have had two mature prune plums completely topple over, due to wind and heavy snow load and inadequate pruning on my part. Prune plums are shallow rooted trees and the above ground growth has to match the underground growth. Gardening 101! I have a Victoria plum that has an off balance growth habit and I think it will be next to bite the dust. That plum is not plumb! The deciduous trees are by and large more protected against snow load by their nature. There is nothing so revealing in the winter than the lovely tracery that the deciduous trees create against the sky. When they are in full leaf they do not reveal their true shape and the unique characteristics and variety of the species. Having a garden or wilderness tramp on a nice day when the snow is off the branches is a visual treat, observing the tree shapes in their skeletal nakedness. If you look down rather than up, you can also read the diary in the snow left by all your little visitors; who they were and where they went.

Copenhagen Bells

The Anglican Church bells in Lotus Island tolled three hundred and fifty times yesterday in support of the Copenhagen Conference on climate change. Other churches on the island chimed in, but we have the only bell tower. The bell ringers came from far and near, including many of the community with their children. All participated! This was a World Council of Churches initiative. When one thinks of John Donne's famous phrasing, " No man is an island, entire of itself------- any man's death diminishes me, because I am involved in mankind, and therefore never send to know for whom the bell tolls: it tolls for thee". The meditation is as gripping and relevant now as it was then! That reflection makes me think of the exchange between Scrooge and the ghost of Jacob Marley, (Scrooge)-- "But you were always a good man of business, Jacob!" (Marley)-- "Business! Mankind was my business! The common welfare was my business: charity, mercy, forbearance and benevolence." It's no accident that the awakening of Scrooge was occasioned by the striking of the heavy bells. He remained awake! As the pianist observed to me, the bell is an archetypal marker that always has and always will signal us to awake!

Laundry

The first two years I was at the University of Manitoba, I shipped my laundry home by baggage for my mother to wash and press. My dad was a station agent in our little town in Saskatchewan so I had a railway pass. I used my pass as a ticket and sent my dirty clothing by baggage, as luggage. My dad would pick it up from the baggage car and when it was laundered send it back by baggage. Clearly there was no cost in this transaction. The transcontinental passenger train didn't normally stop at hamlets between Winnipeg and Saskatoon. It bypassed all fifty odd hamlets on the line unless there was a passenger to get off. When it stopped to unload my laundry, no doubt all the passengers looked out and wondered why the train stopped at a place like this. "Who would be getting off here?" was doubtless on their mind. No one! I think the baggage trick was an abuse of the CNR at the time and if one factored in the cost of stopping and starting the Transcontinental, it was an edgy act at best. My mum always put cookies in my laundry when she sent it back. My brothers, who were still at home at the time, told me recently that they resented the fact that I always got the good cookies and the broken ones were left for them. What a callow youth I was, underestimating the blessings I was afforded! I think now, that there was then, and still is, a sense of entitlement that allows us, erroneously, to take liberties with an institution like the railway. They seem to have lots, and we don't!

Prepared for snow

Lotus Island, on the Salish Sea, often gets two weeks of snow around Christmas time. This is a hilly island and it's tough to get around. Because we are part of the wet coast, the precipitation is sometimes huge. The pianist and I are ready! We are accumulating a reserve of foodstuffs to sustain us and our guests, through a period of sequestration. We have purchased a scoop shovel. Our four-wheel drive SUV has new snow tires. Wood is cut, and kindling is ready for our airtight and our fireplace. Four bags of road salt have been purchased and stored. Candles and flashlights and a wind up radio are at hand. A small generator is in the basement with gas available. The liquor cabinet has been fortified. I have wrapped all the outside taps in burlap and the standpipes have been drained. The lining in our jackets has been inserted. That's the benefit of being an old fart as you have time on your hands and obsession on your mind. Having done all this of course is a guarantee that it won't snow. If you don't want something to happen, prepare! If you want the telephone to ring with an important subject, don't hover around the phone, sit on the toilet and the phone will always ring. I am unlikely to receive much in the way of thanks from the denizens of Lotus Island for preventing the snow from coming, since they don't resort to magical thinking. After all they probably don't believe that King Canute could hold back the tides with his hand either!

Tidy Hair

Appearances are crucial for today's young teenagers. Hairstyles bespeak who you are. I speak only about boys, as I was never blessed with a sister, so girls always had a mysterious quality for me at that age. In our home, hair was a low priority for my brothers and myself. We had a large quart sealer that my mother made up we called "green stuff". It was some sort of gel that was pale green, which she made from a powder mixed with water. It probably was a wave set of some form or another. In the morning before school we would put our hand in the wide mouth sealer, plaster our hair with "green stuff" and comb it. It set in about five minutes. Over time and many cursorily washed hands inserted in the jar, the green stuff became a little more like "grey stuff". It still worked well and by the time we got to school our hair was hard as a rock. Particularly in the winter it caked like cement. In the normal rough and tumble at school, someone would inevitably pass a strong hand though my hair and it would stick up like thatch. There is something quite liberating in that period of life, before Narcissus enters in and self-consciousness emerges. That worry-free period about hair and that sort of thing disappears for years but gradually reappears, too late to be truly liberating again. We carry too much baggage by then. If I mention "green stuff" to my brothers now, they cackle with laughter!

Whitewash cover-up

The pianist and I live on a moraine soil that has a plethora of rocks of all sizes. In over thirty-two years of tillage, digging and raking a large part of this acre, many of these treasures have been uncovered. I never found a rock I didn't like. They are almost always round, since they were ground up and rolled down the mountain in days of yore to create the moraine. I raided the rocks from Mother Nature where she had placed them, and used them "au natural" to bank flowerbeds; slopes for interplanting and to outline my homely little garden features. When I was a boy it was de rigueur on the prairies to whitewash your rocks. Every civic center, all the railway terminals, RCMP stations, centenary parks and many businesses had whitewashed rocks. Rocks were supposed, then, to be ugly in their natural state so were covered up by liming! This was a job I did at the stations we lived in. Whitewash became part of the lexicon for cover-up of things you wanted to hide, even sepulchres. It could be considered an old variety of "lipstick on the pig". As if! Whitewashing structures as well as sins must have extended well beyond our little prairie towns. Tom Sawyer was whitewashing Aunt Polly's fence even before my days of yore. I cannot get over how prissy that convention of whitewashed rock gardens seemed. What's more, one had to whitewash repeatedly, or the truth eventually became exposed.

Two holers and the Honeyman

The science of waste disposal had a local flavor in the olden days. As a young boy I always had an intense interest in this art. In the small towns I lived in as a boy we had outhouses over pits. When I was a young teenager and living as we did in the railway station, we had a two holer. I never gave it much thought but considering it now, why a two holer? I can't imagine a duo sitting and chatting for the duration of their activity. There was no partition. It was a two holer but the same pit. In the winter we had an indoor toilet with a can I hauled out to empty into the two holer. That was my job, as well as cutting kindling and taking out the ashes from the kitchen stove. It may have been a scam, but I was paid by the CNR twenty dollars a month to be custodian of the two holer, put in lime periodically, clean up and make sure toilet paper was available. Eaton's catalogue was a myth. In the medium sized towns we lived in, there was the Honeyman. There were both indoor toilets with cans that you left out for the pickup by the Honeyman with his horse-drawn tank, or you had an outhouse with a back flap to access the can, wherein the Honeyman went down the lane to pick up your waste. In the winter the tank was not very stinky so a kid could hitch his sleigh to the Honeyman's tank, carefully avoiding the brown icicles when he stopped and the sleigh glided forward. I am not making this up! These for me are fond memories.

Eating Beaver

The Scots' heraldry is the Rampant Lion. The Imperial Eagle is the American emblem, as it was for Napoleon and the Roman Legion and the Holy Roman Empire. Canadians have the Beaver. I think we may be the only country I can think of with a rodent, albeit a big rodent, as emblematic of the country. Industrious, hunkered down in the winter, hypervigilant and easily made into hats; is that us? Some time ago the pianist and I went with our son to a festive dinner and Anglican service in James Bay Cree land near Waswanipi in Quebec. My son was the incumbent priest in the district and conducted the service to a degree in the Cree language. As it was, we had an in! It was frankly a wonderful experience and unforgettable. We had a culturally correct meal consisting of, amongst other things, chunks cut from a pit- fired beaver and a bannock topped with bear grease! Our normal capacity to eat lavishly was tempered, but our hosts were forgiving after the first tentative tidbits were tried. Both the Anglican and the Catholic Church proselytized in the north in the early days, including writing biblical translations and hymns in Cree. For us it was a privilege to listen in to the service, conducted with our son's mandolin and a Cree guitarist. I am reminded of similar recent gastronomical episodes in the far north, with our Governor General, and later the Tory caucus, tasting seal meat. Seal may become Canadian haute cuisine, but what about beaver?

Eagle attack

A while back we were watching a bevy of Bufflehead ducks in the harbor with an eagle cruising above them. These are diving ducks. Suddenly the eagle spiraled down and the ducks scattered. The eagle seemed initially to have missed the strike but a lone duck remained, didn't fly off and stayed on the surface. The eagle made a lazy circle over the area and then a long sloping descent onto the lone duck. The duck dived at just the right moment and the eagle seemed to have missed. This scenario was repeated at least five times and each time the duck dived for shorter and shorter periods. The eagle was relentless. It appeared to rake the duck on its last foray and then returned to pick up the duck, which it seemed, could no longer dive. The eagle flew off with its prey in the talons. I felt a sense of horror for the duck. Even though I know this is part of life, I am always struck with the brutality of reality. Predators have to eat and supply their family. Eagles are large birds with big appetites that eat a variety of land and marine life including ducks. Still, I find it sad. I can't be a hypocrite however, since I too am part of the food chain and I am omnivorous. My meat eating is at arms length from the killing fields. Like many others, my action is sanitized. I see it as acceptable since I thrive on denial. Cognitive dissonance!

Dressing down

The haberdasheries of Lotus City in the 60's provided a superb stock of good men's clothing! I can't remember ever seeing a physician at work in that era without a white shirt and tie. Everyone wore a suit or jacket and pressed trousers. Men shaved. They didn't sport a constant five-day beard. We shined our shoes. Even the "suits" these days have morphed into jackets with open dress shirts without a tie. An exception is politicians in Question Period! And hockey coaches! Are we saying appearance doesn't matter? Maybe we are saying "comfort rules". The current crop is clean and smart no doubt! But, why do they dress down? It must be a conundrum in the clothing industry to keep up with this change in fashion. It was always hard with women's clothing, but men? When I go to church, virtually none of my colleagues is in a suit jacket! I've now either given up or given in, I'm not sure which! Lotus City used to have six or seven good men's clothing stores. Now they have one! I still have four worsted suits in my closet that I can fit, but I am retired and there is unfortunately little occasion for them now. I could throw them out but I am still governed by "waste not, want not". I guess I lamented the passing of what I believed was propriety. We used to say, "Clothes make the man." It's clearly not the same today. What's more, it is not even true! Why did it take me so long to figure that out?

Board Games

I'm particularly poor at board games. I never win! Others feel sorry for my ineptitude and try to help. That is even more humiliating! Christmas is coming and when our families gather, board games will be in full swing. I can see it now--all of them poised around the table, eyes darting here and there, perched on the edge of the chair, trembling with anticipation to make the ultimate move. And me, an old duff, sitting in the circle feeling horrid, fearful and worried that the nursing home is just around the corner. The pianist, her grandchildren and daughters and son in law love board games and are good at it. They are not at all unkind to me as they know it is not my thing, but what they don't know is that I avoid board games because clearly there is a part of my brain that either won't, or can't measure up to the competition and I have a certain amount of pride that won't let my guard down. There is a particularly loathsome game called "Bop-it" that involves hand auditory coordination that they are all good at and I am a total bust. I am lousy at crosswords and other similar pursuits as well. I am resigned to be at the edge of this kind of action. Lord knows I've been at the "center" for much of my share of life, so I am not going to whine. In the meantime the pianist will have a splendid gaming interlude with those of her ilk. I'll make the popcorn and 7 up floats!

The Talisman

In the Middle English poem-saga Sir Gawain and the Green Knight, Gawain is given a sash which purports to guard him from death. A form of Talisman! It corrupted the pure honour to be expected of a knight of the Round Table in the encounter with danger. In their early childhood, all three children of ours had little blankets. Each child reposed in safety only when the blanket was in place. A form of Talisman! They had unique rituals with the blanket, which were required in order to give it power. The first born carefully wrapped the satin edging around his index finger and massaged his upper lip with the opposite thumb in the mouth. The second born massaged the nostrils with the satin edging and as well, tickled her nostrils with her hair. The third born tickled her nostrils with a frayed edge of the satin border and later substituted one of the pianists slips for her tattered blanket. The ritualistic application of the Talisman provided a refuge from evil. Think of it! We all have a Talisman in some form. Sir Gawain was not immune to his own human nature. There is always a visible representation to an invisible part of us. When I was a little boy my blanket was a part of me I am told. It was like the others; an extension of my body; an integral part of me. My mother went on a holiday when I was three and left me in the care of my father's sister Mildred. She apparently said, "You are a big boy now Jim, and you don't need your blanket." Mother gone, blanket gone; I must have grieved and faced the danger alone!

Pickwickian

Observing myself in the mirror as I frequently do when going out, there are often food stains on my shirt, sweater or tie that I had previously overlooked. The pianist has a sharp eye for this sort of mussiness, so I am careful to take preemptive action. My shape over the years has begun to approach that of Pickwick and as a result the frontage I display has become more horizontal than vertical. I rarely get food stains on my trousers because of the overhang. The value of the necktie has been largely over looked as to its utility to clean one's glasses, but more importantly to intercept food droppings on one's shirt. The tendency to avoid ties today by "a public man" who wishes to appear like one of the "people" unfortunately resulted in discarding a useful bib. Pickwick was a man of a particularly mild nature as I find is generally the case in the plumper members of the human race. Dickens' genial characters in all his novels seem to me to have always been of a more rotund physique than the lean, hungry and intense nature of the villains or the troubled. Compare Mr. Tubman and Mr. Brownlow with skinny Mr. Jingle. Reflect on Fagin, Bill Sikes and Daniel Quilp; not one of them a fat man. This proposition of course could be a rationalization on my part and on the part of Dickens. But, ask yourself, can a man who loves juicy food, eats with relish and joy and dribbles on his clothing, be skinny and cranky? I think not! There is no one in my mirror with a "lean and hungry look"! Food and satisfaction are aligned in the psyche!

Shred and Burn

Living as we do in a bucolic rural area, the potential to burn or shred the cellulose we accumulate is optional. The noise of my Bearcat shredder doesn't bother anyone and the smoke raised by the burning of larger wooden limbs and trash wood is not offensive to my distant neighbors. I usually burn on the beach. I like the shredded material however because it returns fibre to the soil when composted and supplies useful material for chipped pathways, an advantage on the wet coast. In the wet months I can burn all the paper trash in the incinerator as well and use the ash in the compost for phosphorous. All told this is a pretty good system if you live in the country. I love power tools for gardening. I couldn't shred or use a blower or my weed eater or power washer in Lotus city without constantly irritating my neighbors who were mostly urban green. In my medical practice I saw too many chainsaw injuries to be comfortable with one. I have avoided that useful tool with a bit of reluctance. Four fifths of a loaf is better than no loaf. I hand turn my compost heap but also use a five horse power Honda tiller to mix it when it starts to return to black. Having the capacity to turn most of the biodegradable material back into the ground gives me a feeling of providing replenishment that is somewhat satisfying. I suppose the price of shredding is noise pollution, and burning, nose pollution, but I at least am dealing with my own trash and not relying on others. That gives me some satisfaction!

Sex in the Island

It's spring in Lotus Island and the harbour is abuzz with incipient love making activity! The Oyster Catchers have returned. The couples are never far apart from one another. They always announce their return with high piping whistling. The Blue Herons are battling for tree space for nesting in the same large Douglas fir over our studio. My daughter and her friend counted six herons squabbling, apparently about which branch should be allotted to them. The pianist thinks some of them are yearlings longing to return to a nest and are being kicked out. I'm not sure how many herons constitute a heronry. The diving ducks, buffleheads and mergansers are still waiting the herring return so they can fatten up and migrate elsewhere for nesting. The dabbling ducks (American Widgeons) will eat the eelgrass with even more relish once the herring eggs are on it and the gulls and crows will feed on the loose eggs lapping at the shoreline. All that protein enhances fertility! In the meantime the herring are on the way. The harbour seals are about to take pleasure in one another and later, dine on herring. If you have a dog in your walk on the beach, the seals follow you with great interest. The small birds in the hedgerow at the beach are busy nest building in the hedge. The little males stand a vigilant guard on top of the spent Black bamboo stakes that I leave for them. The pianist is an eagle devotee and tells me they are now in the process of nest renewal and refurbishing and will soon continue their connubial relationship! There is a lot more interesting variety of sex on Lotus Island than Sex in the City.

Collagen or Cojones

The more euphemistic of us would describe a metaphor for the strong and resilient as in possession of "lots of collagen" (fibre). It is not sexist and is a rounded description of the inner toughness of either sex. I don't just refer to " moral fibre", though that also, but collagen is a fibre that maintains and provides strength to our soft tissue structure. It's what holds us together! How really, can "having balls or cojones" provide any quality in describing the inner strength of the beautiful gender, let alone men? I suppose "having backbone" is an alternative that is apt as a neutral expression for both men and women. For the orthopedic surgeon, "collagen and backbone" are part of our lexicon and are preferable to "balls "for toughness or staying power. The orthopedic terms just don't have as much colour. How about "having good ground substance?" Ground substance is the intercellular material in which the collagen lies. We could say the strong and resilient have good ground substance. They are "well grounded"! The other fibre we have in our soft tissue is "elastin". It gives flexibility to the soft tissue in anatomical areas where more soft tissue movement is needed. Flexibility is an aspect that implies real strength. The term "balls " applied to women seems to me derogation, or if not generally considered so, it should be. Having a wife and daughters with strong character, I wouldn't consider saying they had "cojones". Cojones is a choice no man can avoid, and no woman would wish. It's time we stopped lapsing into unimaginative and inappropriate descriptors of the human condition.

Saltpetre, gunpowder and libido

I remember from my youth, two brushes of a totally different nature with saltpetre! There was an abiding mythology in the residences at the university that the food supplied to students in residence was adulterated with saltpetre. That, coupled with the equal myth that saltpetre reduced the libido of the young, was enough to foster a seasoning of mistrust! I was so shy in my first year of university that I would not have recognized saltpetre's effect, real or fanciful. Moreover there is no scientific evidence of saltpetre producing a diminution of libidinous height or its implementation. More likely, worry, late nights, loneliness, maladaption and culture shock of the young, were the proximate causes. We never talked much about the suspicion of adulteration because, in the early fifties we all still did exactly as we were told by our teachers and the institution and believed that they were always right; at least most of us did. The other contact with saltpetre and a more exciting remembrance is making gunpowder in grade eight with my friends. We mixed saltpetre, ground charcoal, and flowers of sulfur in equal proportion 'til the color was a dark and dirty green. I can still see in my mind today the color of our recipe. Little boys blowing up things in the town garbage dump! What was the druggist, as he was known then, thinking of when he gave us those ingredients? In some ways it must have been a much freer time with less supervision. How we could have avoided blowing ourselves up is even more mysterious. Saltpetre sans Libido at university; Brimstone and Violence in the town dump; Naivety following Innocence in the pediatric and adolescent ages.

The hockey referee

My dad in the 1940's was a hockey referee for intermediate hockey throughout the Province of Saskatchewan; one of the cradles of hockey excellence. He was busy with this activity every winter through this period and though the war was on, there were still first class hockey players of an older and largely farm generation that were exempted from war service. You can't farm in the winter in Saskatchewan but you can skate, curl, play hockey, listen to the wartime radio news and watch the Movie Tone News. We lived for sport in the winter. My dad as a referee, knew the hockey rulebook backwards. We lived in Kindersley, which was a hotbed for sports. My dad was one of the smoothest skaters I ever saw and you could see it when he went back and forth following the play. He played hockey as a young man but I don't think he was particularly good, though he would never admit it. Since I loved my dad, and hated it when the crowd booed him for a call he made; I watched the referees as much as the hockey players. If you watch hockey on TV these days, the referees are usually invisible unless they are enjoined in some sort of dispute. Watching the referees is an interesting gestalt. There is a parallel activity going on, with a novel content that no one short of the supervisor of referees probably ever sees. The whole is greater than the sum of its parts. That may be true but it is interesting to deconstruct the whole and look at a part once in a while. This applies to most stuff! Peripheral vision! Try it! I don't recommend it as a steady diet, but it is an eye-opener. In every job there is an under girding that performs an unsung and rarely noticed role! I suppose I would have never thought to concentrate on the referees in a hockey game, except for those recollections about my dad.

Mona Lisa

She had been sitting for a fairly long period and had to go to the bathroom and her leg kept going to sleep. "Can we take a break?" she asked. "Just a couple of minutes." he said, " I'm tidying up something." A trace of amusement passed her face and she shifted slightly to wait. He looked up just as the wisp of amusement was there and it was imprinted on his unconscious memory. He painted it in. He later showed the portrait to His Eminence. "Very average painting " the Eminence observed, "but there is something intriguing about the face." Then later he made a fuller comment on the portrait and observed that the enigmatic smile was significant, as it reflected a depth of both sorrow and joy; that life and death and goodness and sin were omnipresent, as part of the human condition. Centuries later the enigma of the smile continued to confound as gallery travelers marveled at what they were told to see.

So, dear Brutus, let us not be airy-fairy,

If you hear a chirping in the bush,

It's probably a sparrow and not a canary!

Fly Fishing Fiasco

A number of years ago I was captivated by the romance of fly-fishing. The thought of immersing myself in the wilds of nature, wading a small stream with the finesse brought by casting a dry fly to a rising trout seemed an experience "du jour" for a person of my precious sensibilities. Accordingly, I purchased fly fishing tackle for dry fly fishing including the recommended flies for our area. Since I had not done any such casting before, having only experienced trolling a wet fly behind a row boat in the high lakes of the B.C. interior, I resolved to practice casting on our lawn. After several weeks of diligent work I was pleased with my progress and no longer wrapped my line around my head or snagged myself in the trousers. I could cast a fair length and hit a modestly small target area. The pianist and our children arranged a picnic at the Sooke River where trout were known to lurk. Before the picnic meal, I donned my gear for wading and proceeded with my tackle and flies. Resting against a tree in the little park were two farmers in coveralls watching me as I cast to and fro with considerable aplomb. I thought they were probably admiring my technique. It was clearly a poor fishing day and my efforts were not rewarded. I repaired to the family for our picnic. As the sun started to go down one could see little circles appear on the smooth flowing river. The farmers took off their coveralls and waded into the river under the observant view of my children. They cast hither and yon with practiced skill contrasting with my underdeveloped technique. They left with several trout each. I was properly chastened, but love is a mighty thing and I received much approbation for my effort from my family, which lessened the blow.

Memory or money

The pianist and I are becoming decrepit but not demented. We have "stuff" to unload eventually whose value is memorable, not monetary. Whose memory? Mostly ours. That is the trouble with "stuff". Our stuff becomes a legend in my own mind chiefly because it is a reminder of the events of our life; ever present icons of the fragments of our existence. "How", someone might say, "can you worship your stuff as you do? You must be some sort of materialist, placing an inordinate value on 'things' rather than proper life principles." When we acquired the prized possession of old so-and-so, our relative, in the olden days, we wondered why so much fuss was made of this "thing"! I dismissively said, "fuggedaboudit!" Now I know! Most of the stuff the pianist and I will leave has many memories for us, yet it will have little value for others. In the mobile society we have today, and the disposable culture we have fostered, there is not an abundance of genuine heirlooms with intrinsic value that are one's own heritage. Sure, if you have enough money you can buy someone else's heirloom, but so what! It comes without your genes attached. I don't want to burden our children with the icons of my memory, but still we have things that they will treasure that are part of their memory and part of their genes. As I have recorded before and bears repeating, (paraphrased) "Don't be like as ass, whose back with heavy ingots bowed, you carry them but a journey, 'til death unloads you." (Measure for Measure). Easier said than avoided! Memories are light; ingots are heavy!

Gladiolus and Mums

Thirty or forty years ago the gladiolus was a stunning exhibition flower that engaged the best of growers in producing, propagating and hybridizing a truly noble species! The demise of the exhibition gladiolus, and its retreat to third-rate florist varieties, is caused by and accompanied with, the demise of the home vegetable and cut flower garden. The gladiolus was never a suitable plant in a landscaping scene and landscaping is now all the rage. Landscaping sells! Zeitgeist rules! It's the end of an era but it's too bad. Sure, the fall fairs always have a few little exceptions but they really do not rate. In the days of yore my dad could buy large corms of old varieties like Red Charm for $ 4.00 a hundred and Elizabeth the Queen for $5.00 a hundred, from Milton Jack at Hatzic Lake. With that volume you could produce champion specimens. The range of varieties available was huge. There are few, if any bulb farms now solely devoted to exhibition gladiolus. It's the same decline in numbers with the Chrysanthemum aficionados. The Mum group in Lotus City are a small and talented bunch. They grow the most beautiful muted disbuds you've ever seen but their ranks thin every year despite the extraordinary attempts they make to recruit new enthusiasts. Again the popularity falls short due to the need for a vegetable and cut flower garden for champion mums, rather than everything dedicated to landscape. It is sad to see skills sacrificed on the altar of landscape cosmetics. Surely there is room for both styles. If more people were encouraged to grow these flowers again, the cost would be affordable, the beauty pageants would flower, and the standards would be maintained.

Impetuous gardening

A man without a plan is like Don Quixote mounting his horse and riding off in all directions. A man with a bad plan is even less well off! I had a wet spot in my garden that was marshy in the winter and so, some time ago, thought I would plant cranberries there since they grow well here in the Pacific Northwest. The peaty bogs in the Fraser Delta grow beautiful blueberries and cranberries and the fields are spectacular in the fall when they turn deep reddish orange. I phoned a commercial cranberry farmer in the Delta to ask what to do to plant a cranberry bog. He said they mowed the plants after harvest and I was welcome to cuttings since they threw them away. There is nothing better than free. I drove to the Delta farm and he gave me two full garbage bags of his mowings. I built a bed with a substantial soil addition in my wet area and spent a long time planting my cuttings in a bed 5 feet by 30 feet. The cuttings were about 4 to 6 inches high. Most of them took root, but so did the weeds. It was frightful. My little transplants were inundated. The task of weeding was daunting and after a half day of labor and scant inroads I realized I was defeated. Too impetuous; bad planning. I should have summer fallowed for one or two seasons before starting such a project. Too big a hand in the cookie jar! Eyes too big for the stomach! Besides I rationalized, "How many cranberries do you really need?" It was really just the idea! Another fruit to grow! Another idea to try! I transplanted my Gunnera into the erstwhile cranberry bed. Gunnera is much more user friendly.

Unnatural Act

I was removing, with difficulty, a string of outside Christmas lights from the quince tree! Some of the smaller branches were traumatized as the electrical wires clung to them and the freezing cold had rendered the branches rather brittle. As I was working away on the stepladder a small voice said, "You've made me look like a tart!" Then the voice said, "you've spent a long time yapping about Mother Nature, and how organic you are, and you even quoted a poem about me, and now you have made me into a freak!" I must say I was taken aback by this tree's assertion, as I hadn't meant any disrespect! I didn't think it was unseemly to string lights on living bones but now I realize it is an unnatural act and has nothing to do with Christmas either! "I guess you are right that I am a hypocrite", I said," but it was out of ignorance rather than intent." "No way", the quince said,"You have made such heavy weather of your connection to the vegetable world and apparently worshipped the dialogue between us. It gives us the suspicion now that you are a person who talks a good game but really has little understanding or respectfulness for living bones. Rather than your feeble attempt to illuminate me, try to illuminate yourself!" Well, you can readily see that I felt pretty crushed, particularly since she has provided faithfully every year, beautiful quince for jellies and preserves, a home every year for the Western Flycatchers that grace our life, and she never develops powdery mildew. Our quince is sweet! They have obviously discussed the matter in the orchard and I am properly reprimanded. I have assured her that I will not repeat any unnatural acts in the future and will scale down my rhetoric; beating my breast about how connected I am, when they really know better!

The Extra Spoon

We had the usual collection of matching spoons, knives, and forks when the children were growing up in Lotus City. In addition, there was a spoon that was not quite the same configuration as the other teaspoons. It was less oblong and a little squarer! It lived in the same tray with the regular teaspoons. Trivial as it may seem, this extra spoon became "a cause celebre" in our family that generated at times heated discussions with respect to ownership. The children vied to do the table setting to take possession of the extra spoon. It's hard to know where it all started, but clearly once one person wanted it, it became a source of minor veneration. Rational folks, even in the pediatric age group may have recognized the matter as one without merit. Not so our offspring. Matters of the heart and issues of entitlement can raise the stakes! Reason goes out the window. We want something that others do not, or cannot have, even though we lust after the acceptance of the group. Something that sets us apart, but not too much! 30 or so years later, living on Lotus Island I have discovered for some time that we have a different, newer, extra spoon in a different set of matched tableware. It is not exactly like the extra spoon of yesteryear but it is clearly an outlier. It is of no interest to my grandchildren. It has no intrinsic value! It is only of value as most material things are if someone else wants it too. Today the extra spoon sits in the tray with the other teaspoons and I occasionally speak to it, to remind it how indifferent we all are about it. Not, "Deja vu all over again!"

Peripheral Vision

When Hercule Poirot solves a difficult case it is because he sees more than meets the eye. When the radiologist focuses on the center of the radiograph, looking at the condition for which the image was taken and neglects to look at the edges of the film for other things, stuff gets overlooked. The great painters spend much time on the periphery of the painting, not just at the golden mean. There is a lesson here for the gardeners who would be true to their craft. It is not just what is seen that is important, but that which is not clearly seen. That which must be looked for! The boundaries of our plot that we have applied with brush strokes over the years have intimate details and secrets that only we know about. You probably value the unseen, the secret and the inobvious as much as the familiar. If we neglect our boundaries for the seen only, we will not have a private place that one can choose to share, or not share, with someone who loves a garden as much as we do. Intimacy means sharing secrets as well as triumphs or disasters. They come in ample supply in the garden for all of us. Humility is a chastening thing, but it leads to knowledge. I never learned much by my successes, but plenty with the failures. As Hannah, who quoted Leonard Cohen, who paraphrased the Scripture says, "There is a crack in everything. That's how the light gets in." Give yourself a still,small, dark place in the garden that is not for display, but only for those that can see more than meets the eye.

Sex in the Greenhouse

Everyday I water my greenhouse tomatoes, tie them up as they race upward along with the cukes. I fertilize my tomato blossoms at the same time. I have no birds or bees in the greenhouse so the tomatoes have to manage with my brush. The cukes are parthogenetic so can exist without the brush of an elderly eclectic gentleman. The tomatoes need cross fertilizing, but are of the same variety, so they have a lot in common and will give rise to a homogenous crowd of fruit, unlike the potential for new and interesting offspring from different varieties. The little blossoms have responded to my dusting with an enormous production of fruit. There is every reason why tomatoes were originally termed the love apple (pomme d'amour). They respond with gusto! They are fruitful! They were feared to cause uncontrolled eroticism. They fit the bill, "to go forth and multiply." I go down the row, and then up the row, moving the pollen dust to the right and left in order to give best exposure. Just remember these tomato blossoms are captive creatures. I worry about what they think of me. Do they see me as just a pimp, transferring pollen from the unwanted to the disinterested? Or as a member of ménage a trois, sticking my nose into a group where I do not belong? It makes me sheepish! They have an inability to live and thrive autonomously because I have confined them to a pot and limited their horizons. The blossoms have no control of their own life and scope because of the cloistered situation I have placed them in. Since I have not given them the freedom to seek fertilization by natural means, I owe it to them to protect and nurture. I know for them it is second best and I always thank them. Mother Nature also loves them! Respect Life!

Birdie Num Nums

In the ongoing battle to defend one's berry patch against the avian horde, care has to be exercised that one doesn't fatally trap the birdie in one's net. If one is going to grow birdie num nums, prepare to succeed occasionally and fail often. I have given up netting the loganberries on the fence, but they are so prolific the birds always leave enough for us. Strawberries are easier to net and the birds don't get caught. We just lay the nets on the top of the plants. Now that the strawberries are finished, I have mowed the patch to encourage new growth. Raspberries are impossible for me to effectively net. Birds always seem to get in, but the few robins do little damage since the berries come on so fast. I am ambivalent about berry eating birds since we have such a congregation, but I guess it's just about food competition, them and us. I planted the berries but cannot claim ownership! I can't blame the birds as their tune is harmonized to Mother Nature's song, not mine, and I want to avoid raising the ire of the accompanying bird lover's chorus. We have two sweet cherry trees and we never get a cherry! The birds eat them before they turn pink. I have spent the last three days patching holes in the blueberry nets. I'm winning! For the pianist and me, blueberries are people num nums. We draw the line at birds and blueberries. The birds can be voracious over blueberries and it seems mainly the young, speckled breasted robins that think since they were born here this is their place so they are incautious and brazen. The impelling reason to patch all the holes in the nets is because the young birds can find their way in, but not out. I make morning rounds to shoo them out if they are imprisoned. They can get inextricabley tangled in the netting and I don't want a funereal blueberry patch with dead young robins dangling on the netting. It is inharmonious to pick blueberries in the midst of a grotesquerie!

Blueberry nets

We have had large, small mesh old fishing nets, (probably herring or anchovy), for many years. The nets are still serviceable though need repairs from time to time. They are much better than the more rigid plastic garden netting. My grand daughter, my son in law, and I put up the nets on our blueberry patch last week. It's a big patch, 20 by 55 feet and takes a lot of net. The robins are relentless in their attempts to breach our defenses. Tying the several nets together and propping the ceiling net with struts is a major undertaking for the day. If you don't net your blueberries here on Lotus island in the Salish Sea, you will not have any blueberries. They ripen of course, in sequence over a three-month period within the clusters rather than all at once. That is why the commercial berries are expensive since they require being selectively hand picked. Labor intensive! The smart birds would selectively pick, or peck the ripe ones on a daily basis if they have a chance and a flock could keep up with the ripe berries if they were not netted. The first year that I had a big crop in the 80's I didn't net and wondered why my berries never ripened 'til the season was half over. We remove the nets in the early fall since the foliage color is spectacular. The blueberries are user friendly as they do not need spraying and produce from both old and new wood, so pruning is simply tidying. We're looking forward to three month's bounty! The pianist is known amongst our family and friends for blueberry pancakes and blueberry muffins. The piece d' resistance however, is blueberry pie, built with 50% cooked and 50% raw berries, poured into a baked pie crust, topped with whipped cream.

Susan Sibbald

My Grandmother, born Georgina Lyall, was a great granddaughter of Susan Sibbald. Susan was born in 1783 in Fowey, Cornwall and in 1835 came as a widow to what is now near Georgina, Ontario. She built a house and a church on the farm she purchased, which is now a park and historic monument at Sibbald Point, Lake Simcoe. Susan, who was raised in a wealthy family, wrote a book, The Memoirs of Susan Sibbald that was eventually published in 1926, and is presently available since it has been republished! The book is chiefly concerned with her life from 1783 to 1812, though there are later chapters on the Canadian portion of her life at Lake Simcoe. The book is a treasure, depicting the manners, dress, leisure, travel, the panorama of friends and notables and the household life of the wealthy gentry of the time at home in Cornwall and Scotland near Melrose. Curiously, despite contemporary with the time of Napoleon, and Waterloo, Nelson and Trafalgar, and despite the fact that most of her family were Navy or Army with Commissions, her world was seemingly indifferent to these events! It is a remarkable chronicle of an indulgent and shallow lifestyle that was the only permissible way for such a startlingly intelligent woman like her to exist in that stratum of society! Here is an excerpt from the childhood portion of the memoirs; "In passing the kitchen department, what a savoury smell would issue forth, may be a roast Goose, Ducks and green peas, or maybe a Hare for supper, or as greater delicacies still, a Turkey, Guinea fowl or Peacock. We always knew when the jack was wanted by Cook's anxious call for "Sancho", the turnspit, a little yellow crooked legged dog, and many a time we have heard the crack of a whip, a cry of distress, and the jack screaming for lack of oil. For poor little Sancho, being in his treadmill, climbing with might and main, anticipating his feast in the dripping pan, would stop suddenly on hearing our voices, and get from the cook what he did not like to feel, or we to hear." Maybe the past is a different country after all.

Make your bed!

It helps one's equanimity if the bed is made before you leave the bedroom every day! Some say, "Pshaw, why do that when you are just going to get into it again later?" The pianist in her other life was an old time nurse. She could make the bed so tight that you could bounce a quarter on it. There were no wrinkles in the bed sheets. They were tucked in tight at the foot of the bed. When you climbed under the covers at night your feet were never caught into folds of sheet, or stuck out the bottom. The sheets felt cool and crisp. The pillows were all turned and fluffed. The head sank into the fluffed pillow as if it were a cloud. The room was aired, the dirty linen put in the hamper, and the clothing hung up. The room was cool and smelled like fresh air! The "dressed up" pillows were placed over the working pillows to give a sense of elegance, matching the duvet. To come into such a room at the end of day is to receive a warm embrace. No bedbug dare enter and propagate in this mattress that is turned and rotated at intervals. At a certain age, important things for wellbeing are, a good sleep and regular, sit down meals. The pianist has been away for a week. I'm batching! My bed making skills are clearly wanting! The bedroom does not look like the "sanctum sanctorum" we have made it in the past. My effort, sadly lacking, is no better than my cooking! The bedroom has a somewhat jumbled look and is not particularly inviting. Some might say, "You've made your own bed, so lie in it! " I'm going to do better tomorrow morning!

Doomed

The Northwestern crow is normally a gregarious animal. A broken winged crow walked up the road path in front of my window a few days ago. That waddling, bowlegged strut was altered by the broken right wing that dragged on the stones. As I watched, his walk was slow and deliberate. He knew, I think, that he was doomed! He had a stoic look on his face that said it all. I don't understand the entire multiple, complex phrasing the crow uses, but I know body language pretty well, and I know that crow knew he was walking to the abyss! He was silent! I never thought I would see him again and put it out of my mind. I was working in the orchard two days later and there he was, still alive, still hopping from bush to bush, hiding to avoid detection. Hiding from the predators, both his own kind, and the raptors! Still doomed! It doesn't seem fair. You or I may break a leg or arm and it is often a minor inconvenience; rarely if ever a tragedy, and hardly are we doomed. If we were, we would not likely bear our fate with the stoic silence and grim recognition of the injured crow. He gave no quarter and receives none.

Theatrical Eating

The pianist and I, in the halcyon days of yesteryear in Lotus City would occasionally splurge at the Marina restaurant, a deliciously ambient eatery on the waterfront. Being of an age when food is important and cooking superbly, has not dissuaded the pianist from enjoying theatrical eating on special occasions! To experience eating without crowding, and without hurrying, and every course provided with flourish and drama has helped to make us feel special. The Cherries Jubilee, the Baked Alaska and the Crepes were finished at the tableside with flourish! The "piece de resistance" was the Caesar salad! The maitre d' in formal dress with white gloves of course, would bring his ingredients to the tableside. He used a massive wooden bowl with beautiful grain. He crushed anchovies against the side of the bowl, mixed them with a raw egg cracked from a height and combined pressed garlic, pepper and salt, a touch of lemon, grated parmesan, olive oil and Worcestershire sauce! All of this was done with elegant ease. He had done it hundreds of times. Each time was an art form! He mixed with a fork. At the end of it all, he gently tossed in large pieces of crisp unbroken Romaine. If there were croutons, I can't recall. To finish the romance with a flambé of Cherries Jubilee, or Crepes in brandy, or a fiery Baked Alaska, told you your meal was a labor of love and skill! As the sun sank in the west, the eastern islands became illuminated in a suffused pink, and the sailboats rocked gently in a tiny breeze. We lingered over our coffee, the day done. I can't and won't apologize for the periodic pampering!

Canada Geese and Black Aphids

Today, two events of interest were observed as I was toiling in the soil. The egg shakers from the Fish and Wild Life clearly missed two nests of Canada Geese and as a result of this oversight, two sets of parents have finally ventured out into the harbour at Lotus Island with four adolescents each. The adolescents are about half size and are all brown with a slight white backside. They stick closely together with one another and their parents because the Eagles are actively feeding their fledglings. About another fifty adult geese, bereft of goslings, hunker along, trailing after the families. The trailers are victims of the egg shakers no doubt. I guess we need to control the Canada goose population, but the forlorn trailers seem sad. Don't ask me how I know, I just do! For some reason the geese never come up to the lawn these days but stick to the harbour and the sea weed food source, particularly eel grass. That saves a lot of shoe fouling goose poop. They are enormously sedate and hardly honk unless they fly! The other event to report is the heat has really struck here on Lotus Island and that means, with rapid dahlia growth and the humidity, the black aphids have appeared on the early flower bud stems. There are a few Ladybugs around to eat them, but despite that help, the aphid colonies grow rapidly. Black aphids are remarkably easy to deal with mechanically by daily inspection, wiping them clean of the stem with finger and thumb and then top spray with water. The pianist thinks I should try Avon Bubble Bath so I am going to give it a go. A little soap never hurt plant or beast. The aphids seem endemic rather than epidemic, so a daily round and a little early attention is what is required for the dahlias that are afflicted. No poisons are necessary! No other crisis is looming large on Lotus Island today! Good news is not banal! Amor de Cosmos would have fitted in perfectly here.

Scapegoats

In the 556 archeologically identified healing temples of Asklepius in ancient Greece and Rome and in the temples of Israel in the period of the Ancient of Days, goats and other animals including chickens or doves for small sins, were sacrificed to assuage the gods, or God. These sacrifices were "scapegoats". In Ashkelon it was the firstborn child sacrificed and in the Aztec culture, the best looking girl in town. They substituted for the sins of others and paid the price. The concept of Jesus as the "scapegoat" of the world originated later with the construct of atonement, but as far as I can see, he never allowed people to get off the hook for their own actions in his lifetime. They needed to move off the spot for salvation. We still have scapegoats of a different kind. We might even allow them to sacrifice themselves to atone for us. That attribution is, to your parents, your work colleagues, your mate, your friends, your teacher, the other race, your spiritual advisor, or even your dog. They are as much positioned as a scapegoat as the sacrificed in the olden days. Piet Hein said, "What ever doesn't kill you makes you stronger!" We have to take responsibility for our actions, willing ourselves to do the right thing, come what may, and loving our God-given selves for what we are rather than what we think we might have been. We can't forever blame anyone else or anything else! That's not the way out of the morass! As Pogo said, "We have seen the enemy, and it is us!"

Raspberry and Pea pickin'

My dad would never let the children pick raspberries or peas, bless his pea pickin' heart. He was afraid they would tramp on next year's raspberry canes, and they did! He knew they would pick an unripe raspberry with one hand and tear off the whole cluster, ripe and unripe and they did. He also complained that they didn't have soft hands so they squashed the ripe berries. I heard this all my childhood so I have followed his advice. He was right! "The same applies to peas.", he groused, "They pull them straight with one hand and rip the vine from the ground. They have to use two hands, one to hold the stem and one to pick the pod. I don't want dried peas after they leave!" When I was a boy we didn't, as I recall, have the pea varieties that ripen all at once, like the commercial growers want. They pick them once and that's it! Our old fashioned peas, Lincoln, Tall Telephone, and others produced over time, so preserving the vines was crucial. He was right again, bless his cotton picking', pea picker heart. I was picking raspberries today for the first time and thinking back to all of this. My patch has about five varieties planted randomly over the years as "fill-ins". They vary as to both size and color, mellow and tart and date of ripening. Color is OK as an indicator, but for me, because of ripe color differences, texture from a gentle squeeze with such variable berries is more accurate. I'm careful of my new canes, and always pick with two hands. My gentle squeeze is softer than a good retriever's mouth. I've given up on the peas since the California Quail find the sprouting plants delicious and the feral bunnies that have arrived would certainly feel the same if they had the chance.

The Archie Club

When my daughter was 12 or so, the pianist sent her to Simpson-Sears to pick up a prepaid purchase. The mail order clerk asked for some identification and the only thing she had in her wallet was her membership in the Archie Club. There was no hassle from the department store since a member in good standing of the Archie Club would be deemed to have some status and good taste in men. Archie was cool but also beautifully naïve; a characteristic that endeared him to hundreds of young girls. They didn't identify with the sly, the macho, and the slick. The clerk would have recognized a fellow traveler; albeit only twelve. Even though Archie struggled with the usual trials and temptations, he seemed to effortlessly overcome them with a continuing good nature. What's not to love? Certainly the Archie Club card today won't net you much headway at the airport or the customs office, but it tells us where your values are. Even more beautifully naive was Beaver! He was a bit younger than Archie but still had that endearing characteristic that never provoked fear, always comfort. Funny comfort! You could rely on Beaver to say what he thought. He was normal. In my daughter's day the kids were classified as baddy-bads, goody-goods and normals. My kids always described themselves as normals, but I am not always sure they were honest about that. The principal said to Beaver, "Why do you want to be a garbage collector when you grow up, Beaver? " He replied, "Well, you don't have to wash your hands so much, and people don't mind if you smell." Beaver was not ready for Betty and Veronica at that stage of his life, but the candor he displayed would eventually give Archie "a run for his money."

Asymmetry

I was measuring the leg lengths and calf girths of a patient in the office the other day. She said, " Are they the same?" " Nope", I said, "They are never the same!" "How come?" she said! "Well", I said, "God was never an engineer. He has always been an artist, so we are not made with a slide rule." Well, she thought that was the funniest thing she had heard all day and laughed and laughed and laughed. It's not the first time I've used that silly response with a patient. Even a little knowledge of embryology is a great thing. R.I.Harris, the doyen of Canadian orthopedics, measured the leg lengths of one thousand consecutive young army recruits in 1941. Up to 3/4 of an inch of discrepancy was determined by him to be within normal limits. Most of recruits never knew they had a leg length discrepancy. Asymmetry is the order of the day for human beings, unrelated to disease or disorder. If you have ever seen a composite made of the two sides of your face, the nature and degree of asymmetry becomes readily apparent. You will hardly recognize yourself! Of course the extent of variability of asymmetry has to have a baseline of normality. Woe betide the surgeon who fails to recognize or accept the nuances of asymmetry the Creation Artist provided. If something goes wrong in a surgical case where the indications for surgery were marginal, he may find himself up the creek without a paddle. One shoulder is lower than the other, one nut is lower and smaller than the other, and breasts are at different levels and so on. That's what makes us interesting and unique. Vive La Difference!

A clear perspective of your own point of view

In 1969 and earlier, I was on call for orthopedic injuries at a downtown hospital in Lotus City. It was hard work and I was on call every other night, frequently tied up for hours. The Emergency Department had a number of doctor's parking spaces adjacent to it, but often they were filled not only by doctors but also by police who were often part of the scene. I was a bit cocky and felt if the police were in one of the doctor-designated spaces and it was fully occupied, I could park with impunity on the adjacent street. I got a lot of parking tickets which I ignored as I was convinced of my own rectitude in the matter. One day when the pianist was particularly busy with children she received a visitor from the police department who told her I was under arrest for failure to pay multiple parking tickets and should appear at the station. I hastened down to the station, was informed of the charges, booked, fingerprinted, and jailed. The desk sergeant said I could make bail. Since I was a doctor, and given the situation, I believed they were unfairly dealing with me. Still, I was my own worst enemy and down deep I knew it. I made bail and later, as I appeared before the judge, I argued my case as I thought it was a good one. The judge smiled and said, " 50 dollars or ten days, and all your ticket arrears are to be paid." I smiled back and bit the bullet. Never walk loudly and carry a small stick! I learned my lesson!

You are your Name

In 1979 several of us took on the mentorship of a Vietnamese boat family that had spent 2 years in a Malaysian camp before they came to Canada. The father of the family spoke to me about 2 weeks after they had arrived to tell me that the name recorded by the immigration at entry was incorrect. They had reversed his name. Moreover, it was misspelled as well. I said to him, "No problem. We'll just go down to the customs and immigration office and clear it up." Given that this was a busy time, he and I waited in a lineup for over an hour 'til we could be processed. I explained the situation carefully to the official at the wicket. She looked at me and said, " I'm afraid it is too late to change that name now. He has been through customs and the name he has been provided is now his name." When I tried to explain the importance of his concern she treated us as if we were daft! Well! She didn't know that you are your name. When Jacob wrestled with the proxy for God, and was given the name of Israel, he became Israel. It was the ground of his being and important to him. Canada Customs and Immigration is not God, so it isn't the same. Our name is the label whereby we identify ourselves and our tribe and where we slot ourselves in the human race. It may not seem important to some but it was important to him. About all that man had at that time was his name, and a suit of issued clothing, and me. We left the office and I phoned my MP, Don Munro and got him in Ottawa within minutes. I told him what happened and he said "That's bullshit! Leave it to me! Go right back there now! " I know it's a bit sinful of me but I felt a small surge of triumph that day. It's not often that you can win against the bureaucracy. I forgot for the moment that it was all about him and his name, and not about me!

Mouse

Every house including ours has night sounds. It's been particularly cold on Lotus Island this week and the temperature gradients between the inside and the outside make the beams and studs shift and squeak and crack a little, the wind shakes the house an infinitisimal degree, to which it nevertheless objects, and the boughs of the cedar, brush it gently. The sleeper who is hypervigilant also hears his ear and head contact on the pillow, his tinnitus, the bruit of the carotid pulse at times and the crow on the roof. These sounds we have become accustomed to and are unique to our house. Another's house sounds have different singularity. At 4 am this morning I awoke with a new and unaccustomed sound. Was it the icemaker dropping chunked ice, an intruder, or something else? As I went down the stairs into the kitchen where the sound was coming from, it seemed to be a metallic sound originating from the tile floor. There had been a suggestion that an uninvited visitor had arrived the day before and I had set a mousetrap that night on the floor beside a baseboard with bait of peanut butter. In the trap was a mouse and it was alive and struggling. The metallic sound came from the thrashing around on the tile. The mouse probably ventured further into the trap than usual to gnaw at the bait so his head was not crushed and he was caught in the trap by the body. I have always had a primal fear of vermin, a legacy from my mother and the Middle Ages. I could deal, albeit difficult, with a dead mouse but a living, wiggling, squiggling, leg and tail waving mouse that is in agony is a different matter. I went back to bed to await its death and silence. I couldn't sleep however; assailed with thoughts of the waning life force and with the reminder from the continuing sounds emanating from the kitchen floor. I took my courage and went back and put the mouse outside on the deck. Silence! This morning at 8 o'clock he was dead and had struggled for a further 18 inches, dragging the trap from where I laid him on the deck. I'm sorry! I must kill! Rest in Peace!

It's how you say it!

My youngest daughter's first job was a Pink Lady at the hospital in Lotus City. She was 15 years old but had talked them into hiring her by simple persistence. It was a summer job. This was 1978 and the nurses still wore white uniforms and there were other working groups of Pink Ladies, Yellow Ladies and Blue Men. Pink Ladies were the ward cleaning staff and my daughter really felt she belonged because our family were hospital people and were connected by both the pianist who worked there as a nurse, and me, on the wards every day since kingdom come. I think the cleaning staff had a very good union agreement at the time since the pianist constantly grumbled about how much our 15 year old was being paid in contrast to her, a registered nurse! But that is beside the point. My esteemed partner came onto the cardiac ward with a mild heart attack and was being actively investigated on the ward where our Pink Lady worked. She chatted with him every day as she cleaned around him since she knew him as my senior friend and he appeared to be doing very well according to her nightly report to us. Then one morning I got a distressed phone call from her to tell me that he had died! She had been sent by the head nurse to clean up the room where he had been. The bed had been stripped and the side tables emptied. She inquired where Dr. G was and the nurse said, ostensibly in a doleful voice, that Dr. G was "gone"! Then the nurse looked down at her feet. Body language! After the Pink Lady called me I phoned G's wife to give solace and to invite myself over to commiserate. She said cheerfully that she would love to see me. Then she said so would G as he had been discharged! Dr. G was not a "goner" at that time. Words associated with inappropriate body language have the power to mislead. Body language, even in the presence of a completely foreign tongue will communicate. The face, the hands, the eyes, the tone, the posture, the animation, will usually tell the aware what they need to know. We hear with the eyes as well as the ears. That's a real anatomy lesson!

The 50th wedding anniversary

The pianist and I are going to a 50th anniversary of long time friends this weekend. Most of the people we are going with are also 50th anniversary veterans. We have been to about six celebrations in the last five years including our own. Practically all of our friends are enjoying or enduring codgerhood or cronehood together. What is this? Is it a generational thing? We all, I think, promised to live together for better or for worse, for richer or poorer and in sickness and in health. Certainly, all those issues intervened from time to time, or enduringly so. Our children were key figures in the celebrations we attended, including our own. If it weren't for them, ours would have been a spartan affair. The blessing of children and grandchildren separates the gathering from anything else that one could experience. As my son Robert pointed out, this has more to say for them about the congregation and lineage of a family and the relationships that are fostered, than about longevity of the union. It was always called our celebration, as it is undoubtedly, but it really is, for the pianist and me, a celebration of those who have been part of us. I wonder if fifty years from now, will people still be doing this or will the institution of this kind of union, that forces the growth, fun, companionship, resilience, forgiveness, persistence, and love of every sort, still last? I hope so!

Prayer and profanity

In 1978 my 15 year old daughter and I came out to the cottage on Lotus Island in the Salish Sea for the evening. It was November and a looming dark, cold, and misty night. We came out for a short stint, me after work in my good suit and her, in school clothes. There was still a little daylight and she said to me "I'm going to row out and look at the crab trap." "OK " I said. As she left, I could see the tide was carrying her away from the trap. It suddenly started to rain and became darker. As I squinted across the harbour I lost sight of her, but I could clearly see the little islands, The Three Sisters, in the harbour beyond where she would have been. I was certain that she must be in the water! I raced over to the neighbor who had a boat, only to fall into a creek on the way , loaded with blackberry thorns and three feet of water. I struggled up the bank of the creek, praying mightily, covered in mud, with my trousers torn from the thorns. No one was home and the boat was nowhere in sight. I ran in a panic to another neighbor's door and l knocked loudly. He came out of the bedroom stark naked with his lady behind him, also close to starkers. I didn't notice! I said to him that my daughter might be in the water. He assured me my worry was groundless. Who knew? We went down his rickety steps to the beach and his rowboat. The tide was fully in and we were all standing in three feet of water, neighbor, lady, and me, all of us yelling into the mist. Suddenly, I heard the splashing of oars and a stream of invective. She hadn't drowned! That stream of profanity was in response to what she thought were young people making fun of her. I can't tell you how deliciously wonderful that swearing was. We must have been quite a sight! All shore people in mud, rags and less; daughter in good form. She seemed to have come up from nowhere!

Low threshold criers

When I would leave home to go to university, either after the holidays or the summer, my father would cry. It used to embarrass me because it didn't seem manly at that time. I certainly didn't cry. My father would also bawl every Christmas day that I can remember, ostensibly because his mother's funeral was on December 25, 1932. Every Christmas he said the same thing, word for word, "You boys don't know what it's like to lose a mother!" Not much later in life, I started to cry. Sometimes it was maudlin I am ashamed to admit. A sad, or happy movie with a poignant ending, an endearing embrace, bagpipes, Amazing Grace or sweet sad songs will do it. I have to take tissues to weddings and funerals. I have three brothers and two of us are criers! The two of us were never able to do a eulogy for our parents because we bawled our heads off and choked up. My other two brothers were at least as loving, but didn't cry, so were useful in all similar circumstances. The pianist and I have three children. The youngest displays my crying capacity. If we go to a movie there is always something to at least sniffle about. What is this curious dichotomy? In the practice of medicine, I encountered the saddest of events and crises in people's lives but my effectiveness never allowed even a trace of tear to pass my lids. My crying daughter is a nurse and experiences the same events in her work; related crises and sad events. She doesn't cry at work. I guess, in our jobs, the role we play accepts the nature of the work without a qualm. We wouldn't be useful otherwise. It seems however that the response that some of us have inherited, in our case from my father, allows us to wring out the feelings when it is safe to do so. There is something comforting about tear jerking activity. I don't get embarrassed anymore.

The California Quail

This Edenic patch called Lotus Island is within the most northern range for the California quail, a species of which we have in abundance! They are without doubt the most picturesque addition to any garden. Here, they seem to have several sets of chicks throughout the season and the chicks resemble little walnuts scurrying around, always close to cover near the underbrush. Several adults can be seen guarding a family of up to a baker's dozen little walnuts; parents and aunties all clicking vociferously if danger lurks or cover is needed. Lots of thick cover will assure you of a cavalcade of these feathered friends in your garden. I guess I really don't care if they eat all my new pea shoots in the garden. The quail have very little protection from the predators, crows and raptors. We have many eagles, hawks, crows and ravens. I hate to see the carnage but I suppose it's the way of the world. On the one hand, most creatures, including us, are engaged in eating one another. On the other hand, Al Capp invented the Shmoo that love to be eaten. In my opinion the quail is the closest thing I know that physically resembles the Shmoo. Given the hypervigilance of the adult quail, and the obedience of the offspring to the clicks, it's unlikely that the California quail is enchanted with the prospect of being eaten! The quail along with the bunny has the survival capacity as a species to endure by way of their procreative ability. Lucky for us!

Reading, ought and want

Ought and want have always been a dilemma for me. I have that deep seated little voice that says," You ought to know this for your own good," versus the other that says," Enjoy yourself, it's later than you think." Well it is late, I confess! Time is limited and the hours expended by reading a book that is uninspiring is time wasted. If you prize time, the need to be selective is important. It drives some of my loved ones crazy that I often read the first ten pages and the last ten pages of a book to decide if I will put in the time to read it. It's a little like wine tasting or sampling the food. It's not often that one goes wrong with this technique. Do I read Paradise Lost, a classic that I feel I should know, or John Grisham's novel, which I know will keep me awake? One is exciting, can be read in an evening and makes a good movie. The other is ponderous and difficult, but something I believe I ought to read once. On the other hand I will never read a John Grisham novel twice, because it's easy to remember, but the complexities of Paradise Lost will need to be reread. Cognitive dissonance! Milton would probably be better in the weekly book group I attend where we read together, monitored by our mentor John, a Middle English scholar. His style is Socratic and therefore promotes interactive learning. All good literature from any age is contemporary in mind and heart, but you have to learn the style and language to discern the nuances! With Middle English, the style and the vocabulary are a struggle though good translations abound. I must confess that good literature is some-times too taxing for my brain if I read alone. If we read as a group together in short segments and then deconstruct the segment we have read at length, the work becomes alive and immediate! I'm not always sure what good literature is! That is a subject that we have discussed and definitions are not self-evident. I think, forget the critics! Good literature for me is what makes me cry. That gives me joy. That enlarges my soul. What one remembers later and may dream about. Thoughts that tax my mind and stay with me. That changes my attitude and my action. That touches me. I think there is room for both the oughts and the wants in one's lifetime of reading. If I stick to classical literature with the help of good groups, and contemporary literature that I vet by author or sampling, I will minimize my wasted hours. Any age can be an age of enlightenment and enjoyment!

Summerhill revisited

The pianist and I were part of a group in the 1960's that embarked on establishing a progressive school for elementary children based on a Scottish educator's school-- Summerhill. The essence of the schooling theory of A.S.Neill was that education should, rather than be coercive, be provided at the initiative of the child. The theory proposed that education was a natural outcome provided the environment promoted enthusiasm and play as a major part of the programme. Our two eldest school age children were enrolled. We initially had a jewel of a principal who was a prime mover and brought her teaching concepts from the Berkley campus, of course! Unfortunately we lost her, and her drive, and never found another who could effectively implement the concept. We waited for the fun and playtime to end and the teaching of the three R's to begin; insinuating itself when the intrinsic enthusiasm for these skills would spontaneously arise. Two years elapsed and that blessing never occurred. Continuing play and fun were the order of the day. These were the 60's and remember, flower power and freedom were the Zeitgeist. The demographic of the classes was carefully selected by us to include a mix of income groups and ethnic heterogeneity, consistent with our philosophy. No government subsidy was provided, due to the "uniqueness" of our quest. My teacher friends thought we were crazy. We had monthly meetings to listen to the parents and the teachers going on endlessly about goals and objectives, the iniquity of assessments and the issues of simple order and hygiene that took second place to freedom of expression. We probably thought we were "avant garde" but in retrospect we were "rear bedraggled". Interestingly enough if one analyzed the parents in this "forward" looking group, they were virtually all from highly regulated, success driven, ultra formal educational environments. Why does that not surprise me now? Fortunately our kids caught up quickly when we gave up the utopian idea and moved back to regular school. I think the secret to success of any school, including the Summerhill clones, is the capacity and strength of the teacher and that was the downfall of our experiment rather than the concept. My daughter, who became a teacher in BC, was enthused about a teaching innovation with some of these elements called the Year 2,000 Programme, now abandoned. She was involved in its implementation and promotion, but was sorely disappointed when the teachers and government disavowed it. I can't help thinking she was coloured a bit by her Summerhill experience.

Summerhill revisited again

Our zeal for the alternative approach to education with the Summerhill template became of an almost cultish nature. The time and effort and money the pianist and I put into the organization was substantial. We, as a group of parents fed on one another's enthusiasm. The deconstruction of conventional child-raising activity was in process. Love and freedom replaced regulation and discipline. We swam against the tide. In our living room we had a monstrous bowl of junk candy from the corner grocery store that the children could help themselves to at any time. They did so freely. The theory was that they would spontaneously come to realize that candy was unhealthy and they would seek only nutritious food. It never happened. The building we rented as a school no longer became available to us so the pianist and I and four other families bought a house, to house our precious school. We put a new carpet in the house among other changes. The parent's committee took exception to our wish that the children not wear muddy shoes in the school as an infringement on their freedom of self-expression. We also made the house we purchased available to the principal and his father to live in, in return for janitorial duties. The house had oil fuelled, hot water heating with hot water radiators throughout. The pair went away for Christmas without telling anyone and the oil tank ran dry. It had snowed the day one of us went in to check and found all the radiators had been frozen and then split with a thaw. They were leaking water all over the new carpet. I remember that evening my friend and I digging around in the snow and the frozen ground trying to locate the buried oil tank somewhere in the yard. I said to him then, "No bloody school is worth this. This is the last straw for me!" We sold the house. A dismal end that had nothing further to do with principles of education for the pianist and me; an education nevertheless!

Symbiosis is not Co-dependency

I do the dishes in our house and the pianist does the cooking. This is highly satisfactory to both parties with few exceptions. The reason symbiosis is not co-dependency is the presence of " intelligent design" if you'll pardon a borrowed phrase. The pianist is a good cook, as her mother was. I take pride in a relatively clean kitchen at the end of it all. I am reminded "relative" is the operative word. Clean counters, a place for everything and everything more or less in its place. You should be able to put your hand on anything in the kitchen in the dark. I don't mean to be insufferable. It's just that if I have this role in retirement, then I have a right to an opinion about it. My one complaint, always ignored, is that the pianist invariably leaves food on her plate, no matter how much, or how little she initially took. Even this morning, the one piece of toast she ate had a tiny bit of crust uneaten, measuring 8 millimeters in diameter. I cannot understand the critical threshold of an appetite that is so finely tuned that couldn't cope with such. She states that her family taught that to eat everything on the plate implied that you were "greedy". I was taught in my family to eat everything because the poor starving people from elsewhere in the world would be sorrowful to see such waste. The upshot of this is, I always have to go to the garbage first with her plate to scrape, whereas my 'greed' driven approach is one move less. I can't emotionally put dirty dishes in the dishwasher. I have to rough wash them first! Don't ask me why? Probably blame the operating equipment room mentality. This kitchen activity has extended to many other aspects of our shared existence. It's symbiotic in that when in a pinch the roles can be reversed, not seamlessly, but without a disaster of great magnitude.

That's the fall back position in retirement. You can still be cheerfully, "a Jack of all trades and a master of none." The price of always licking your plate clean and never going to the garbage is tight trousers. I am not Jack Sprat! I wish we had a dog again!

The Grinches and the Olympic Flame

It's Halloween on Lotus island and the Olympic flame is arriving here at 2.30 pm by seaplane. It will be here for half an hour or so and many young people and families will be able to see it and be thrilled by it. However, we have a large number of home grown Grinches on Lotus Island. We are not "Whoville"! The Raging Grannies; the Marxist Leninists, the disaffected and the tax revolters may be out in force competing for the annual award of the Cup for the most Churlish. "A waste of money", they say! " What about the arts, the health, the climate, the war and the corruption?" All probably true, but please, let's at least have a little joy. I was going to go down to the dock to watch the floatplane come in the harbour and cheer, but I'm afraid the protesters will just make me cross. I'm staying home, making Jack-O- Lanterns for tonight and putting new batteries in my "Singing Fish". The pianist has made about 20 candy-coated apples with our label on them so the mothers will not worry about razor blades. What a world! The pianist thinks my "Singing Fish" might be scary but that's what Halloween is all about; All Hallows Eve! The following day; All Saints Day, the small children continue to be protected and hallowed by the saints called Parents.

Contract to tease

When my children were small I told many bedtime stories in which they were often the principal character. The events of the story were not pre-thought but simply unfolded at random; generally had a happy ending in which the characters had a somewhat heroic role. The stories often began with the generic, "Once upon a time ", and the contract to tease initially went like this! " Once upon a time, (Pause)," when the pigs chewed tobacco and the hens drank wine!" (Laughter). "No, come on, tell us a story." " OK, now I will. Once upon a time," (Longer pause) (tantalizing smile), "when the pigs chewed tobacco and the hens drank wine." (Loud laughter). Then the story would truly begin with "Once upon a time". Then later, " Tell another story." " OK I 'll tell you a story, (Pause) about Jack Mc Nory, and now my story's begun. I'll tell you another about his brother and now my story's done." (Laughter) "Please tell another story." "Ok, this time I will. There once was a calf, and that's half. They hung it on the wall. And that's all." (More laughter and pleadings), Then the second story would begin. At the young age they were, the familiar teasing was always funny and though totally predictable, was an expected ritual. If it was not done in this way there was a sense of loss. The teaser and the teased were bonded in the silliness of it all. Thank God for silly.

Moxie (Savvy) (Street smarts)

Elderly eclectic gentleman may be too prideful an eponym. Doddering old fool would be too much self-abasement. Being at the mid-spectrum of these poles, the development of moxie is essential. In matters of money management how the old are advised needs intelligent dissection. The television these days rarely programs for the old, but incessantly advertises at the old: alarm systems, bathtubs with doors, Chip mortgages, chairs on rails on stairs, and funeral insurance. We are beset by a constant bombardment of telephone salesmen and charity requests. It's easy to be dismissive about advertising and pressure selling, but I know times are not easy for many, and people are scrambling. My dad was very short of income when my family moved to Vancouver in the mid 50's. He worked in the daytime as a telegrapher in the CNR station, 8 am to 5 pm. To make ends meet he took another job. This is what he said in his memoir: "I worked in the Vancouver Herald for a short while to supplement our income, selling subscriptions over the phone. About fifty of us were in separate cubbyholes, and were given a sheet out of the phone book. You called each one with a sob story about paying for a crippled children's Easter Bunny bus and the like. You got 15 cents for each subscription sold and the manager got 5 cents for all subscriptions sold by the 50 cubbyhole occupants. The hours were 5 pm to 9 pm. I got home at 10 pm and ate. I caught the bus at 7 am next morning to go to my regular job. I made 15 dollars a week selling subscriptions." Every time I answer a "telephone pitch" I can't but help thinking of my dad, coping as best he could with an income shortfall. I'm ambivalent about the boiler rooms and the hardship of the sales persons because of my dad. We are called to value connectedness and avoid judgment. We can't really say we are able to walk in anyone else's shoes. I say to myself, "Just shut up and do your best!"

The Tortoise and the Hare

This morning the tree men came. They scampered up a 40-foot high plum tree that had many dead branches that thankfully could still be identified from the live branches, as the leaves had not all fallen. The dead and dying branches are also identifiable by the growth of moss called Aaron's Beard. That probably makes it appropriate for me to deal with the branches at my stage in life. I was impressed with the agility of the tree men and had initially worried about damage from large branches dropping on the rhododendrons under the tree. They took the heavy dead branches off in incremental portions and not a rhododendron was crushed. Then they did a tidy up of some of the very tall western red cedars. Tree fallers and limbers rarely clean up the mess. They are high flyers! They finished their work in less than an hour and now the elderly eclectic gentleman has to cut up the debris with his loppers and tote it off to his shredder. It's going to take me two days. I enjoy shredding! I prefer to shred rather than burn the branches, as it seems more organic. Cellulose gives body to the compost though it decomposes slowly. If you think this is a plaintive commentary it is not. It's just to celebrate the contrast between the young and the old, the strong and the feeble. I can celebrate that! At the same time we all have our strengths .One of mine that I have learned the hard way is time and patience will accomplish much. I can celebrate that as well! The tortoise and the hare!

Fauna change

Today the Oregon Junco has returned en masse to Lotus Island. They are slipping and flitting everywhere, exploring the locale. Next will be the Rufus sided Towhees. They, like their cousins are one of our winter birds. They fly so close to the ground in the underbrush that I have momentarily mistaken them for a rat. Startling! The Black Tailed Mule deer have lost their smooth caramel coats for a heavier grey brown. The young bucks are starting to rut and have already slashed my declining Gunnera to pieces and soon they will sharpen their horns on the bark of various defenseless young trees. The pianist and I watched a river otter run across the lawn from the harbour yesterday and it flushed out a bunny that it startled. I don't really think an otter would eat a bunny, but the bunny obviously wasn't taking chances. The otter with a long body and tail and short legs runs in a sinuous, ungainly, loping fashion. The California quail walnuts are now large but still clinging together and listening to mum and dad. There are a few runty fawns still around, late gestations, and I fear for them this winter as they have little flesh. In the winter there is often a corpse under the tool shed or the leaf piles. The deer here are endemic as there are virtually no predators. We have all adapted to the deer and they to us. This is a great spider season. The webs in the morning, wet with dew are fantastic and if you don't duck there is a risk of a face full of web. We are careful around the old woodpile for the "Widow and the Brown Recluse". We finally took down a large empty wasp nest from the top of a pear tree; wasps long gone. The nests are beautifully made. The fruit flies in the fresh compost generate at an unbelievable rate and it is not surprising that the ancients believed in spontaneous generation. Thank goodness the fruit is soon finished;

it can be overwhelming; however there is an interesting observation to make. Our own fruit in the kitchen fruitbowl has a myriad of fruit flies, whereas the supermarket fruit section has no fruit flies. Tells you something doesn't it?

Rink Rats

In the olden days of the late forties there were no Zamboni's. The rink rats, a tribe of which I was a member, were proud to be noticed as we skated up and down the ice with our ice scrapers, caroming against one another, pushing our snow load to the big door at the end of the Kindersley arena. We cleared the ice of snow between hockey periods and after the game. The biggest rat shoveled it out the door. We were allowed to watch all the hockey games free. The Kindersley Klippers were a great Intermediate B team. We all were proud to be identified with them. I lived on 3rd Avenue east, a half block from the rink and like all small town rinks it was available most of the time. Rink rats did a lot of other little go-fer jobs as well. The entire management was of a volunteer nature. It seems in retrospect that we practically lived in the rink in the winter. Kindersley had Peewee, Midget and Juvenile hockey teams so the rink was always busy. There was frequently shinny when the rink was occupied, usually on the icy street near the rink. I don't remember any junior teams of ours at that time. If we had anyone that was good at junior age, they usually went to Moose Jaw. Hockey was as natural for us as skiing for an Austrian and swimming for an Aussie. There was little money in those days for the players who made it big. It was love of the game. Players like the Bentleys and Geordie Howe and the Huculs would have made more money staying on the farm. What was it that drove us? The pure love of the game and the sure knowledge that it was our game and still is in all of small town Canada. It had everything to do with participation and dreams. We played it in our sleep.

The aftermath of war

My father's mother died on December the 23rd 1932 and was buried on Christmas day. She left his youngest brother, who was 15 years old at that time to be raised in a family of adult brothers and father. It was the height of the depression and these were hard times on the prairie farms. He joined the Canadian army after schooling and was shipped to England as a corporal in the Canadian 2nd Infantry Division. He was part of the Dieppe raid on August 19, 1942 and was captured by the German army after 4 days inland. He was to remain a prisoner of war in Stalag 8 b for the remainder of the war. I must have written to him when I was 8 years old, because he wrote back to thank me for the carton of cigarettes and the chewing gum. I still have the letter from Stalag 8 b with the censor stamp. When he was repatriated he tried a variety of jobs in the Okanagan where his brother and sister lived, but he was rootless. He became an alcoholic. He had a serious car accident when he was drinking and driving. His friend in the car was killed. He was convicted of manslaughter and jailed. He was jailed again for cheque passing and forgery. Throughout the time we knew our uncle he was sweet and kind to his nieces and nephews and always interested in us. There was a Jekyll and Hyde quality to him in retrospect. He eventually came to realize that he couldn't cope with the "civilized world of the 60's" and he learned to cook and spent the rest of his life working in the mining camps of northern Alberta and the Yukon. He wrote to us at Christmas and more often to his sister. My father received a letter sometime in the 80's from a friend of my uncle in Edmonton who reported that he had been in hospital with TB and had died several weeks earlier. He left no possessions of value and he had no issue. He had enough money to pay for his burial. His family had eventually despaired of him and came to try to forget, as much as one can. Post Traumatic Stress Disorder was not defined in my uncle's time. We were black and white people in those days and wondered why they didn't, "just get on with things!"

The anatomy lab

I entered first year Medicine in September 1953. The first year of medicine at the University of Manitoba and in the Canadian schools at that time, entailed long hours in the anatomy dissection laboratory. Our class of sixty-five had twenty-one bodies to dissect and it required a full academic year to do so. The first day we entered the lab room was a daunting event. We saw twenty-one cadavers, each on a separate table, encased in Vaseline and wrapped, appearing like a mummy in muslin. The enormity of it was awe-inspiring. Each group of three students was given one body to dissect for the year. We started on the back muscles. Prior to beginning, the Professor gave us a lecture on the need for decorum and respect for the persons who had donated their bodies to science. The ethical responsibility he stressed would serve us well in practice, to learn to be respectful of both life and death. He was well aware he was addressing a collection of spirited twenty and thirty year olds. The teaching of Anatomy has completely changed with the evolution of virtual reality, modeling, imaging, and anatomy linked with pathology, clinical work and other disciplines. The volume of required medical knowledge has increased considerably since my day, and I am sure the current methods of teaching anatomy are geared to more rapid and comprehensive learning. What is lost, I suspect, is the intimacy and connectedness one developed with a once living human creation. The doggedness that is necessary to display a perfect dissection and teasing out of anatomical structures common to all of us. A respect for an authentic person we called a cadaver but knew that once there was a life. The patience required to persist in dissecting, slowly and carefully, laying the groundwork for a surgical career. Most of the science in Medicine is rapidly subject to change. What you learned ten years ago is often altered with new knowledge gained. Gross anatomy does not change. You learn it once for all time. Ethics don't change. They were first instilled in us in the anatomy laboratory!

Gandy dancer

In 1952 and 53 my summer job was working as a section man on the CN railway. The official title was a "Maintenance of Way" employee and the job was to maintain the track and right of way in good condition. The jobs included correcting the inevitable heaving of track on the mainline due to winter and summer extremes, changing deteriorated ties, and constant inspection for track defects. It was hard and heavy work and in that era the bulk of workers were of middle European origin. The job was critical to the smooth running of the railway. The track at that time was aligned by educated eyeball. Many of the section men lived in railway bunkhouses in the small prairie towns we lived in. The wage was small but adequate for bunkhouse living if that was one's fate. I of course was still living with my mum and dad and brothers so I had a family and all my needs met. I tried sharing the bunkhouse for a few days at the start since it was more convenient to the workplace but I guess I was spoiled living at home. I was content to walk the 5 miles back home after work. The name "Gandy dancer" seems to me an unintentional derogation provided by someone who wanted to give it a romantic spin. It seems it arose in an earlier time for black railway workers in the south and Chinese workers in the west. Neither of those groups would have believed the job had a romantic spin. For me it served a useful purpose in that I knew what I didn't want to do. Why is it we try to color reality a brighter picture than it really was? It may have devolved from Jump Jim Crow. It may have arisen as a reflection of John Henry, the steel driving man. The railways were built on the backs of men! Gandy dancer indeed!

Homemade wine

Today is Thanksgiving Day in Canada. It coincides with the Christian, Harvest Festival. My daughter is a nurse and worked a twelve-hour shift last night. She will work again tonight, so her family, who usually come to Lotus Island for Thanksgiving, are unwilling to leave her alone in order to feast with us. Well, Mohammed this time will go to the mountain. The pianist and I are going there with the cooked turkey and all the trimmings. It's a bit complicated as it's over the pond by ferry. Food transport of a critical warm mass is a consideration. Our daughter asked if we would bring some of our homemade fruit wine from the cellar. It's not rotgut, but it is not stellar either. I usually serve that wine with family, but why is it that we often take the people we love best for granted and don't always provide what we prize most? Why should we reserve our quality wine for the dinner party with friends who we like but do not love, and settle for less with some of the most important people in our lives? The answer to that is obvious. Because we can! Perhaps we should reevaluate where we put our first fruits. It's kind of a useful question to pose as a Thanksgiving Day thought!

Runcible spoon

Just to contribute to the conjecture on the nature of the runcible spoon; I have a few thoughts. It seems to me that Edward Lear may well have loved the sibilant quality of the word since he meant his poetry to be recited, as well as read. Primarily spoken in my view! The hissing sound in runcible, spoon, pussy, mince and quince, has that vocal distinction one would hear from a pissed off pussycat. Certainly the owl and the pussycat would require a special tool to eat both mince and quince at the same sitting. If you have tackled a quince you will know they are as hard as rocks unless mercilessly cooked, so a sharp serrated edged spoon coupled with a three pronged fork tip of a broad nature, might be just the ticket to carve the quince into fragments, spear them, and chew. Lear does not address the nature of the quince, whether cooked or raw! The spoon like component would at the same time contain the mince so it would not fall through the cracks of a fork. The wide spread use of runcible of course was not confined by Lear to the spoon. I can only think the word produced a sound that pleased him. What do I know? Etymology is not my bag! Phonation also, not my bag! I have never allowed lack of knowledge of the facts however, to prevent me from giving my opinion on a variety of subjects.

Fromaway

In this small island in the Salish Sea, one of the questions frequently asked is "How long have you lived here?" That passing conversational gambit, innocent enough, places you in a category. When, if ever, does one become a "local"? If you were born on Lotus Island, you are a local in island terms, but some places may require generations of you as a necessity to be a "local". Otherwise you are "fromaway". Much as I love this place I am glad to be a "fromaway". Thirty- two years here does not entitle me to use the term "local". When we moved to the island there were barely four thousand people here and now there are over ten thousand. Some of the fromaways are part-time residents, as we were for many years. Houses that are part-time country homes often remain empty for extended periods but bring welcome respite to the "fromaways" when they return. When they do return they are reintroduced to the magic of island living. The influx of "fromaways" has contributed enormously to the welfare of the island and it's cultural mix, bringing diversity and economic wellbeing. "Local " may in fact be better described as the degree of engagement and contribution to the welfare of your community, rather than the time you spent on the cracker barrel! In the meantime, my best nature suggests I celebrate the commingling of the locals and the "fromaways". A drink blended well, is worth celebrating and will bear repeating.

Nitpicking nattering nabobs of negativism

William Safire died a while back and The Economist obituary recorded some of his lexicographical tidbits that I have taken liberty with. He analyzed nabobs, nattering, and negativism. He may or may not have seriously studied nitpicking. Certainly in politics at the federal level in Canada today, the opposition, all three of them, are guilty of a certain degree of this. I don't think the present government was any less guilty when it was in opposition. In fact politics at all levels are guilty and the media thrives as a result. Gloating is good? Schadenfreude is splendid? When you are in the business of government or opposition of whatever stripe, it is so easy to fall into the habit of the four N's. Both the media and the partisans promote these! What if, wonder of wonders, electability was put on the back burner for a period of time in order that the public good may be served by positive and collaborative action on the part of politicians. Things are bad enough for many Canadians that selective criticism, with a bent that can lead somewhere cooperatively would be a blessing. They may have forgotten the true definition of "politic". The voting public is less and less enamoured these days with nitpicking nattering nabobs of negativism. Just a thought!

The mixed hedgerow

The hedgerow that separates our property from the beach was, to my knowledge, always there. All the hedge shrubs are indigenous to this area. They consist of snowberry (Symphocarpus albus), ocean spray (Holodiscus discolor), Nootka rose (Rosa nutkana), Big leaf maple (Acer macrophyllum), red alder (Alnus rubra) and common hawthorn (Crateagus douglasii). We only remove the new growth when trimming so as to avoid disturbing the birdnests in the hedge structure. When this hedge is pruned annually or twice annually at four feet on the property side and twelve feet on the beach side it still has a look that belongs, rather than appearing cultivated. The diversity of plants however does provide a certain amount of chaos and informality that a diverse population of people would also display. Plants with varying growth rates, both in time and season, varying production of flowers and fruits, both early and late, deciduous leaf color changes and leaf drop at different times give a changing kaleidoscopic aspect to the hedge. The presence of a diverse indigenous mix provided by Mother Nature, rather than a monoculture we might have provided, gives a greater durability than we could achieve. I have resisted the temptation to "monkey" with it. "Don't just do something, stand there!" The hedgerow, I think, represents the strength of the population in a country like ours and especially a province like British Columbia, where strength, durability and color is present in all of its diversity. It just takes a little more work to manage than a monoculture.

Poignancy

"Poignancy"

The photograph of two of our children looking out to sea from the beach was taken at St. Ives, Cornwall, a Sunday morning in 1962. It is one of my favourites! Little children were taken by the hand and transported by us, not necessarily where they wanted to go: but home for them was wherever the pianist and I were. Home for us was out there, somewhere in that direction. The photo depicts for me, the vulnerability, the aloneness, the immensity of distance, the clinging to the companionship of the known and the longing for something inexpressible. Almost 50 years later it still evokes strong feelings for me of a time when we all struggled to retain our center! They are looking out onto the Bristol Channel to the west, as it widens into the Atlantic. The same route was taken by many to the new world, and first by the explorer-navigator John Cabot in 1497 for Henry VII. We had taken the weekend off but had driven too far to get back to Plymouth that day so we had to stay in St. Ives overnight. Not having central heating, our car was the warmest enclosure we had, so we often went driving in the winter, escaping the cold council house where we lived. Money was tight but we found a bed and breakfast in St. Ives to tide us over. I remember the weekend as if it was yesterday. We had spent much of the Saturday morning at Land's End, the closest place on the Cornish coast to Canada. The pianist and I were doing what we needed to do at that time in England, but the realization of the poignancy of the feelings we came to own still lingers with us. As we look again at the Bristol Channel we might have wished we were on the sailing ship with John Cabot.

Mother Nature's Fruits

The indigenous berries produced on the prairies, where cultivated fruit is rare, provided a wonderful bonanza in the fall: a gift from Mother Nature for the taking. I'm not talking of the cultivars that have developed from these plants by the plant developers at the universities and experimental farms, but the original plants that we harvested berries from in the olden days. Low bush blueberries (Vaccinium agustifolium) from the Hudson Bay Junction area. Your fingers were blue from the bloom on the berries and your back sore from the stooping. Your ears were alert for sounds of bears in the patch and your legs ready to run. High bush cranberries (Viburnum trilobum) were from the same area, but not related at all botanically or horticulturally to the common cranberry (Vaccinium macrocarpon). These high bush berries made a tart and piquant jelly. The pin cherry (Prunus pensylvanicus) also was a favorite for the jelly maker. A tart and delicious jelly was created, particularly good for meat and game. My favorite as a child was chokecherry (Prunus virginiana). The flavour of jelly from this berry was unique. A slice of homemade bread, slathered with butter and chokecherry jelly was ambrosia! (Food for the gods)-- from Saskatchewan! Because it took a long time to pick enough of these fruits since they were so small and thinly distributed, the preserves were special, a treasure trove, and treated with great care. The Saskatoon berry (Amelanchier alnifolia) was wide spread throughout the prairies. The pioneers named the city after them. The berries made very nice pies and were easy to pick. Saskatoons were the prairie Icon, possibly less for the flavor than its ubiquity. The cultivars that have arisen as a result of selection have improved the production of all these little trees undoubtedly, but they will never supplant the fruit flavours one remembers from one's youthful taste buds. Mother Nature has provided indigenous fruits on the wet coast as well. We have abundant cultivated fruit on Lotus Island, so we often tend to ignore the indigenous offerings. Moreover they don't compare to the prairie berries in variety. I don't include the Himalayan Blackberry variants or the Rowanberry because they are not indigenous. The Trailing Pacific Blackberry (Rubus ursinis}, that little squirt that tangles everything you plant, produces a quality berry jelly, very different from its mellow Himalayan cousin. The salal berry (Gaultheria shallon} and the Oregon grape {Mahonia aquifolium) produce berries that our long time neighbor used as a wild flavour addition to most jelly and jam preserves. The Thimbleberry (Rubus parviflorus) and the Salmon berry (Rubus spectabilis) are for the birds, and best left to them. There are many good publications on more of the wild fruits that may be worth trying! I can't say! Not in anyway to derogate the abundant cultivars that are the anchor of the fruit industry, it's worth trying a little of what our early ancestors had available to them, freely given, if only for the novelty. A paean to history and Mother Nature!

Loss of Innocence

When I was about ten my dad took me to watch Whipper Billy Watson, Hardboiled Haggarty, and Chief Thunderbird "wrestle". My mother wasn't at home or she would have never let me go. My dad met up with his friends, so I sat and watched these large men punch and kick one another endlessly in what seemed to me as a little boy, like a life or death struggle. I still remember the feeling walking home in the dark on that winter's night in Kindersley, on the glittering hard packed snowy road with a newly found sense of dread! I thought of this when I watched Wendy Mesley yesterday on CBC interviewing two "experts" who have studied evil and the media's compulsion to cover it. The experts concluded that the extensive coverage and all the abundant crime shows, serve a "useful" purpose to inform the naive that evil is around and protection is needed! Bosh! We all have a shade, including yours truly that compels us to watch, however dreadful, the sad, the sick and the evil that is around us. The fear and discomfort it arouses has a titillating presence. It doesn't take a psychologist to note that we all have a shade of darkness. It's one thing to recognize it, and another thing to pander to it! We, like Pandora, opened the lid of Pandora's box and the Evils flew out. There is an interesting analogy here because at the bottom of the box only Hope remained after the first opening. The second opening of the box by Pandora occasions the emergence of Hope! Interesting where this all leads, n'est pas?

Touching

I was at supper in a busy restaurant on Lotus Island with my granddaughter, her uncle and two colleagues, when the upbeat waitress, who couldn't remember what my order was, put her hand on my forearm to get my attention! "I'm sorry, " she laughed, "I was so discombobulated I forgot what you ordered!" After I confirmed my order, the granddaughter and my colleague looked aghast! "She touched you" both of them said at the same time! My reaction was bewilderment. So what? All I noticed was nothing more than a friendly and an apologetic gesture and a gentle grip on my arm. My grandaughter, who is 25 and about the same age as the waitress, said, "They never do that!" I've thought about it since! Teachers don't proudly touch children who turn in good work any more! Your avuncular old pediatrician never gives a precious squeeze to his little patient. Grandad never bounces little Mary or Johnny on his lap. What is going on here? Not everything is sexualized! The world is in a spin of phobic correctness. Maybe it's my age but there was a time when you could pass peace with those you knew and that mutual cherishing was accompanied by a comfort hug. Old friends cheek kissed as a matter of course! People who conquered the mountain together gave precious hugs to one another! It still happens, but all too often the approach is tentative and hesitant. We shouldn't forget that children are also people! We seem to have entered a time when tactile expressiveness is guarded. I suppose it is for good reason at times, but it is a sad thing. For expression of simple enthusiasm with one another, we only have our voices and the five senses to utilize including touch!

Avoiding Vanity

In the olden days I played defense for our hockey teams. I wasn't all that bad a defenseman. I wasn't the best skater on the team for sure and I wasn't rough and tough. I was a "stay at home" defenseman, moved the puck forward well and stickhandled skillfully! Whenever I had a really good game, my dad would say, "That Jackie Smith is a terrific forward!" Tantalizing, since the string was pulled out of reach! Whenever I brought my spelling test home my mother wanted to see what I had spelled wrong! I'm not complaining, I'm just observing. The carrot was held just in front of my nose! I tried hard to munch! Later when I was the new boy in a prairie medical clinic I often showed the senior guy my good results. I was looking for affirmation. Eventually he said, "Jim, I know you are a good surgeon but I'm too busy to keep patting you on the back all the time." Gulp! The head of the clinic once said to me, "If a patient gives you splendid feedback, suck it up, because you'll be able to withstand the brick bats more easily!" Good advice! Is this reluctance to praise the praiseworthy fear of instilling vanity into the big striver? It certainly made me work harder to eke out that scintilla of praise that came. King Solomon, who was a very smart guy said, "Vanity of vanities, all is vanity." It sounded like danger to the devout! The residual Presbyterianism in my parents may have taken that to heart. They praised with a faint damn to our face, but waxed on about us to their friends. Somehow we knew this and that had to be enough! Today's parents are supportive and effusive about the children's success to their face. I'm not sure that the new approach is any more effective frankly, but it is more pleasing. Even slight praise from the constipated provides a small hard thing to be savoured!

Fellini Satyricon

The dying Grandee said, (I paraphrase), "If you eat me you will partake of my bounty." So the last, or perhaps the penultimate scene, is the compromise by the Lustful, all sitting around the large table, or perhaps a large marble entableture (it's so long I can't remember exactly), at what appears a campsite, munching doggedly on the corpse of the deceased! Fulfilling the requirement of the will, to obtain the promised largesse! They clearly are not enthralled with the means to the end, but it just goes to show where Fellini would put the bounty hunters. In the meanwhile, the final scene shows the rest, those Uncompromised, the Enlightened, now the Non-inheritors, down to the beach about to sail to unencumbered freedom. How much, money seems to rule! How much misery it has caused! How much sacrifice it has driven! How little stability it really provides! How much joy has it erased? How manipulated those who receive! Of course it is not money per se that is evil; it is the love of money that leads to destruction. Money can provide ease; the love of money provides dis-ease. There is a pointed character on CBC that says, "I love money". "Greed is good." I don't know how serious he is. He may be partly a provocateur! His counterpoint, a female with a strong animus, serves to modify his point of view, but marginally! Our values have become so skewed by reward that it is difficult to carve a path that combines the growth of the soul with the necessities of the flesh. People give up trying. They become cynical. Anger arises at the fetters that have become bonds and chains. Ambivalence confounds even the gentle.

Agonal bloom

As the groundwater rises and the light shortens, the dahlia patch enters the period of agonal bloom! The old plants have become exhausted, partially due to "seed production interruptus" from yours truly! Each time they produced a perfect bloom in order to entice an insect to assist it to produce a new seed, it was plucked. If it escaped the plucking when prime, it got deadheaded well before seed set! Now, in the approaching agony the plant throws itself into a desperate budding frenzy to reproduce to no avail! Feeble little curlicue stems, petal deficient flowers, stem rot, color fading, nodding blooms, and a proliferation of unsightly "sports" are the end game. "To everything there is a season…a time to plant, and a time to pluck up that which is planted", (Ecclesiastes 3). It's inevitable I guess, that we interrupt the natural history of the plant, or nature, or for that matter maybe of ourselves, in order to produce other gain. That's progress? No one asked the plant if it wanted to stay rooted in a spot that was drier in the winter and more clement, or if it wished to produce some serendipitous seed from a fancied dahlia colleague to create a new variety, as well as perpetuating itself from it's tuber. Instead it may have been pruned by a would be exhibitor to one or two lonely stems for gain of another inch of bloom breadth and a millimeter of increased stem width. Or it became the bride of a chosen groom by a plant marriage broker, the bloom shrouded in a chastity belt after fertilization until seed production! Or it was allowed to flower 'til "untimely ripped" for a vase when in full pubertal beauty! We are plucking up that which was planted on October 25th. The bulbs will be buried in a straw cloister for the winter and frustrated again next summer! In my hands, they are always the bridesmaid! Sorry, mea culpa!

Godot

Many years ago the pianist and I went to the Belfry Theater in Lotus City to see Waiting for Godot! I was mystified by the play, found it opaque and blamed myself for not being "with it"! What is it about that play that has stuck with me? At 76, am I able to see through the opacity that bedeviled me when I was 35? Maybe! Why Beckett wrote it in French, and whether at 76 he understood more than he did when he wrote it in his 40's, I do not know. Whether he took a swipe; mocking what he considered the gullible, and their absurdity waiting for The Man, I don't know! Maybe the French were more atune to existential thinking than the Irish, but I doubt it. He might have thought it would do better there! There are lots of things I'm dumber about at 76 than I was at 35. It's just that I know it now. I do know that the play has been dissected over and over again. What Samuel Beckett thought, and what his interpreters thought is interesting, but what it says to you is the crunch point. We went to Olympic City last weekend to spend time with four old friends who were an integral part of our wedding party in 1957. We have all grown old together and walked similar, but dissimilar pathways! Together we have a total of 157 years of marriage. The play no longer seems absurdist. At forty I was impatient and certain that I would amount to something! It seemed terribly important! Amounting to something was clearly defined! In my case, defined by others. Rabbit ears! Waiting was agony. Waiting is still somewhat agonizing but expected now. Living with uncertainty is easier now. Amounting to something is no longer as important and not now so easily defined. Godot will appear when he does. It is certain, that he will appear when you least expect it. If he doesn't appear, then the faithless were right! Being part of the woodwork and watching that march of humanity waiting for a blessing, is a blessing in itself since the woodwork no longer has to perform if it chooses not to. Both cream and shit float up to the surface!

Trip to Fairyland

In 1947 my dad went to Kelowna for a holiday to see his brother and sister and their families. He took me along for company. Another younger brother had just arrived there after a long period as a prisoner of war. When I say " took me along for company", I am using the phrase ironically, since when my dad was away from home and his responsibilities he became a free spirit. I don't remember seeing him much during the weeklong holiday! Bonding wasn't in! No matter! I had acquired the company of my cousin Joyce, and her friend, Linda. Kelowna in those days was like a fairyland to a boy from the bald prairie. Both of the girls I was hanging with for that week seemed like princesses! And they liked me, wonder of wonders! I had no real, "time of communion" experience with girls previously. They both had boyfriends, but they set them aside for the week to devote their time to me, a new object of interest. The three of us were sitting in my cousin's back yard, a fairyland of lawn, flowers and a small clear stream. Our conversation was innocent and intimate. My aunt was busy, hanging clothes on the clothesline. "Jim", she said, in loud and ringing tones, "You didn't bring enough clothes. I'm hanging up your underpants that I washed and you only have this old yellow sweater as well." I could see the underpants swinging down the line with my only sweater, designated as old. I could envision my newly found princesses assailed by horror that I, a boy, would have somewhat well worn underpants. The humiliation was intense. It's easy to be humiliated at 13 years of age. They however didn't miss a beat. I don't think they even noticed! It was a year when I realized my "anima" for the first time and came to appreciate the gifts of girls. It was one of my best holidays ever!

Heritage Dahlia

Bishop of Llandaff, some times listed as (Landorff), is a heritage dahlia, first created in 1924. It is by modern standards very venerable, like it's namesake. Llandaff is the Scottish Episcopal Seat in Wales where it was first developed. It cannot be purchased locally, but is available through friends, as is the one currently in my possession. My friend Sue, who gave it to me, tells of her parent's garden in Comox BC, which was then a commercial Rhododendron nursery, but had some Bishop of Llandaff available. Her mother wrote to the Royal Horticultural Society in England to offer Bishop of Llandaff to them, since the society had written an article describing their loss of this treasure following the Second World War. They stated that the dahlia had disappeared in English gardens due to displacement because of the war effort and the priority of food gardens. The pianist tells me her "nana" grew it in her garden in Regina. The plant is a small, semi double dahlia with a red core and rich red petals. The foliage is green black with small but attractive crenellated leaf margins. This is the only heritage variety I have, as most of the dahlias I own are modern hybrids produced by a limited number of committed hybridizers. The season this year has been exceptionally long and the dahlia are still in good bloom. I am looking forward to growing Bishop of Llandaff next year! A dahlia that has remained with quality morphology over almost eighty years and has an affectionate following among knowledgeable growers has outstanding worth! It may not have the lushness of today's varieties but it has character and history! A lot depends on which characteristics you prize!

Legal Wrangling

I was in court as an expert witness, testifying at the request of the insurance company in a personal injury case! The plaintiffs' lawyer was cross -examining me on the basis of my previously rendered report! I had examined the plaintiff earlier and had reviewed all the documentation germane to his medical condition, consisting of records both before and after the accident. This material included the hand written notes of the emergency room physician at the time of the car accident. This particular physician had quite terrible handwriting but we were accustomed to deciphering one another's script or scribble, so it was do-able for me. Cipher was a good term for it though! In the copy of the emergency physician's note I had circled two words, though I didn't refer to them in my report! The plaintiff lawyer showed me the copy of the emergency report from my chart and asked, "Is this your circle around these words?" "Yes", I said. He then asked me, "What are these words?" I said "Hyperventilating and circumoral numbness." He paused, so I said, "Do you want to know those words significance?" "No," he said, "I asked you just what the words were!" After he concluded his cross -examination the defense lawyer rose for a re-cross examination and asked what the significance of those words were. All hell broke loose as the plaintiff lawyer appealed to the judge that the question was improper since he had not opened the question of "significance". They argued the point for about ten minutes and the judge agreed that the court would not address the significance. I swore in court at the beginning of my testimony, to tell the truth, the whole truth and nothing but the truth! I'm impressed that due to the arcane logic of the lawyers, the whole truth is often not addressed. The whole truth means consideration of all evidence, favorable or otherwise, rather than some truths buried by arcane rules of evidence. As a physician I couldn't make a good assessment without all the evidence available! Why not find out everything? Why suppress anything? Making argument, making judgement, expert witnessing should in an ideal world be peopled by those completely indifferent to the outcome. The only interested parties should be the plaintiff and the defense! Adversarial perhaps, but based on the whole truth, not half-truths; whole facts, not half facts! Law reform in British Columbia needs to go well beyond exclusive Duty to the Court with promises of unbiased, independent expert witnesses. It's just a good start!

Inherent Vice

Years ago my father-in-law purchased a car load of walnuts from Chile. He owned a packaging company that wholesaled to retailers. The walnuts were prepaid. When they arrived and at the time of packaging it was apparent that a hatch of worms had occurred in the bulk walnuts. "Inherent vice" could have been the label applied. Neither the carrier nor the insurance was liable in his case. My father in law had no knowledge of the term inherent vice at that time. He just knew he was out a big bundle and had no recourse! This simple phrase reminds me of joint replacement and implant surgery in general, an activity in which I was immersed for many years. Inherent vice, this strange term, is defined as, "a hidden defect (or the very nature of) a good or property, which of itself is the cause of (or contributes to) its deterioration, damage or wastage." The evolution of quality surgical implants is highly dependent on the research capabilities of the bioengineering firms that manufacture the implants. Inherent implant defects were not uncommon in the pioneer attempts to restore joints, immobilize fractures and reconstruct major physical defects. Although the surgeon undertook careful case selection, and product safety was paramount, the test of time is infinite, not finite. Some products, despite best efforts in the early days, displayed inherent vice. It was an ethical tightrope to choose. It's a curious thing that until recently I had never heard the term inherent vice despite my long professional career inserting surgical implants. I only learned of the phrase when, in a literature group we were reading The Faerie Queene and encountered the characters created by the magician, Archimago; faux humans who were really Sprights: a product described by my esteemed insurance colleague as, "inherent vice"! It just goes to show, no matter what you know, there is always something to apply to your area when knowledge is cross fertilized!

African Violets

In May of 2007 the pianist and I celebrated our 50th wedding anniversary! Our daughter bought a large number of African Violets for the table settings! They are still blooming for us! African Violets are beautiful, but fussy and if you are to keep them in good health the care is rigorous. We ordinarily couldn't be bothered maintaining plants that are not user friendly, beautiful notwithstanding. However, given the circumstances, these are keepsakes. Having a greenhouse and a potting shed is an advantage in maintenance of houseplants during their rest period and the necessary pruning, splitting and repotting, but the real secret is care during the bloom period. The violets are the pianist's wards and she is as fussy as they are. They are bottom watered and the leaves gently stroked with warm water. She maintains them by situating the plants with a good view of the east. They are fed lightly every 10 days or so and unwanted growth and spent blooms pinched to extend the season. She does the same with the second cousin of the violets, a Streptocarpus that was given by a good friend years ago and therefore also a keepsake. We still have after 3 and 1/2 years, most of the African violets and their offspring. I could never do this labour of love, since I am too impatient. Plants of a keepsake nature are nurtured not only because they are beautiful, but also because they have meaning, history, and relevance to the ongoing relationships in our family. Embrace the present!

The Turkey Fish

I picked up a free range turkey from the farmer this afternoon. A Thanksgiving dinner years ago came to mind! An aunt and uncle, with whom we had a chequered relationship over the years, came from Winnipeg to Lotus City to stay with us for Thanksgiving. My aunt was keenly interested to go salmon fishing with me. I lucked out that morning as she caught a fighting spring salmon of about 15 pounds. When we got home, she phoned her daughter in Winnipeg to set up her customary dinner party for their medical clinic friends and colleagues. We then settled down to a family dinner of turkey and all the trimmings attached to that festive occasion. My aunt was ecstatic about her catch and fully engaged as well, since she was particularly fond of our children. The stay was stretched to the last minute before the necessary ride to the plane for Winnipeg. The fresh fish was packed in ice in a double bag on top of the freezer, ready to go!. The pianist has always operated on a "waste not, want not basis" and had bagged the turkey carcase for soup making in a double bag. You know what happened! The bagged turkey carcase was packed in the rush to leave and discovered in Winnipeg when she proudly opened the bag at home to display "her fish" to her daughters. The pianist and I had an enjoyable salmon dinner party with our friends and colleagues later! That winter my aunt died of a head injury when she fell from her horse at the roadside in Winnipeg! She was 56 years young! That Thanksgiving a relationship was restored! It never fails to remind me at Thanksgiving, of the healing, humour, blessings and sadness we are given!

Wood Burning

The pianist developed, over the years, expertise from her wood burning, fast fire, outdoor kiln. Her choice of wood was cedar and fir, split fine, which we have in abundance on Lotus Island. She managed over 60 firings of high-fired, ash- glazed ceramics in the years when we were young and sturdy. We however, were never attentive to the woodburning alternative in our house until this year. Since the onset of the cooler weather of fall, and a desire to be green, the fireplace and the Vermont airtight have become fully employed. No more base board heating for the present in this house! We are novices in this house heating matter, but are keen to learn and experiment with wood of various kinds. Our base wood for jumpstarting and push is alder. This is primarily used in the airtight. Ceiling fans and room-to-room fans distribute the warm air after a fashion. Laziness must be over-come in the early morning to take the ashes to the compost daily and reset the airtight for a new fire later each evening. The fireplace, on the other hand, is large and though the Alder is the starter, Cedar and Fir split logs that follow the alder are abundant in the ancient wood-pile. The fireplace is set at night for the early morning wood fire when the pianist and I gather for our coffee and a vegetative period. Care needs to be taken with handling this older wood to avoid the "Brown Recluse" and the "Widow". They are unwelcome in the house! We also have in the old woodpile, hard wood from the orchard trees that we had felled or trimmed in the past. Both Italian prune and apple wood logs are available. They provide an even and spark free heat. I have a number of year old, evergreen magnolia branches and logs that are also a hard wood and burn slowly and well. Some of the very old wood the woodcutter described to me as "punk". He looked at it with disdain and observed it had no BTUs. The etymology of this description of "punk" escapes me. It is certainly lightweight and becoming sawdust, so maybe that is it. It certainly ignites and burns fast, but doesn't last! Maybe that's it! Maybe "punks" have no BTU's. This exciting phase of our life is beginning to take fire, learning to make smoke in the face of global warming, conflicting with saving electricity! Whatever!

Ponce de Leon Syndrome

Juan Ponce de Leon, in his search for the mythical "Fountain of Eternal Youth" discovered and mapped much of southern Florida. He never achieved the immortality he sought since his search for the fountain was interrupted by a Seminole arrow. His contribution of the discovery of Florida was however, a useful secondary goal. The recent genetic discoveries of telomere shortening in the ageing process and the role of the enzyme, telomerase, in reversing the cellular aging in vitro has led to new speculation. Extending life with enzymatic treatment, or alternatively extending cellular health through a normal life span, has been an engaging idea for some scientists. It has also piqued the interest of some entrepreneurs. Certainly Ponce de Leon had a healthy entrepreneurship in mind. Maybe we are talking about a phenomenon like "The Wonderful One-Hoss Shay"! It lasted in perfect shape for one hundred years and then it all fell apart at once. As I understood, it was an abrupt and complete system failure. We are more and more avidly in pursuit of physical health and longevity, which is somehow equated to happiness. We seek freedom from illness and stress, and so we often exercise without goals other than achieving or maintaining self-health. No problem! Now however, the new emphasis will be on increasing your telomerase levels and checking on the rate of shortening of your telomeres. The problem? Potential cost! For what? "The Fountain of Relative Youth!" High achievement is often associated with unavoidable high stress. Exercise with the additional goal of producing a product, or a service, will have two benefits; one to you and a secondary benefit to mankind. Those of us who were long in the health field and long in the tooth were often beset by the demands of the patients with "Ponce de Leon Syndrome" and were never able to fully provide the satisfaction they required. The many physicians from Lotus city over the last twenty years that volunteered to work for six months to a year in the primitive surroundings of Vanuato will recognize that the "Fountain of Eternal Youth" is a self indulgent fantasy of the affluent world! The scientist who tries to touch this star towards immortality shouldn't say, "I'm doing it because it can be done!" They should say, "Why am I doing this?" It's undoubtedly fascinating research, but why is it that technology always seems to drag ethics well behind it? Lengthening our telomeres is a long way off anyway and of no earthly use to an elderly eclectic gentlemen.

A Good Egg

You might say of a friend that they are a "good egg", or a demanding boss is "hard boiled". An intelligent friend could be an "egghead". And, if we were arguing, we might be "egging one another on". I don't have useful etymological thoughts on all these weighty matters, but I know a good egg when I taste one. I know a good egg when I find one. They are not always hardboiled; they are not necessarily smart; and they are not typically argumentative. The pianist is an expert at the craft of cooking eggs. Poached, with the addition of vinegar to the water, the surface white is congealed early so that it neatly contains the yoke due to the vinegar altered surface tension. The egg remains lightly congealed on the inside. She times 3 minutes 10 seconds for me, and 4 minutes for her. This timing of course is at sea level. That timing delivers a good egg and mirrors the characteristics of our good egg friends, soft, contained, and delectable. It's easy for us to treasure a good egg. Perfect hard boiled egg timing in the hands of the pianist consists of 20 minutes of immersion, off the element from the initial boiled state, and then a cold water bath. Unfortunately, the over boiled egg, timed beyond this period, develops unsightly grey margins at the center. This is unattractive in person and egg, giving a grey shade to the derivatives; potato salad, deviled eggs, doing business, meeting people and charitable acts. The grey shade will not occur if a cold shower is applied in timely fashion to the hardboiled! As always, in love and war and eggs, timing is everything!

The Great Depression

My father was not interested in farming as a boy and after high school he learned the Morse code and joined the Canadian National Railway. This was 1929. The market crash did not fully bite on the prairies until the dirty thirties. There was virtually no work for my father. The farms failed, including the farm he grew up on. He tried growing mushrooms, sheep and potatoes in the early thirties, but it was hard, and no one bought his produce. His sheep got maggots; he poured his potatoes down the coal chute into the basement where they rotted and the mushrooms wouldn't produce as advertised. Spawn sellers scammed him. By 1934, when I was born, he had somewhat steady relief work on the railway, but traveled extensively to the short term jobs, so my mother and I lived with my maternal grandparents for a further three years. The great depression introduced fear into people of that generation that is ill understood today. My father throughout his life had no use for healthy people who did not work. He paid a bill in cash the day it arrived in the house. He never had a bank loan and never would have had a credit card. He took a two week holiday every year, but rarely traveled. He rode a bicycle to work for years because he couldn't afford a car, not because it was politically correct. He smoked a lot, but rolled his own and used Zig Zag papers, because when you laid the cigarette down, it went out and you could relight it without waste. How could you avoid being raised by this man and not value work!

Sunrise Lost

On Lotus Island at the end of September, the sun rises behind the cedars to the southeast so we will no longer see it rise in the morning from our vantage point in the living room. What we will see is simply the dawn of a new day. We will see the sun rise again in late March. The wall of Western Red Cedars buffers us against the November gales as they come from the southeast, so the trees are a blessing. The harbour depth goes abruptly from the 20-fathom mark to a 7-fathom mark a bit out from us, so the large rollers generated from the rise in the harbour depth along with the wind, are bracing. There is always lots of interesting flotsam thrown up to intrigue the curious. A massive rock wall, piled to move with the waves, protects our bank. Those who flee to the desert in the south may be pleased to avoid the season's change, and the rain and wind, but the pianist and I would miss it, though a couple of weeks in Maui wouldn't be a turnoff. Getting through November to Christmas is the dreariest time. The winter ducks, American Widgeons and Buffleheads return through the winter, 'til April. They choose to come here. The Widgeons are dabbling ducks and stay close to shore. The Buffleheads are diving ducks and feed further out. They fatten up at the March herring spawn time to enhance their fertility and prepare physically for their long migration. The ducks don't seem to mind the wind and rain. The day in March that we see the clear view of the sunrise from the living room, for the pianist and me, is the hallmark of our new season.

The Altar Guild

I take great pleasure in the elegant displays of the altar guild women who, amongst other things, provide flower arrangements for the Sunday service. For the months in August, September and October, dahlias are often used along with russet peony leaves. The leaves are a great complement to the dahlia colors. When they pick from my dahlia and peony patch it is an honour for me that I share in the worship that they give. I suppose in one sense we all have some icon we use to center worship, in or out of church, but Jesus used all sorts of worldly examples, props, and referred to all sorts of contemporary elements to illustrate his teaching. I suppose there is a certain ego satisfaction in supplying flower arrangement for the services, but beauty represents an act of love and duty on the part of the altar guild women; a form of worship combined with a sense of unavoidable pride. My orientation always leads me to see the arrangement as a first connection. We take so many things for granted in a church or any other organization that depends on volunteer labour. The people on the ground, doing the regular hands on work as a matter of commitment, are the people who really make the organization work. Some of the most unsung of groups are in fact the connective tissue of the church. You only notice when they are not there and then it's a catastrophe. The care and skill of the arrangements provided by the altar guild are a reflection of their Spirit. Take the time to thank them for the beauty they provide, week-by-week.

Michaelmas

The Michaelmas daisy, which is really an aster, is a blessing that blooms in the late fall, in time for the Feast of Saint Michael and All Angels on September 29. My daughter who lives nearby gave me a clump of her asters several years ago for a vacant spot. What a color complement to the chrysanthemums and split leaf maples! I have a number of planter boxes adjacent to the house. I ruthlessly removed the rangy summer blooming flowers, snapdragons, lobelia and alyssum and replenished the soil with compost and planted chrysanthemums and daffodil bulbs together. Two birds with one stone! Hopefully the chrysanthemums will bloom till mid December and the daffs will carry on in February. The town boulevards on Lotus Island are alive with color in the fall from the annual chrysanthemums and the Red Oak trees with their spectacular leaves; a welcome prelude and antidote to the winter drabness. The holly berries are now turning deep orange so they are on the way. If we want holly for Christmas we have to pick it by Dec 10 because the birds eat the ripe berries after that. It's a curious thing that my neighbour has a hybrid holly hedge loaded with berries that the birds never eat. Our blueberry bushes have started to turn red early this year and we still have a final pick available since they are all bird netted. My big job over the next few days is to get rid of the old raspberry, tayberry and loganberry canes and string up the new vines. Routines like this give one lots of time to ruminate and talk to one's self. I hope my lips don't move! The garden is still alive at Michaelmas. It takes a rest at Christmas!

Halloween party

For many years the pianist and I went to Gabriola Island to celebrate Halloween with old friends for the weekend. We have known our host for 40 years. There is usually a gathering of some twenty other friends. At least there was, before time began to take its toll. We party, drink a bit, eat well, and continuously talk. These were friends from another era that keep in touch once a year and we never run out of things to say. We don't exercise. We of course carve pumpkins. The pianist always made Sunday breakfast of bacon and blueberry pancakes using the last berries from our patch. The clean up is as much fun as the "dirting down". We say goodbye each year hoping it is au revoir! Years ago our host showed us the large cored holes in a granite tumulus near her cottage. There were dozens of them, measuring four feet across and five feet deep. The large round intact grindstones extracted from the granite were transported to the Vancouver Island pulp mills to grind pulpwood in the old days. By Halloween the holes are full of water and in attempting to traverse around them I was less nimble than my host. I fell in to a hole up to my armpits and eventually struggled out. As I was falling I had that split second thought that the holes might be 30 feet deep and that I was a "goner". It is hard for an old fellow with gumboots and a thick, soaked parka to extricate himself from such a situation. That night at the party, my cracked rib, the heady atmosphere and the libation caused me to faint and, since my fellow celebrants were also less than perspicacious at that time, they thought I had no pulse and called the fire department. The firemen had just finished their fireworks display in the harbour and were in need of action. All was well. It was an inconvenient way to be the center of attention, but we were invited back the next year in hope that I would provide further excitement.

The Green Tree Frog

As I was coiling up my hoses I heard the little green tree frog with his mighty voice summoning all or any females to his side. They are very cute. Telus uses them in their ads along with lambs and lizards gamboling about. My friend, a greenhouse man, puts them in his green house; I suppose to eat the insects. I'm not sure the "amourian" is in the appetite mode for anything but a lady frog. Certainly those of other species, including our own, in a state of unrequited love are not very hungry for food. I never had much luck with my friend's greenhouse tactic. He told me he enjoys the frog music, but I found it was quiet when I was with my prisoner that I captured for the greenhouse. My transplanted frog in the greenhouse withered on the vine, as it were. I think there was pining and a wasting away because of unfulfillment. You have to face the music and leave the frog alone. The rule probably is, "Don't muck about with Mother Nature too much". To employ a frog to do your dirty work in the guise of being organic is no excuse. Think of his feelings. He is a brief enough candle as it is, what with working for Telus, seeking and procreating; just surviving the environmental degradation to which he is so vulnerable. As you know he is the canary in the cage. He won't live beyond his allotted life span outside or inside the greenhouse but so what! Toiling in the workhouse is probably worse. There isn't anything fundamentally wrong with a short but happy life of freedom. Let it be!

The Scythe

Last week my friend asked if she could borrow a tool to cut her long grass, because her grass and brush were too tough and long for a weed eater. She said, "Do you have a sickle? I know you have a lot of tools." I don't have a sickle but I have a scythe. The scythe is not only an ancient tool, but it ranks in importance with the binder and the combine in the march of agricultural harvesting technology. I lent her my scythe and a stone. You can maintain a scythe's sharpness with a hand stone, but from time to time, if not used much it needs a rotatory grindstone. Nowadays sadly, the sythe is not used much! The important thing about the scythe is to keep it sharp. The stone has to be used in the correct way! It takes time to learn to sharpen the blade to make the job easy. No job, however so humble, is simple. To cut effectively one develops a rhythm much like a golf swing with the back stoke equally important as the cutting stroke. The swing becomes relaxing! The blade of the scythe leads at a 15-degree angle from your coronal plane. When I was 17 and 18, I worked for the CNR as a section man in the Touchwood Hills. Our June job was to cut the long grass on the right-of-way. Five men would move along, each cutting the measured interval between two telephone poles, and then leapfrog ahead to the next available interval. After each cut we'd roll a cigarette of course! The right-of-way has a downward slope on either side and we, being responsible for six miles of track always cut on the downward slope, up six miles and back six miles. It took us two weeks. Once you got going in tandem there was some irregularity in "smoke time", determined by the fastest man. Of the five of us, no one wanted to be the slowest man but after an hour the pace evened out. When you have six miles out and six miles back the only time you hurry is the last 100 yards or the last ten minutes in any job day. I haven't seen my friend since she borrowed the scythe but I hope she enjoyed it. There is no finer feeling than a sharp tool slicing through long grass, which lies down in geometric windrows at your bidding.

Dog Show

I was 14 and visiting my grandparents in Winnipeg when my mother phoned me from our home in Saskatchewan to tell me that my Irish setter had been poisoned and died of strychnine seizures. He was a gift from my aunt. My family made it up to me by purchasing an Irish setter puppy from a well-known breeder. I was convinced my new Irish setter, Rusty, was a dog show winner. He had a beautiful red coat that was darker than usual. When he was 9 months old I entered him in the Ladies Kennel Club dog show in Saskatoon. We had practiced standing and heeling for months. We were bonded. I had fancied I would one day become a professional dog handler. I had a subscription to the Canadian Kennel Club Magazine and read what I could about dog handling. We lived about 200 miles from Saskatoon on the main CNR line and the passenger train came through the town about 4 am every morning. The day before the show I washed my dog thoroughly. The day of the show the train stopped for us in the early morning and Rusty and I both traveled to Saskatoon in the baggage car. He slept on one side all the way in to Saskatoon but unfortunately he was still slightly damp from my doggy bath and sleeping on one side for that many hours was a disaster in the making. He was curly on the damp side and fuzzy on the other side. His glistening coat was dull and free of natural oils. My debut in the doggy show world was a disaster and being 15 years of age, the humiliation was intense. I believe that seminal moment led to a change of my choice of vocation. I dreamt of revenge on the Ladies Kennel Club. Don't ask why revenge! They didn't do anything wrong, except in the doggy world competitions there is no charity good enough to assuage felt disaster at that age. I consoled myself on the long train ride back home that I would become rich, buy the best show dog in the world, and win Best in Show at the Ladies Kennel Club of Saskatoon. I never did. I hugged my dog and he licked my face!

Loss

My young Irish setter Rusty, still less than a year old, was across the tracks near the Pool grain elevator. I didn't know he was there. It was a favorite spot for a dog because there were rats as a focus of interest around the elevator annex. He was still young enough that he lacked savvy and had separation anxiety in new situations. I first noticed him when a freight train was standing, waiting for orders at the platform. I heard the freight start to move with that characteristic squeal of axles mobilizing and as I looked under the boxcar that began moving at a slow walk pace, I could see Rusty trying cross the tracks under the boxcar. He made several tentative passes. I yelled at him to go back to no avail and as he tried to slip under the moving boxcar to the platform where I was standing, a rear wheel caught him in his midsection. I watched in horror as each wheel of a long train passed over his body. I ran into the kitchen where my mother was. She comforted me. Bob, the Pool elevator operator and my dad stayed outside after the freight train pulled away. Then my dad came in the station and said, " You have to pick up your dog and bury him." My mother and Bob said, " He can't do that!" My dad told me I had to do it, that it was the only way. So I picked up the two parts of my dog and put him in the wheelbarrow and went about 500 yards down the right-of-way and buried him near the tracks. I'm not sure what my dad was thinking or why, but then I'm not sure that he was wrong. I guess no matter what, we have to face our grief head on. We cannot sanitize the events of our lives. Doing what I did probably allowed me to participate both in the life and the death of something I loved. At fifteen I suddenly took a further step towards becoming a big boy. I never had another dog 'til much later in life. Living beside the tracks on the main line, with 10 or 15 trains a day, is not the place to have a dog. I think in retrospect, I'm grateful to my father.

Changing of the Guard

Dr A was an early pioneer in the "Morgantaler" initiative. She had studied under him at his postgraduate course and encountered with him the ferocious opposition. She was committed to change and weathered untold adverse criticism from various quarters, medical and non-medical, in that era in Lotus City. Dr. A had the drive and zeal of an evangelist and stuck to her guns through and through, year after year 'til the winds of change blew! She worked in the public short stay surgical suite with the rest of us who were doing the less controversial surgical bits and pieces at the time. Even if you disagreed with Dr.A's actions there was no one that questioned her professionalism or her tenacity to follow through! She knew how to get things done and invariably provoked a certain envy at her capacity to take a stand and weather a storm. The surgical change rooms at the time were labeled "Doctor's Change Room" and "Nurse's Change Room". The male orderlies changed into greens in the doctor's change room and the female doctors and other female staff changed in the nurse's change room. One "eight am" morning, the anaesthetist, Dr B, came barreling out of the doctor's change room as I was going in. "Dr. A is in there changing," he said. Well, I wasn't going to be buffaloed like him so I went into the change room and there she was in bra and panties. She said, "I'm damn well a doctor and this is my room." I went to a locker and dropped my pants and shirt. She quickly dressed in greens and fled. I think the sight of me was disgusting enough that she wasted no time. This is all beside the point because the following morning the signs on the change rooms were altered to read "Men's Change Room" and " Women's Change Room". Just as it should have been of course! Real change sometimes just requires a nudge. Activism has a broad and often pertinacious reach. Dr A was an expert at it!

Telling the truth

When I began training with the bluntest man I ever met, he said to me," I know you don't know any orthopedics and don't pretend you do. If you want to stay here there are only two requirements; be on time and don't lie! If you screw up a surgical case tell the patient the truth. They deserve that! That way you never have to remember what you told them. You have an insurer to look after your interests. It's his problem, not yours." That may have been blunt but it was good advice for me and served me well in my career! The orthopedic service in the 50's in Olympic City was one of the better-organized services but the system was run like a military establishment and you obeyed orders or you didn't survive. There was little room for free spirits and no room for sluggards. If you had a family with children and your wife needed a little down time with you, it was a challenge to escape the taskmaster. We probably would have been better to adopt a celibate monkish existence for the training period of five years. How the pianist ever survived that period of neglect is a wonder. The Chief, at the end of each training year dictated where you were to go the next year. No one ever said, "No". Unfortunately I did, as my putative year was to be the traveling year. I had 2 children, a wife and no money. I said I couldn't do it. I went from golden haired, to close to persona non grata for a time! Despite that confrontation we carried on. Senior surgeons came privately and upbraided me for daring to say "No" to the Chief. Even then, as a lowly second year surgical resident, I could not get over the willingness of talented senior surgeons bending to the rule of one man. What's more, as I think of the first interview and the Chief's observation that we don't lie and we can offload the responsibility to the deep pockets of the insurer, I believed even then, that there were other reasons to be transparent and tell the truth. I can't deny however that having an insurer is handy. I spent 12 years in medical committees frequently adjudicating patient complaints about doctors. One of the more prominent causes of complaint was lack of transparency. People do not expect perfection! They do expect respect! If we screw up a case we can be forgiven by most patients, most of the time, if they know we were there for them, on time, and we didn't lie.

Bonding and fishing

When my son Rob was 9 yrs old we bonded over fishing. I needed a father and son activity and at that time, he was working away with little boy efforts and rudimentary equipment to fish on a lakeshore without much luck! I had neither the interest nor past experience with fishing and if it hadn't been for his enthusiasm I would have never started. I began fishing in the interest of a father -son relationship and in the process I got hooked! Our initial fishing trip was to the high Okanagan lakes for trout, then stream fishing on the way back to the coast and finally fishing the bay at Port Renfrew. Just the two of us for two weeks! We caught nothing but the bug. So we bought a twenty-six and a half foot, wooden, diesel cabin cruiser. My daughters and the pianist entered the pursuit as well. We all became keen and fished together. It's not so easy for the novice to catch a salmon and it's also scary for the novice to take responsibility for the safety of a family, even in inshore waters! We spent days in fruitless pursuit, but even empty-handed there were lots of adventures and the family bonding was good. Then, miracle of miracles, we caught a 13 inch salmon grilse. When we put into the marina, Rob said, "Dad, can I gut the fish?" Part of the pleasure of gutting the fish was being observed by an abundance of tourists at the Lotus City Marina. Interest and questions were often asked of the "fisher folk", since our prize now demonstrated we were part of that celebrated group. In a few minutes the little guy returned to the boat, crestfallen! As he began to gut the tiny fish, and answer the questions, and display his prowess, the slippery fish squirted out of his hand and slid down the drain hole of the fish basin. A seal quickly gobbled it up. That fish sure was small. What to say? "The drain hole must have been too big! There's always another day." Over the next ten years we all tasted fishing success thoughout the southern coast! Yield is not all that counts as much as doing things together. Getting skunked is almost as interesting as limiting, but different! Fishing has stuck with my children over the years but when they left home, I did not fish again. Fishing with them when they were growing up is among my most prized memories and a source of endless stories, but I remember our first fish best!

Cigarettes and whiskey

My paternal family had for many generations a romance with John Barleycorn. It was spirits for them, because they were of Scots and Irish origin and in the olden days, oddly enough, wine was for "foreigners" or "winos". Grain alcohol was more available where the product was grown and it also could be homemade. Old John B. didn't stop them from working or being productive but it made it more difficult. We also, over the generations, provided large personal subsidies to the tobacco industry. To be dominated by one's addictions leads to guilt, remorse, salvation, relapse, and shortness of breath, all of which serve to diminish one's self image. I believe genetic makeup predisposes to the addictive personality. This is never an excuse. It had been a struggle for many of my family and was always a cautionary principle for me. Still, we cannot walk in anyone else's shoes and make judgments because love of family conquers all in the end. Cigarettes and whiskey are no longer celebrated these days. The young have just changed what they are habituated to. The old have got more interested in living longer! I have often said facetiously," If I live to 90, I'm going to smoke again because I loved it and the stream of smoke and conversation that floated on it." It wasn't called a "peace pipe" for nothing. Augment that with a glass of spirit and everyone becomes a conversational genius, except when you haven't had a drink and you have to listen! It is hard being a killjoy and pretending you aren't. When a member of your family stumbles the bell tolls for all. Tough love is not as tough on the loved as it is tough on the lover!

Slugs

It's raining today, so it is a good day for dispatching slugs. I no longer use toxic materials added to solid bait as it is also toxic to furry and feathered friends. These chemicals were always highly effective and the liquid slug bait is still safe if used sparingly. The best organic method is to cut them in half; a rapid and humane way to eradicate them and then leave them to recycle 'in situ'. We have blacks, browns, grays and the ubiquitous banana slug. If you tally your kills you will be able to assess the efficiency of your control mechanism. You can even plot; number killed against cutting days and come up with a nice Bell Curve if you are so inclined. Slug killing methods are contentious here in Lotus country! An incredible fact is; even killing slugs is mildly contentious. That is because a zealous few see the active and ongoing digestion of organic material as nature's catalyst. Thank heavens they are not my neighbors! In respect to methods of execution, some advocate animal friendly methods such as ferrous compounds. These are not toxic to animals, at least in modest amounts. The crows here however eat ferrous pellets as soon as they are spread as they look like seeds. The company doesn't tell you that on the package. Those with small gardens advocate copper wire or copper impregnated fibre strung about the periphery of the garden. I'm not sure it works but if it does it would require constant adjusting. Various baited trap and drown systems are also available. One year I collected a full garbage bag of hair from the barbershop sweepings since someone told me slugs would not cross over a hairy strip. I decided however that dandruff, old hair and vegetables didn't go hand in hand! Since slugs will cannibalize the corpse of their fellow creatures of any stripe, half of a dead slug is the best bait of all for another slug. You can return with your trusty secateurs and slice the cannibal in half while he is enjoying himself. Two for one day! This keeps them occupied and away from your plant. Certainly, of the organic control options this is the most effective, surgically satisfying, accountability accurate and consistent with good non-toxic recycling principles. It just means you have to get up early before they go under a rock. My tally today was, 110 slugs, including one banana slug.

The Snowplane

A reinforced, fibre covered vehicle on skis, with an automobile engine and propeller in the rear was the transport of choice for our country doctor in the dead of winter in Saskatchewan. The snowplane, manufactured in Saskatchewan, must have been an early forerunner of the Bombardier. Dr CM had a driver, and could treat emergencies over the twenty-mile radius he served. The snowplane ran on otherwise impassable roads and on snowdrifts over fences. The romance of that activity proved a great cachet for a teenage boy! The thought of a medical practice that depended entirely on your own resources, even today, fills me with admiration. He also had a new "bustle back" Oldsmobile-- probably 1953. That Dr CM could afford a new car was a further source of awe. Dr C.M. left his general practice while we lived there to undertake a surgical training programme at the Mayo Clinic. He had a family as I recall; a wife and two children. Banks and bank transfers were less utilized at that time and he showed me his savings he was taking to look after his family while training for the four years he needed. I had never in my wildest imagination thought I would see fifteen thousand dollars in bills in a roll. I think he was proud of himself! I believed those three things were the original stimulus for me to study medicine. Years later, in interviewing prospective candidates for the medical school and listening to the "reasons for applying", it strikes me that I would have had to sacrifice honesty for expediency at that earlier time! As it happened, there was no interview when I entered medicine so I didn't have to restrain myself from blurting out my three reasons. As I reflect on the matter now, I know that when we are young we identify the tangible more easily than the intangible. What Dr. CM really represented for me was the skill, dedication and incredible creative resourcefulness that a good medical training can provide to the right kind of person with the right stuff. That's what I would have wanted to emulate, though I couldn't articulate it at the time!

The Botanist

The first year I was at the University of Manitoba the botany examination was a week after the rest of the final exams. To save money and relax, I gave up my boarding house room and took the train home for the week, intending to come back in time to write the exam. My dad was the railroad station agent so I had a train pass and my transportation was free. The night before the examination day, I stayed with my nanny and grandfather. I was ready to write. When I got to the university in the morning I found that the examination had been held the previous day. I was in a panic. I had misread the examination timetable. I had done badly enough that year despite my best efforts. Culture shock bewilders! Botany was my best course! I thought my putative career was dashed. Nanny said, "Why don't you phone the professor and tell him what happened? He's a nice man and he goes to our church." I called him at home, told him my circumstances and left the stuff out about my grandparents and church. "Well", he said when I phoned, "I'll write you a new test and you can come to my office for invigilation today." " Mind", he said, " You won't get a really good mark." The relief I felt I can still feel today. Botany was a small class and he knew I was an interested student. My family and I were lifelong gardeners and I was also interested in the flora of the Whiteshell. The professor spent his summers tramping the lower reaches of the Canadian Precambrian Shield, of which the Manitoba Whiteshell was a part. Despite being in his 60's, he didn't differentiate his vocation and his pleasures. They were one. It is the hallmark of a happy man. The blessing that kind man gave me was a precious gift! When you are close to the edge as I was that year, the little things are important.

Road apples and ketchup

In 1943 I was nine years old. My father worked in the railway depot in Kindersley as a telegrapher on a shift known as 3rd trick; from midnight to eight am. He was always home at suppertime. The war was on and so food was sometimes scarce or choices limited. My mother was a quick cook with no frills. As you grow up however, you develop a taste for your mother's cooking that knows few bounds. That was, and still is the case for me though she is long dead and the western world has become eclectic and international in scope with respect to food. The exception to my mother's cooking would be that she made a tomato soup with canned tomatoes and milk and never bothered to remove the tomato cores. I hated that soup. I hated the soft, sloppy, slimy, tomato gobs attached to the tomato cores that floated in the soup. I would sit and gag for hours over it, but got no relief. My parents would not bail me out no matter how long I sat. I said to my dad after a particularly long session, just to give him an idea of the seriousness of my situation, " I'd sooner eat shit!" I remember this as vividly as if it was yesterday. It was the dead of winter. He went out to the street and picked up three frozen road apples. He brought them in the house, arranged them on a plate, put ketchup on them and said, "Take your choice." I ate the soup. There is now, almost no food I will not eat and relish. The pianist makes all our soup from leftovers, but there are no tomato gobs or cores. Frozen road apples were used to mark goalposts for road shinny and as a puck. I had never before considered them useful to encourage eating in childhood! In the meantime as they used to say in the country when a contrived and undeft argument was being made," Don't eat that Elmer, that's horse shit!"

Work Habits

I have two daughters of middle age. When they were something like eight and ten they did, among other things, the dinner dishes since at that time we did not have a dishwasher. The two of them would horse around for hours doing a job that could be completed in twenty minutes. They sang and danced after each dish, argued about who would put the dishes away, argued about who would wash and who would dry, (washing was deemed best since you could quit earlier), flicked wet towels at one another and raised a genial hell. If I heard "Henry the Eighth, I am, I am" once, I heard it twenty times a night. Finally, because this drove me crazy, and they knew it, I would go out and say, "Finish this job in the next ten minutes and do it QUICKLY, QUIETLY and WELL!" Of course they not only expected this reaction, they waited for it and savoured it when it came. At least we were all consistent and there is something comforting in the expected. You recognize that this is who we are! It's important for young women to make a stand early in their life career and they safely experimented with their father. Quickly, quietly and well may be a good credo for a surgical operation but it's a bit stiff necked for parenting. They knew it instinctively. The pianist tolerated horsing around better than I did. Today as I reflect on the work habits of my daughters I can see that they carved careers with work habits that arose out of goals, not pedantic clichés of mine. They both work quickly and well today and are impatient with those who don't. They are however, not quiet, and that's because our family always had a lot to say, some of it sensible. It's the way we are. I have just left the hospital following pneumonia and I received a "get well" card from one of my grandchildren. The quote is "Dear Grandaddy, We would like you to heal QUICKLY, QUIETLY and WELL.!" What goes around, comes around!

Currants

Someone once told me, or I read, that the Queen loved red currant jam and the company that supplied her with jam, provided a few jars with the seeds handpicked out of the jam specifically for her. Red currant jelly, though delicious, doesn't have the wherewithal of jam. Whether this seedless jam is an apocryphal story or not, I am sure it would have been a "dainty dish to set before the Queen". Frankly, seedless jam would be too fussy for me. Get a toothpick! Our currants this year have an abundance of tresses on both the red and white. The cousins, gooseberries and black currants, are not berried in such abundance. I know of no other way to avoid currant maggot in these precious little fruits other than carefully staged spraying with Malathion at flower time. There are wild currants and wild gooseberries on Lotus Island so the maggot is endemic. No amount of good husbandry will eradicate them, though with care you can minimize the damage. Slight infestation of current maggot is however, like slight pregnancy. The crop is still tainted. If you label your jam or jelly product to state that you have used Malathion at flowering time, you ought also to say on the label that these currant and gooseberry products do not contain "essence of maggot"! Don't be dissuaded from staging three spray sessions of Malathion, at flower time. It's a nuisance now since the "greening wave" has meant I have to travel to the agricultural outlets to get the spray. The nurseries no longer sell it. These four little fruits harken me back to my Manitoba roots with my grandparents. It may be that the Manitoba winters were often too cold for the currant fly pupae to survive in the soil. Those were the days without poisons!

Hair today, Gone tomorrow

In the early 70's my hair was thinning. The pianist was off on a trip with the children and I was having dinner with my parents. My mother said to me that I might look better if I had a permanent wave. I had a few colleagues who had recently adopted curly long hair. Big hair for men was becoming a statement. My mother knew nothing of that; she had just noted my bald spot. Mum said she had a friend who did Toni Home Permanents. "Sure"' I said feeling cavalier, "why not?" The next day I had my perm. When I was sitting down being worked on, looking into the mirror with big curlers in my hair, I realized for the first time how much I looked like my mother. My perm worked out pretty well, curls, but not too tight, a bit bigger hair, and giving an appearance of being slightly risqué. Some people said to me "Are you having mid-life trouble?" When the pianist got home she was thunderstruck, but amused and reflective. She wasn't sure she should go away too often. I took a good look in the mirror and realized that I was on a new course. I had joined the youth movement. I remembered that the ancient Jews believed Samson's power came from his hair. People may have resented hair in Samson's time for it's supposedly regenerative power and production of singular strength. Certainly Delilah destroyed the power of Samson by ordering his hair be removed. "Gotta "mean something! It took away his confidence. Samson got sheared like a sheep. I always thought the initial appearance of the sheared sheep embarrassed them a bit. Now in this enlightened period, virility is displayed by shaving the head. Bald is in. In the 70's we only had Kojak and Yul Brynner for virility. Bald is power now! There is no telling what man will do or undo next. I went back after a year of my locks to my mouse colored, thin, conventional hair style when my 14 year old grew his hair below his shoulders. It was all too heady for me!

Cherry pie

Montmorency cherries are sour pie cherries that are hard to find because the industrial processors buy them all. Stony Creek Winery in Ontario used to make a nice Montmorency wine. Some fast food restaurants have sour cherry pie turnovers but they are mostly glairy filling with red colorant. Montmorency is a yellow-red sour cherry and is much more reliable on Lotus Island than the Morello which is red and prettier. It's still a fact that flavour trumps appearance, though the consumer sometimes becomes seduced by appearance. We have a productive 30-year-old Montmorency tree and the birds, unlike the sweet cherries, leave the sour cherries alone long enough for us to pick them ripe. With the sweet cherries, the birds are voracious and eat them well ahead of ripening. Today I made several deepdish cherry pies and cherry filling as well. The biggest problem with cherry pie making is stone removal. It is tedious, but the tedium can be lessened during the picking of the ripe fruit. If a little eccentric pressure is put on the fruit when you pull it off, it will leave the stone on the tree. A certain finesse and dexterity is necessary! Speed of processing is necessary as the cherry juice darkens (oxidizes) quickly once the stone is out. I always warn dinner guests to chomp the cherry pie softly since I always miss a couple of stones. You have to microwave fresh Montmorency cherries well, before you make the pie filling since the fresh cherries don't cook down well unless pre-softened. Cherry pie is a lot of work! There is no way that charming Billy Boy's intended could make or bake a cherry pie, quick as a wink, talented or not!

Grandparents

My grandparents were married in Vancouver BC in June of 1906. The San Francisco earthquake and fire was April 18 1906. My grandfather was a Londoner who came to Winnipeg about 1900 and eventually worked as the accountant for Acklands, the hardware wholesaler. My grandmother was an Ontarian who worked in Winnipeg as secretary to Mr. Ogilvie, of Ogilvie Flour Mills. They were married in Christ Church Cathedral Vancouver, then honeymooned by train to San Francisco, Salt Lake City, and Minneapolis-St. Paul before returning to Winnipeg. I am the curator of my grandparent's album with some great pictures of San Francisco after the earthquake, the showers from their friends in Winnipeg, the menus on the trains and hotels in San Francisco, Salt Lake City and St Paul. They were an adventuresome pair and remained that way throughout their life! I said to my mother one day, " Why did they leave all their friends and come to Vancouver to have a wedding where they knew no one?" I thought it very mysterious. She said, "I have no idea. I never thought about it." My mother was born on March 29 1907: that is, she was not born yesterday, but still, she seemed remarkably incurious! I have clearly a more curious mind than her. She and her twin sister were born 9 months and 10 minutes after the wedding. Still a mystery! Because of the great depression, my mother and I lived with her parents for 3 years after my birth. If you live with your grandparents for the first three years as I did, there is a lot of bonding. From time to time my cousins and I still visit the big country house they built 90 years ago at Little Britain, by the Red River, north of Winnipeg. The land between the Lower Fort Garry and the Upper Fort Garry on the Red River is replete with history! Little Britain, Old England, and Canada's oldest intact fur trading fort, Lower Fort Garry! All a parcel of Lord Selkirk's ill-fated settlement, The Hudson Bay Company, Louis Riel and the Red River Settlement! My grandparents were special! They were part of the mix of the English, Scots, French and Metis that were the remnant of the building blocks of Rupert's Land.

Loganberries

When the pianist and I moved to Lotus City in the 60's, the adjacent farmland was dotted with loganberry farms supplying the fruit wine industry locally and the jam factory on Sinclair Hill. Now the jam factory is an unused heritage relic and the Logana Winery is converted to a heritage structure housing an upscale steak eatery. Soft fruit jam is available only from industrial manufacturers except for minor cottage industries. Grape growers and vintners, primarily large franchise holders, have displaced the local loganberry farms. This part of the world was prime country for loganberries and never was prime country for wine grapes. They produce pretty fair wines from specialized stock in this area but they will never compete with quality wine worldwide. We grow world-class quality soft fruit varieties. Why don't we stick to what we can produce of excellence? Tastes have changed. Still, we could compete better in the long term with what we do best, not second best! I suppose we have to live with industrial farms and industrial food manufacturing! But hey, what the heck! Yesterday I made 13 jars of loganberry/tayberry jelly from our berries. I guess we are our own cottage industry. I missed the jell-point and bottled too soon so I had to dismantle the seals and reboil. It's a bit harder to jell loganberry juice than some fruits, as the loganberries have little pectin. My grandmother and the pianist's mother never added pectin to jellies but they could assess the critical jell-point to the second. "Lightly jelled" was the mantra for optimum achievement. The industrial jelly makers always add pectin and chemicals. I also made 20, 2 cup-bags of logan/tayberry juice for freezing. The pianist makes a loganberry juice meringue pie after the manner of a lemon meringue pie. It's a delicious and pungent dessert treat. Loganberries and tayberries are easy to grow if you have room on your fence. It's satisfying to know you have a year's worth of eating from your own ground, by your own hand, in your own cottage, with the sure knowledge of the contents!

Robin, Canadian of course

Every day for two weeks the pianist and I watched daddy robin attack the window of the pianist's pottery studio. He'd stand on the car's side view mirror and stare at the studio window. I guess "glare" would be a more accurate word. Then he would fly at his mirror image, traveling up and down the window repeatedly, screeching as he flew. We thought he was crazy 'til we saw he was nesting in the Kiwi bush adjacent to the window. We moved the car so he couldn't see this "adversary". Despite having moved the car, he continued to perch on the mirror but peered at himself upside down and pecked at, and fouled up the mirror and the side of the car. He intermittently tires and gets busy with worms rather than fighting the phantom. Dear me! He has seen the enemy and he is he. My neighbor is a car buff! He has robins as well and the behaviors are the same! He however "has no time" for bird shit on his cars. His ploy is to simply cover the side mirrors with little plastic grocery bags, securing them with elastic. It works, but his beautiful cars always look like they have a perpetual bad hair day. I look in the mirror from time to time these days and recognize my shade. I have to deal with the taunting from the shade about retirement agitating me, but I'm not going to cover up the mirror to hide my "adversary"! I have to see and take direct action at my shade! The robin adapted and busied himself with worms but I'm not partial to worms. Our fledglings have flown so there is no fledgling to protect. I suppose I should wash our car. Maybe I will write stuff!

Dr A's Daughter

I'm delegated to cook today because the pianist is glazing her pots and the measuring of chemicals for the glaze is tricky. It requires concentration. I'm not adept at cooking, but she has laid out, in sequence, all the "materia foodica" required for me to amalgamate into some sort of pottage along with handwritten instructions in plain English. Lunch and dinner! Feigning ignorance is a ploy that can gain one certain advantage only for a limited length of time, but eventually it becomes ineffective. This reminds me of Dr A, who must have played his cards right, or else his wife gave up from exhaustion. He was an old time surgeon from Second World War days and was in his heyday when I started work in Lotus City in the 60's. His daughter was an OR nurse. One day when we were chatting, she told me her mother had taken a holiday and left her dad 10 meals for dinner; frozen and labeled. Her mother also set the table for 10 places so he could rotate around, distancing himself from his dirty dishes. Egad! I'm not that bad! Dr A's daughter rejected that leaf from her mother. The apple had dropped much further away from that tree. She brooked no missteps from the surgeons and freely pointed out our sorry sides! I had been in Maui for a holiday with the pianist and bought a checked, blue and white seersucker jacket, lemon yellow trousers, with a yellow tie and white shoes. I can't remember the socks. My ensemble had a certain sartorial splendor in Maui. The first day back I walked to the OR change room in my resplendent attire with white shoes! Dr. A's daughter bumped into me in the hall and slowly looked me up and down with a glint and said, "You look like a well dressed Bulgarian. What national flag is that jacket? " What cheek! For the Bulgarians and me! I probably deserved it! It was tough for the newly arrived like me to fit in behind the Tweed Curtain. I should have stuck in those days to tweeds with leather elbow patches! Lotus City savoir-faire! Dr A's daughter kept you on your toes!

Osprey

I have been watching the Osprey fishing in our harbour today. They nest across the harbour by the Three Sisters islands. The water is deeper there, so the bird fishes on this side, where the water is shallow and the fish are nearer the surface. The osprey appears to dive head-first into the shallow water but comes up with the fish in the talons. They must make an abrupt turn at the surface of the water after the dive, in order to seize the fish with the claws and surge up on the wing through the surface tension of the water. They are so fast you can't tell just by watching. The Osprey is a beautiful bird and more easily adept at hovering and diving than the Eagle, which swipes the water when it fishes. The Eagle's technique is more in keeping with picking up ducks; its more usual fare. The Osprey is far less commonly seen than the Eagle in our area. Later in the season the Kingfisher appears and fishes in the same spot as the Osprey, hovering in the same way, diving in the same way, but beak first, and comes up with the fish in its beak. Hover and dive and breaking surface into the air in one fluid motion requires strong wings, strong necks, patience, accuracy, buoyancy, and good knowledge of the best fishing holes! Both the Kingfisher and the Osprey are an object lesson in elegant ergonomics! The Osprey picked up a fish today right under the nose of a Blue Heron. Success in "one fell swoop".

Newspapers

The newspaper as we knew it is slowly becoming obsolete. Not soon, but sometime! For a medium that is said to provide crisp analytical insight, the newspaper industry missed the boat in predicting their own survival. They didn't read the writing on the wall soon enough. What we are doing on the Internet is as immense as the industrial revolution. Instant information has and will revolutionize civilization and will put the giving and receiving in the hands of everyone. Nothing, including television, has ever before provided the transactional nature of information we are now blessed with! Dare we say, "The medium is the message"! Interactive per se does not guarantee good content. Power to the people requires the development of mature structure. This is the challenge when technology is so far ahead of content! Whether content will make that information useful, productive, open, and solve many of the world's problems, is another matter. It may be a step in the development of the "oneness" of humanity. What we have been getting for years are opinion pieces from a select few. Guidance is given with oversight of the facts; usually interpreted by the presenter of the facts! Entertainment can overcome accuracy. "News paper" at times may be a bit of a misnomer! Ask yourself how often the subject of an article that you have an in depth knowledge of, is superficial and slanted. That may apply widely don't you think? At least, with the burgeoning Internet sites, the dispersal of information by social media allows for much more resource to be available to the reader! I drive regularly past the pulp mill in Crofton, BC. I think to myself, "if there is one thing I will never invest in now, it is pulp." The newsprint business is going to fade! We are in for a paperless universe! The large logs that traverse the Island roads every few minutes of the day for processing, the barge loads of chips and sawdust entering regularly, and the major ship loading docks are ultimately in jeopardy. The demise of the newspaper as a major force is inevitable! I think the whole thing is somewhat sad because there is a loss of the tangibility that newspapers provide; but "it is what it is". Maybe we don't need something to hold. Let's hope human beings can do their own filtering rather than always having it done for them!

Wealth

DUKE: " If thou art rich, thou'rt poor; For, like an ass whose back with ingots bows, Thou bear'st thy heavy riches but a journey, and death unloads thee". Also, "and when thou art old and rich, thou hast neither heat, affection, limb, nor beauty, to make thy riches pleasant" (Measure for Measure). Why is it we learn everything the hard way? We all have something I think, of Gordon Gekko in us, at least I do!. He is aptly named, almost spelt like the lizard and appropriately located "on the Wall". I've looked in the mirror over my time and it's not all good. I have periods of being empathically challenged! Wealth has taken a beating these days and maybe it's a good thing. Maybe we should adopt the "Year of Release" every 7 years when all debts are forgiven and we start again. Fat chance! I really don't believe that anyway! It might have worked in the tight colony of the ancient Hebrews! Maybe we should have a "Year of Jubilee" every 50 years when land is returned to the dispossessed. The Dukes of Sutherland would thereby have left a nobler legacy, but then most of us wouldn't be in Canada! If you really believe Shakespeare had it right, it still "cuts no ice"! Some still cling to what they have 'til the agonal state arrives. At that time, little is plenty. I belatedly realized my only wealth is around the dinner table at Christmas time or the summer holiday! Why don't I continue to remind myself of that every day? Human Nature!

Rhubarb, the First Fruit

Rhubarb is the first fruit of the season. Some say that Rhubarb is infradig. What a heavy trip to put on a beautiful and ancient plant! I think that comes from the fact that it is too easy to grow. They said " If you can grow it on the prairies it can't be much of a feather in your cap!" Practical people have got out of the feather and cap business. Do what works! I think there is something of vegetable and fruit snobbery in the food business these days. People often want something exotic they can't grow or won't grow. With rhubarb, this may be because urban people don't have a big patch to plant perennials, or else a limited knowledge of cooking from the garden. Rhubarb freezes beautifully with or without sugar. The variety I have is "Victoria" and it's easy to grow, provides a lot of product, is immune to disease and is free of pests. It's a gift to the novice with a deep dirt patch and a good compost pile. We lift and split the roots every four years and replant in a different part of the plot.

The pianist and I make 12 to 14 frozen deepdish rhubarb pies in cake pans every year. Picking and preparation time is easy and rapid. Timing is everything for harvest as it quickly extends into Currant and Gooseberry season and the stalks decline here after June. I could never keep the rhubarb plump enough to combine it with our strawberries when they ripen. Some like the combination but we haven't tried. I suppose we could use California strawberries. The pianist likes the small stalks since her mother was of the opinion that the rhubarb sauce was redder. I like big stalks since they are faster to process. We work it out! There is nothing nicer than a rhubarb pie at Christmas for you and your children and grandchildren. When one is born on the bald prairie at the height of the great depression, one never totally escapes the dread induced in you by your parents that without basic food that you can grow or store you are somehow naked and exposed. Rhubarb gives you a big bang for your buck if you grow it yourself!

Nutrition

A farting horse will never tire; a farting man is the man to hire!

My pioneer family's homely refrain was a reflection of the nutritional needs, and the assurance that things were in good working order, at a time of deprivation. A hearty meal for horse and man, eaten quickly, provided jet fuel for hard work. Possibly the publicly flatulent are less restrained and therefore in the eyes of the jingle writer, more "gung ho". Such a view needs further research. The volume of intestinal gas is increased with a high carbohydrate diet such as would be expected in pioneer days. Moreover the "poor man's food", Brassicaceae and beans, would have contributed mightily to this gas! There is high correlation observed of intestinal gas and caloric intake when investigated. Mean total volume of intestinal gas produced per day in a healthy adult averages 705 ml. and this includes both bolus gas (swallowed), and gas from colonic fermentation. Swallowed gas would be increased in the trencherman. The speed with which the trencherman "fueled up" on these foods increased air swallowing. The rate of daily emission of flatus is variable but was enhanced by heavy ploughing and digging as the pioneer hired man and his horse toiled in the soil. The pioneer diet also provided a significant, sturdy obesity that served as a base of reserve when the 6th and 7th stages of man could leave you atrophied. Sort of getting a physical head start in life's race. Low carbohydrate diets, associated with high fibre meals, reduce flatulence considerably, but at the expense of energy; not desirable in the case of the hired man! Moreover, there was no mechanization to speak of on the farm at that time. Petrol was of no use. You literally couldn't work the farm without your hired man and horse," running on all cylinders ". It's no surprise the horse and the hired man lived apart in their own quarters.

Hippocratic Frame

"The Hippocratic Frame"

The drawing shows a frame popularized by the Hippocratic School of Medicine at Kos in the Aegean about 400 BC. The portrayal of the reduction of the dislocated shoulder is still an acceptable mano-ever today, but now we just stick a stocking foot in the armpit and pull like hell. It's still called the Hippocratic Method. I was privileged to perform orthopedic surgery for over 35 years in Lotus City and to have worked shoulder to shoulder with so many fine surgeons. The advances in surgical techniques over that period of time are immense. Curiously the refinement in operative techniques, though important, are overshadowed by the tremendous developments in bioengineering, implant technology, computer generated imaging, fiber-optic advances and cellular physiology that have contributed greatly to the excellence of today's orthopedic techniques. The manifest importance of cross-fertilization is clear! We owe a great deal to the non-surgical disciplines for the range of treatments now available. No longer Jack-of-all-trades and Master of none, today's crop of orthopedic surgeons has concentrated their work into sub-specialties of excellence. The training of young orthopedic surgeons has become so comprehensive now as to turn out a highly skilled individual, unlike the training available in my day which was as extensive, but not as well organized and less directed by formal programming. It was up to us to seek out jobs that we thought would build up our skills. It was still, even then, a rigorous apprenticeship! Life long learning is a blessing, conferred by teamwork and group interaction. Old guys like me could fly on the coattails of the young. The Hippocratic Corpus-- (the ancient body of knowledge), is replete with observations of an orthopedic surgical nature that reveal that musculo-skeletal surgeons have been around a very long time.

Struck by Lightning

Our family of four was struck by lightning when anchored just offshore in the Salish Sea. The pianist and I were in the cabin cruiser with our 13 and 11 year old. The youngest of 8 was onshore in a tree house with her friend. The weather had been unsettled that day and we were sleeping aboard at night when a savage storm struck with both forked and sheet lightning. Our family friends in their cottage rescued the tree dwellers and watched us through their windows as the storm surged around them and us. They said with each lightning strike the entire bottom of the bay was lit up. The four of us, trapped in the cabin, held hands and prayed. It's a certain sign of extreme anxiety when you can get a 13 year old and an 11 year old to pray aloud and fervently for salvation! The roof leak in the cabin cruiser drenched us, but we didn't notice. The boat was anchored in the bay on the mud floor with a heavy chain since it was pretty shallow anchorage. At the height of the storm we were struck by a bolt of lightning and heard an instant clap of loud thunder. The boat shook! We shook! There was an instant smell of ozone throughout the boat. The anchor chain must have grounded our boat. A fresh downpour made us wetter by the minute. It would have been dangerous to try to make shore in a dingy in that storm. We simply had to wait it out. In the morning we observed the drinking water in our galvanized tank under the floorboards had gone from clear and clean, to the color of 2% milk. In the aftermath, all of us, and our old boat, were undamaged. Our friends said as they watched us in the storm, they thought we might be "goners" because they saw the lightning strike the boat. Our 8 year old was safely out of the tree house but was terrified for us. A number of trees were downed in that storm and a nearby cottage destroyed. Though this happened almost 40 years ago the dangers of the sea and the weather, and the power of prayer are etched in our collective memories!

Tilling Fallow Ground

In this week's Economist, the book reviewer, in reference to elegiac writing says, "…the very possibility of death's approach gives a new urgency and a new energy to the apprehending eye. Everything to be seen and heard becomes precious and surprising". It strikes me that it's not too late to recreate the time needed to unwind one's life and address the world anew. It just takes a bit of work. It's tempting to hide inward rather than work at change because there is so much emphasis on bad news these days. It may tempt you to weave a web of spit around yourself and hang upside down and let it harden. If you make a cocoon for yourself it won't work and you will still eventually emerge unchanged. I'm "long of time" these days, so have taken the elegy to heart and will tackle a job that has been put off for years with new urgency and energy. It will be worthwhile since the subject is precious and surprising. Fifty years of photographs, slides, 8-millimeter movies and stereo slides; some in a state of relative disrepair and often not well edited are crying out for care. If we don't tackle the job now it won't get done as all our offspring and their children are too busy. We are also the custodians of the older generation's pictures. We are now the only ones who can identify many of the people pictured from our prior generations. Who else has time and the apprehending eye for this sort of stuff other than a geezer? This is fallow ground that needs urgent tillage and the more I look at these images the more enthused I get about putting them in order for those who will follow. These seeds have been sitting in the cupboard for a long time; they'll still germinate, but the remaining number of Springtimes for us are running out. I have to stay out of the cocoon for a while.

Squirrel scraps

The little brown squirrel that is co-owner of this ground is not easily taught to clean up his mess on top of our barbeque. In the fall he spends a lot of time pulling off the scales on the Douglas fir cones and eating and hoarding the seeds, leaving the scales strewn about. Now he has clearly opened his storehouse of last year's maple husks, resurrected them, cracking them open and eating the seeds. Home for the little brown squirrel according to my neighbor was in our woodpile. Not the new one but the old punky one that we have given up on; the one that is slowly slipping back to nature with a mix of bugs. Why does the squirrel store in one place and then transport them up to our barbeque to eat under the barbeque cover? Maybe he prefers not to eat in the old woodpile with all those bugs. I don't blame him. He is very social so maybe he likes company. He can eat and talk at the same time! He is very saucy too. He gives us the "ole' eyeball" as he eats and scolds, almost saying, "You don't frighten me buddy boy! I can move like lightning if I want, skip and fly; but I don't want to yet! So there!" I love his attitude but I worry because we have a lot of raptors that enjoy squirrel. What I find are the scraps he leaves behind, all the seeds removed, husks littered about, and he neither cleans the table, nor wipes up after himself. His table manners seem atrocious. I clean up after him at least once a week. It's worth it for us to be his buds!

Gospel music

Last Saturday the pianist and I went to a performance of Chor Leoni. They are a noted Canadian men's choir from "Olympic City" and usually sing classical music, what ever that is. The pianist says, " Within the common practice period." I like that term better since my tastes are more eclectic, or maybe more vulgar, I'm not sure which. Whatever! We often get good musical performances at Lotus Island since our theatre is excellent and performances are well attended. Chor Leoni gave a program of Gospel music that was outstanding. It got me thinking widely about Harriet Beecher Stowe and Stephen Foster, the compelling nature of Gospel music and that genre of thinking, and the ovum that is buried in Everyman that seeks to be penetrated by a chord of truth and beauty! I went away from the performance thinking that there is little or no distinction between the secular and the religious in many ways. Stephen Foster in his short and desperate life provided soul music that lifted his nation and struck a chord in Everyman. Harriet Beecher Stowe wrote a story that shocked and revolutionized an attitude that cracked barriers forever. Technically, they may not have produced so-called great literature or music, but they touched the spirit. Both were criticized mightily in their lifetime, and Uncle Tom's Cabin was shunned up to modern times. How would these two have known that the influence they provided has lasted up to this time? When you walk away from a performance with a warm glow in your heart and resolve for the umpteenth time to crank up your "anima", you can celebrate both classical and classy! Religious is, as religious does!

Canoe River BC

In November 1950 a troop train transporting Canadian Army troops for embarkation to Korea was in a collision with the Continental passenger, eastbound. Twenty-one people died in that collision, mostly troops of No.1 Royal Canadian Horse Artillery from Shilo, Manitoba and four railway employees. The collision occurred at Canoe River BC in the Rocky Mountains. The army and railway eventually charged a twenty-two year old telegrapher with manslaughter on the alleged basis of failure to transmit accurate orders. I remember the crisis in our family at that time because my dad, a station agent, had copied orders on that same troop train earlier on the day before and it was not clear at that time where the fault lay! Remember, at that time orders were by telegraph. They were transmitted to the engineer on a paper slip attached to a hoop held up from the station platform as the train passed through, slowing down at the yellow light which indicated new orders were available, for which "meet", and which "siding" to take. There was always the potential for disaster! The dispatcher in Winnipeg phoned my dad directly after the accident telling him to seal his copy of the order for safekeeping. He was subject to immediate assessment by the railway inspectors. To the relief of all of us, my dad's orders were all right! This tragedy was subject to a trial in BC. John G Diefenbaker assumed the defense of the young telegrapher, gratis. Mr. Diefenbaker paid 1500 dollars in order to become a member of the BC bar for this occasion and went through the bar examination where it was said that the only question asked of him was to define a "tort". John Diefenbaker succeeded in defense of the client whom he portrayed as a scapegoat for the prosecution. The death of so many was an incredible tragedy, but he succeeded in laying the fault on the systems rather than the employee! In our family at that time, and after he became Prime Minister, we thought no one could be considered greater than the man who freely gave his time to serving persons like us; ordinary Canadians. When Mr. Diefenbaker died, the people in our towns along the main line lined up for hours to salute the passenger funeral train as it passed by. The common touch is what distinguished him and the things we valued!

Clam digging

Today my neighbor and I dug clams. Actually we raked clams, as they are only a few inches below the surface. Butter clams and Little Neck clams are abundant on our beach since there are very few people that care to harvest them now. I don't know why that is so since they are delicious in chowder which I am about to make. I picked up 50 clams in a nine square foot area with about 20 minutes of work--if you don't add in 40 minutes of talking time. I'm soaking them in water now to encourage them to get rid of the sand. I'll steam them up in order to facilitate shucking them tomorrow and then make Manhattan clam chowder. The pianist doesn't like clams, so it's all for me. Once you start to collect clams there is a natural tendency to take more than you really need. Some restraint is good, only because you can get yourself in a mess cooking in factory like volumes, chopping vegetables, straining the liquid, packaging, labeling, freezing and washing up. Now that I think of it, maybe people are smart to avoid clam digging. This is the first week in three months that we have had daytime low tides. Despite the fact that my neighbor and I could never make a good living manufacturing clam chowder, it is a satisfying pursuit to cycle what we think is our own resource. Of course, calling it "our own resource" is nonsense. We return the shells and adductor muscles to Mother Nature's beach for recycling. In Canada, the people "own" the beach just to the high tide mark. Forgive me for saying, "own". It's only a manner of speaking! We really lease everything in this life anyway!

Osmosis

When the pianist says, "No one ever taught me how to cook. I just learned by osmosis by always being around my mother. I learned unconsciously by absorption": I say, "Tell me more!" Osmosis is simply described as the transfer of water across a semi permeable membrane from a low solute concentration to a high solute concentration to establish equilibrium. The transfer of information by osmosis from the less dense to the more dense will gradually move toward equilibrial density. These osmotic transfers of water and information take place with low energy expenditure. When I worked as a surgeon over the years I did many things that worked well, and I knew what I knew, but often I didn't know how I knew it! With experience of years, much of what we learn is intuitive and gained by osmosis. This knowledge seeps in through the semipermeable membrane that you exposed to the world. If your membrane is impervious that osmotic transfer doesn't occur! For the pianist and me there needed to be, in addition, a high energy expenditure as well. Both of us needed a high energy expenditure for the physiology of our bodies to maintain the necessary osmotic pressure gradients necessary for life, since passive osmotic processes are not enough. Both of us needed high energy expenditure in the active learning process which is volitional and identifiable. Osmosis is not enough! My aunt Mary always said, "Your little daughter is a bundle of energy!" She was righter than she knew, since thermodynamics and molecular science tell us that we are simply molecular energy bundles! Energy= Work+Heat. The conversion of energy to work is always imperfect and the excess energy is given off in the way of heat. Study is directed work, provided by energy, and is also imperfect and is accompanied by an energy loss. Intelligent study will render energy conversion to work more efficient and lose less heat. Or if you are like me, a lousy woodchopper, you will convert that energy to highly inefficient work, and get bloody hot in the process. We can't depend only on passive osmosis and permeability in our intellectual or physical world. Active learning augments osmotic transfer by the addition of fostering selective osmotic gradients that require energy, transformed to work plus heat, to maintain life and intelligent life!

Orange Marmalade

It's mid-January on Lotus Island and I hustled to the supermarket to get the first of the Seville oranges that have just arrived. They are not a hot ticket item anymore so they often languish in the bin at the store and dry out. We hardy few who look forward to our bitter marmalade preservation every year mark the calendar. The Seville oranges come from boulevard trees in Mesa, Arizona. Mary, Queen of Scots would have had her oranges shipped from Spain. A patient, years ago, a distant Chivers relative, gave me his three-day recipe that I have faithfully followed. Since some of the people I care for do not like marmalade with large peel pieces I have dispensed with tradition and use the Cuisinart to chop the peel more finely. One does what one has to. My oranges today are clean and plump. Sevilles are amongst the most ugly of the orange varieties so don't be dissuaded by their lack of beauty! Don't take offence at the bitterness of the fruit. Ugly and bitter will transform into sublime in the hands of the lover. Gentle patience is all that is necessary! Here is the recipe. I make a double batch.

Day 1, 8 large Seville oranges, 2 lemons. Halve these and remove the fruit. Leave the pith on the skin. Place the fruit in a muslin bag. Chop up the orange and lemon peel with the pith. Place all the material in a large container. Make sure your muslin bag doesn't leak or you'll have seeds in your marmalade. Add ten cups of water and soak everything overnight.

Day 2, Boil contents for 45 minutes. Let cool and rest for the balance of the day. You may need more water than the recipe calls for, I have found. Keep a sharp eye.

Day 3, Take out the muslin bag and squeeze well. Add 1 and 1-quarter cups of sugar to each cup of your product. Boil for 45 minutes from the time of rapid boiling. Simmer longer if the marmalade does not jell well when dripping off the spoon. Fill jars and seal when hot, in jars oven heated at 275 degrees. Quality of the jelling in my opinion comes from the thickness of the pith. The marmalade darkens over the year but quality remains. No pectin needed: no citrate compounds: no treacle! Bon appetite!

Scum, skim, and fuzz

When I boiled my marmalade mix in sugar today for the requisite 45 minutes, I created scum on the surface margins of my product. Some call it fuzz, and others, froth. If you want your marmalade in the jars to be pristine, without little gobs of scum, skim your scum from the margins of the pot before pouring in the jars. For skimming I use a flat edged spoon. The scum or froth or fuzz is good to eat and I saved my scum in a little bowl for immediate eating. My mother always allowed us boys to eat all the scum from her preserves, on bread and butter. It may be that the particular amongst us would turn up their nose at scum. They might say that it was infradig to eat scum. I am sure however that the same person probably relishes the froth on their cappuccino and the other epicurean concoctions available in the cardboard cupfuls! I skimmed my scum today and have tried it on 2 slices of whole-wheat toast. My marmalade is sealing and snapping as I write. Why we ever allowed these pejorative terms to describe a delicious side product of the jam business that has all the attributes of goodness without the prettiness of the retail product, I do not know. Beauty trumps flavour in the real world! Enjoy your cappuccino fuzz. Skim the fuzz off with your spoon before drinking, or you'll have fuzzy lips and a white mustache!

Garden Bones

The bones within the established enclosure we call the garden are dry bones and living bones. The mighty conifers, old orchard trees and venerable ornamentals have "ruah" and are living bones. If they are well placed it is unwise to disturb the skeleton created by Mother Nature. They carry their own sinews and flesh and lift them up as a risen testament to life. The dry bones are another matter. Not withstanding Ezekiel, these dry bones will not rise again; they will not be covered with their own sinew and flesh, and they are expendable. The thoughtful gardener will work with the living skeleton to complement its beauty and only flesh out the bed on which it rests. The dry, man made bones of terraces, lattice works, fences, new beds and structures can be changed or modified to suit the palate of the current garden custodian. You can add sinews and flesh to these structures, but they will never grow sinews or flesh themselves. No mighty tree can be replaced in a gardener's lifetime. No birds of a variety will frequent your enclosure without trees. No sweet or otherwise songs will fill your air with passion! Your exhilaration in meandering will be muted. "Thus there are two books from whence I collect my divinity: besides that written one of God, another of his servant Nature, that universal and public manuscript, that lies expansed unto the eyes of all; those that never saw him in the One, have discovered him in the Other" (Religio Medici). Don't change what 'aint broke! There are an infinite number of shorter-term things you can do to put your own imprimatur in place on the page. Just don't change the parchment!

An Ugly Boat

Our family owned what was one of the more ugly boats on the wet coast. It was a wood planked, twenty-six and a half foot semi-planing hull with a smoky and loud diesel engine. It was a single- screw and it ran at seven and a half knots at best. I bought it for two and a half thousand dollars in 1968 and we had it for twenty years. It was the kind of boat you could hammer a nail in anywhere, to hang anything you wanted. The pianist made curtains and nice mattress covers for the bunk beds and made it homey as best she could, but much of it remained "dressed up ugly "! We were very fond of our boat as a family of five and used it constantly, so it never let us down. A boat in constant use remains a faithful companion. If you don't "use it, you lose it". Every time I went down to paint the boat at the marina, I went fishing instead. When it needed caulking, I was a fast caulker so the cabin continued to leak, but we had more fishing time. We went for a summer cruise in the Salish Sea for a week and the weather was squally. We were caught at sea in the squall and our clothing became wet with our cabin roof leak. The pianist jury-rigged a clothesline and we hung our clothes out to dry when the sun came out and put into Bedwell, the nearest harbour. Bedwell is aptly named, as it is a secluded refuge for overnighters. As we pulled into the harbor we could see a flotilla of large, white, sleek, beautiful boats, with a clutch of glistening people in whites, deck shoes and big hair, cooking steaks on the Hibachi at wharf side. My 14-year-old son said, "Shit, we should get out of here!" I'm sure he spoke for all of us, but by then we were committed. As I eased our smoking, ugly stinkpot into the moorage, the disdain from the boaters was palpable. Certainly the pianist's clothesline added to the picture: the flags of the Salish Hillbillies. I did think however that in all probability we were the only people moored who owned their own boat! Maybe the only ones that could manage a single- screw!

Cucumbers

I have been laboring under the illusion for years that gynoecious cucumbers produced cukes without the need of male flowers. Apparently that is not so! I am now given to understand that the seed sellers include a marked, male flower producing cucumber seed, or two, in the package with the females, to grow up to be a big boy and fertilize the gynecological crowd. Cucumbers labelled as gynoecious have female flowers primarily but still need a pollinator male! This seems eminently more sensible but why didn't I clue into this before? I think it is because when I ordered seeds of Carmen, a cuke that has performed well for me in the greenhouse, it costed out at about $2.00 a seed and there were only five female seeds in a packet. There was no male seed in the package! The answer I learned is that Carmen is a parthenogenic cuke! There is no male seed needed. What we have in some plants, some lower order animals, and some experimental species, is a looming crisis to the "drones" of the world. It's been coming for a long time slowly and inexorably. Boys, you had better get to work to find your niche before it's too late! You may have thought the sperm bank would be your nemesis, but there is now an even larger cloud over the horizon; Parthenogenesis! And moreover the offspring of these cucumbers, Carmen, are all sweet females. Prolific and not bitter!

Gophers (Prairie Dogs)

My brother Ken told me he took his son to the Saskatchewan prairies several years ago and they stopped enroute and shot prairie dogs as a part of Ken's nostalgic return to the past. Gophers, as we knew them in the olden days and still now, are pests to the farmers. The number of varieties of species of gopher are quite overwhelming but for us as children they were just "gophers". The current measures of gopher control in Saskatchewan include various poisons like Strychnine, and shooting as a sort of control sport. We were too young for guns and too innocent for poison when we were children. Living in the then small town of Kindersley, the bald prairie was close at hand and in the spring the sloughs were full of water. It was easy to haul a pail of water from the slough to the burrow hole, fill the burrow with water and guard both the front and rear burrow entrances. When the poor bedraggled gopher emerged we would club it to death and cut off the tail. We got one cent per tail and deceitful or not, if the tail was particularly long, we cut it in half. Our family left Kindersley when I was 13 so this was a little boy business. The tail production was not substantial but a penny is a penny. It dismays me now that the rather grotesque nature of our work seems to indicate that we were bereft of finer feelings. I think now of the seal hunt and the animal rights group and harken back to that earlier time. Certainly there is no distancing of the act of killing when one drowns or clubs a little animal to death.

Bird Feeders

My Italian friend I studied with in Plymouth, England, liked to eat small birds. It apparently was a custom in Milan. He and I studied together in the same house and when he studied he set a food trap for small birds, starlings and the like. He'd then hang them in the basement for a few days 'til the meat "matured", cook them whole on a spit and invite his friends for a dinner party. Our family with two small children lived upstairs in the council house and were aghast at this barbarity. It was contrary to the pianist's teaching that "God sees the little sparrow fall." I attended once by myself, when invited to the meal and found it interesting but unusual. Of course the English neighbors found this small bird feeding custom offensive but my friend persisted. It reminded me, however, of my culinary endeavors as a boy in Kindersley, Saskatchewan in the 1940's. We had a dam adjacent to the town and it was a favorite place for 10 to 12 year olds to play. The dam was the only water source around in the arid, bald prairie, so it attracted much bird life around it and in the spillway. My friend had a Red Ryder BB gun and we shot, over time, a few small birds, sparrows and red wing blackbirds and cooked them at the dam site. Our stove as I recall was an oilcan turned upside down with wood and brickets as fuel. We boiled the breasts of the small birds in a little pot. I also remember cooking fried eggs on the flat surface of the oilcan. I cannot remember the taste of our product, but it probably left something to be desired. I cannot remember any other small bird dining parties. What we small bird feeders have to answer for!

Bad Breath Soup

A variety of soup the pianist occasionally prepared much to the objection of some of our children was a variation of ham and split pea soup. The children named it Bad Breath Soup. The soup was a derivative of the previous meal that was always New England boiled dinner. This consisted of a large ham, boiled with onion, cabbage, carrots and spuds and then the soup was made with the leftovers and with the "held over" boiling water. A big dollop of split peas was added to the soup, as well as seasoning. The boiled New England dinner is served as big chunks on a large platter and gave a visual image of plenitude. The chunks were later diced more finely for the soup. There was always enough to freeze several soup packets. The nose and tongue, though aligned and working in concert, are neurologically autonomous. The tongue taste buds are mediated by the 7th, 9th, and 10th cranial nerves and the olfactory role of the nose by the 1st cranial nerve. What an object smells like is a scent that is somewhat different from how it tastes. The wine and cheese tasters know that is so, but they may not know why! The soup that derives from the boiled dinner may not have the visual appeal but the taste and the smell certainly appeal. Bad Breath Soup is a misnomer. A more apt name would be Strong Breath Soup. It smells like onion and cabbage, both hearty and pungent vegetables that give a superb scent. The quality of the delicate taste is a blend of all the ingredients; the sensations conducted by an orchestra of cranial nerves ,separate, but in concert. As adults, our mature children have developed a keen relish for Bad Breath Soup, as it continues to be called by its traditional name. Our children learned to eat this soup by the admonition that, "Bad breath is better than no breath at all!"

Gravy

When my mother died and we planned her funeral, my brother Ken was elected to do a eulogy because the rest of us would have cried. He said in his remembrance that she was famous amongst her friends and acquaintances for her turkey gravy! We, her family, didn't know that! Sure, we knew her turkey gravy was good as we had eaten it many times but we did not know that its fame had known few bounds. Ken said she was also somewhat less famous, but not much less, for her small soft buns and lemon curd tarts. When I married the pianist years ago, she made gravy like her mother did. The pianist's mother was a careful cook who followed a recipe exactly and was vigilant to avoid ingredients that could lead to obesity or heart disease. She was well ahead of her time. Her turkey gravy method was to spoon off virtually all of the fat and add pre-mixed flour and water to the turkey browning. Then she boiled the gravy vigorously while stirring, adding her vegetable water and seasoning as required. My mother, never to my knowledge followed a recipe. Her construction of turkey gravy consisted of adding the dry flour to the browning and drippings without removing any fat. She would stir and scrape the molten mass into a brown, boggy glob, whereupon she added plain water, stirred more vigorously, boiling to reduce. She only seasoned with pepper and salt. Of course, the gravy flavour arose not only from the turkey but from the dressing as well. The pianist is now well known for her turkey gravy and has adopted the excellence of both of her mentors. She gets rid of much of the fat but adds the dry flour directly. Best of both worlds!

Road to Beulah

My father's family farmed in Isabella, Manitoba from the later 1800's. A town near them was Beulah. This area of Manitoba was the best farmland in the province. The Assiniboine River deposited deep dirt from the prehistoric flooding of the area. Our pioneer family came to northern Ontario as part of the Clearances in the earlier 1800's and then homesteaded in Manitoba later, in search of more and better land. My dad often made fun of Beulah with us because in the heyday of these towns Isabella always had a better hockey and baseball team than did, hapless Beulah. Both Beulah and Isabella have disappeared with the changing times. The first pioneers who homesteaded in Beulah would have named it as the community developed. It must have seemed full of promise to the landless that built the first sod houses in the area; hence its name. I have an early picture of my great grandfather by his sod house. He doesn't look like he is in heaven! The road to Beulah is long and winding with many side roads. The pianist and I are on the road to Beulah. We have taken a lot of side roads at one time but there are fewer roads now we wish to travel. After 54 years of marriage we are not interested in playing hockey or baseball. The deep dirt will still be there, but the sod huts are gone. Beulah may be small but it was never the wilderness. I'm just hoping that there is still a place for us in Beulah!

Foods of yesteryear

When one looks at today's foods, the ethnic cooking, the diet cooking, the cosmopolitan choices of ingredients available, the pre-pared foods, the restaurant meals; the foodstuffs of yesteryear are frequently forgotten! The things we ate during the Second World War, the pioneer food and the poor person foodstuffs are of some interest, at least to me. I have tried some of these recipes to take a fresh look at what we ate in those days. Raisin pie was as common as apple pie when I was a kid. No one I know eats raisin pie today but I was reminded what a good old taste it was when I made one. The drawback is the pounds it will add! How about Shoofly Pie? The pianist and I tried it once. Brown sugar and molasses! When that was what you had, that's what you used. I tried Irish Soda Bread once and cooked it in the fire-place on a grate insert over woodcoals since I didn't have peat chunks. It wasn't bad for a cook without yeast. Just a bit labor intensive! I never tried Colcannon but I grew lots of kale one year and mixed it in with mashed potato. Delicious! My mother made Mockapple pie a few times during the war, with soda crackers, lemon juice and sugar as a substitute for apples. I tried it once experimentally. It's a poor substitute for apple pie, but it is surprisingly deceptive. If we were still hungry after supper my mother would say we could have bread and milk. I remember eating bread and milk laced with sugar. I tried it the other day. It was filling. I had never eaten Brewis 'til we went to Nova Scotia last year and I ordered it at a restaurant. It wasn't too bad. I can't make it here on Lotus Island since salt cod is not readily available. I guess when some people talk about plain cooking, at least in those times the plain cooks cooked, which may not always be the case today. It seems to me the more shiny copper tools hanging from the show kitchen rafters the less cooking is being done. Maybe this churlish assumption is my hang-up! I admit it! Let's just say that a standing rib roast with gravy, tarragon oven roasted potatoes, broccoli cooked "al dente", and deep dish Gravenstein apple pie, cooked in a country kitchen is not plain cooking by my definition!

Whither Fritz Perls?

I often wonder what remnants of the sixties still can be found in the litter of today's world and its ethos. If one throws enough mud against the wall, will some of it stick? Was it all in vain? Did anything that Fritz Perls talked about at Big Sur result in any long-term influence, or change our present way of looking at relationships, or was it just jargon going nowhere? Did Easy Rider, Fellini Satyricon or Blowup give a kickstart to a change of perception that lasted? Did Alan Watts, poor man, make any sense to the world, grappling with his identity issues and ours? What about Robert Bly and his male concepts in Iron John? Did this speak to any males seeking to redefine themselves? Is it only Leonard Cohen that is left carrying an old torch? I think not. He still speaks to many. Are there still subversives that see a way out of the polarized and hugely "structured in the box" thinking of today? Yes! What ever happened to love when success took over? What ever happened to peace when gratuitous violence took over? What ever happened to freedom when regulation ramped up? Sure, there was a lot wrong with all that earlier stuff. Some people would say, "You must be an old hippy." It was often impractical but it had some of the "right stuff". I think there is still mud on the wall. It included seeing the divine in your neighbor for all his and your own warts, and caring about it. I hope we can look at the mosaic that is the world and pick out bits and pieces of it that we can say, "Here is, 'I have a dream!'" The church I go to tries to get out of the box and seek the core values of loving your neighbor as yourself, and the neighbor is the world and the whole community. It's a start. We want to be part of an emerging mosaic. We are beset with fetters of our own making in the church these days. Whether we can work out of our packaged ideas and open up to life hinges on our capacity to acknowledge all parts of the elephant, though we be partially blind!

Tickle your bum

When I was five years old and after my brother Ken had been born, I went from good to naughty. I was no longer the center of my mother's universe in 1939. We lived at that time in Melfort, Saskatchewan and my father was frequently working out of town. My mother had a daytime girl to help with the household. The outhouse was at the back of our lot by the lane. The outhouse was a one holer and not over a pit but rather over a can that was emptied by the frequent visits of the honeyman. The access to the can was a flap that lifted up on hinges, at the back of the outhouse. The daytime girl who helped my mother came to the outhouse to do a bit of "business" when my small friend and I were playing in the lane. The scene I am about to describe is as vivid in my mind's eye now as it was at the time! When the daygirl was in the outhouse, my little friend and I lifted the back flap and held it up while we inspected. I can see that big bum hanging down through the one holer as if it was yesterday. I tickled it with a long piece of grass and then we ran. I can remember her racing out of the outhouse and yelling, "I'm going to tell your mother! " I don't remember the outcome. Memory is selective.

Witching

The phenomenon of mind- body interaction is mysterious. When the pianist and I bought our piece of ground on Lotus Island the first job was to look for water. We had use of a jointly owned well, but we needed a backup plan. We hired a witcher. There is a reason it is called witching. It may be more accurate to call it "bewitching". Moreover, I had seen the movie, "Mr. Blandings Builds His Dream House". I had some knowledge about the fruitless search for water from the dowser in the movie, which was not encouraging! Our dowser came with his witching rod of willow and dowsed on our plot in the most likely of places. I expected the process to be amusing and primitive. Sure enough, his dowser dipped and water was found in an area near the surface. Actually, it was too near the surface to be of use, other than as a cribbed shallow well for watering the plants. We never bothered to crib it. However, I was intrigued about the mysterious process and started on my own to dowse. I tried forked willow, forked vine maple and a wire coat hanger. If I approached a part of the lot where water was possible, each of my witching tools would dip easily and strongly, including the wire coathanger! What was this phenomenon? I do not know. As a scientist it is easy to be skeptical, particularly about other people's inexplicable experiences. One can say," What benefit will accrue to this other person if they are convincing, or is it worth their while to fudge the truth?" Or, one can say, "Is this other person sincere but credulous?" Or one can accept that there is a realm of phenomena for which we have no logical explanation. Speculation is not a substitute for explanation. I wasn't committed enough to drill several dozen holes deep into the bowels of our ground to investigate whether I was crazy or not! A mind-body phenomenon! I am convinced that though my mind said this was nonsense, the body responded as if it wasn't. Cognitive dissonance!

Mother Nature's Garden

In the more bucolic parts of Lotus Island, Mother Nature's handiwork is in full display this spring morning. The Indian Plum (Oemleria cerasiformis) is in full flower. This small tree or shrub is the first of Mother Nature's to flower. The plum is widespread throughout the island and like us, is not spectacularly beautiful, but is plentiful, durable and fruitful. The Red Alders are abundantly present throughout Mother Nature's plot and the red catkins are in full bloom. Though the Red Alder (Alnus rubra) is so named because of its red bark, the male catkins, when a grove of Alder is seen from a distance, give a beautiful red brown hue to the landscape. The western view from the Fulford harbour ferry is fantastic. The wild American plum, (Prunus americana) is also in bloom, white flowered, beautiful and abundant. It might be more of "an escape" than Mother Nature's baby. In a way though, I suppose we are all "an escape". It just depends when rather than whether! Over our painted deck the three Western Red Cedars (Thuja plicata) have been dropping their cones for the last two weeks." The tiny cones stick to the deck because of the little irregular scale like shape. They don't seem to provoke interest from the Oregon Juncos that are making the rounds right now. "The air is thick with pollen", the pianist commented to me on the walk yesterday. It has to be the Alders and the Indian Plum as the Maples and Cottonwoods are not in bloom yet. Last year's maple seed cases winged their way onto our shingle roof in the fall and have split and produced hundreds of seedlings growing in the shingle roof. I hate to disappoint the seedlings but the first few dry sunny days and it's curtains for them. Thank goodness!

Knowledge and Judgment

When I was a young doctor and came to Lotus City to work I was singled out by some senior physicians after a while, who told me that I may have current knowledge but that was no substitute for experience, from whence comes judgment. They of course had experience! I toiled away and by hook or crook, got experience. We surely learn more from our mistakes than our triumphs and it is a leavening experience if one avoids operating by denial. Now that I am old, the young men that surround me are kind but insist that experience is not as useful as current knowledge. What goes around comes around! At the moment I am reading Harvey Cushing's "Life of Sir William Osler". It was a labor of love since they were physician contemporaries in the late 19th and early 20th century at Johns Hopkins, Baltimore. The detail of Osler's professional life described in the biography is profound. Osler addressed the relationship of knowledge and judgment in this aphoristic style. He said, "To study the phenomenon of disease without books, is to sail an uncharted sea, while to study books without patients, is not to go to sea at all." One could substitute disease, with farming, building, designing, or any other work. We used to say in assessing physicians for registration that they should, " HAVE the skill and knowledge necessary FOR the practice of medicine". At some point in order to assess judgment as well as knowledge it became necessary to change the phrase to read, " BRING the skill and knowledge necessary TO the practice of medicine". A subtle word change but immense in application. I can recognize the point of Osler's metaphor at my stage in life. I now need to sit on the seashore or drydock and watch the other sailboats negotiate the charted seas.

A place for everything.

My dad was a railway telegrapher responsible for train orders. They needed to be accurate and timely so orderliness counted. If my dad said it to me once, he said it a hundred times," A place for everything and everything in its place!" Since I am now old and haven't much to do, I am finally able to follow his advice. In fact I am now able to deliver the same message to others without a scintilla of shame. When I was young and busy, I often didn't finish a job fully since the subsequent demands seemed more imperative. I thought I was doing everyone a favor. Things and objects got left behind or lost and the efficiency of my work suffered accordingly. No one was getting a favor! The very tool one needed or the essential report that needed finishing disappeared into the woodwork. Once I found it I didn't need it. The ability to lay your hand on any object, at any time, gives a head start that is invaluable. It can only be done if we avoid fragmentation, learn to say no, and value our time and output. We can only do so much well and that requires focus. Work habits are as important as knowledge. They go hand in hand. That means work smart. That means, " be prepared." Lord Baden-Powell told us that and it was true, but it became so trite you needed a barf bag every time you heard it. Prioritization and finishing the job at all cost will give great success. I have seen executives with a desk top full of papers that looks like a hurricane has gone by, but they seem pleased to display how impressively busy they appear. I know how busy they must be just sorting out what they should have already done. If the surgeon doesn't go through his records at night in preparation for the following surgical day, trouble will loom. I have seen many an Emergency Room Physician so burdened with competing demands that they become fragmented and make mistakes. In that situation the answer is to slow down, not speed up, triage and keep your cool. Don't let yourself be pushed where you don't want to go. You will end up being the fall guy and no one will thank you. There were no train collisions from my dad's watch in his lifetime!

Rags to Riches

When I was about thirteen my father gave me a copy of "Jed, the Poorhouse Boy ". He found it in his father's possessions after the funeral. Horatio Alger Junior had written dozens upon dozens of similar formulaic stories with the theme of rags to riches, or at least rags to wellbeing, achieved because of goodness and decency. The modern expectation of "entitlement to advance" is the antithesis of the Alger tales. The Alger theme is embedded in the human psyche, deeply evocative and satisfying concerning justice and reward. Many of us are moved by rags to riches stories and want to identify with them; usually perilously close to fibbing about our origins in order to connect. I remember competing with my colleagues about who came from the most straited circumstances; almost a badge of honor. Who walked the furthest through snow to school and who had the most spartan lunch, or for that matter who had lunch at all! Who struggled despite adversity and conquered! It was all more or less sham. There were few Abe Lincolns amongst us. Living in Canada, the adversity is only relative. The characters in Horatio Alger's books typically included a wealthy older man; an avuncular figure who selected a young boy to give assistance to, over other ragamuffin newsboys. One might have considered, given the thematic nature and repetitive story lines of needy boy, generous, hovering, older man, and women not part of the narrative, that Horatio Alger Junior might well have had pederasty as an unconscious sub theme. Living vicariously! We know he took Greek at Harvard. It is pretty certain historically, that he battled his own demons! Still, at thirteen, I loved the book!

Jesus and Joe Btfsplk

Bad news sells! We all love dirt! "The Inferno" has always been more interesting than "Paradiso". Schadenfreude was conceived by the Germans but practiced worldwide! I don't excuse myself from any of this! Canadians may be particularly bad at well wishing anyone who soars! Of all the deadly sins the most self-destructive is envy. It's more destructive and negative on the envier than the envied. Actually the envied rather like being envied! What is it about the Joe Btfsplks and the Eeyores and the Chicken Littles these days! Eeyore always found something wrong with Pooh's optimistic ideas; the constant rain cloud or the sky cracking beset both Joe and Chicken Little. Is it bad news, or other people's sins, or an immanent sense of disaster that provides some form of extreme vitality to an otherwise pedestrian and mundane life style? I can't bear to watch the news anymore: it's so negative. Something came from the sky for Jesus too, as well as Joe and Chicken Little. A voice gave thumbs up to Him and life! The Jews of Jesus time were looking for a warrior to beat up on the Romans and their proxies but they got a peace maker and an optimist who didn't flinch from all the negativity he got at that time and still doesn't flinch! It's difficult for me to behave as well as I want in this world since I am such a human being! I still rain on other people's parade. My committee colleagues still call me Eeyore. I still, in the recesses of my mind, fear that the sky might fall down! I'm old enough that I should know better, or not admit it!

The Legatee

Dr X was a prominent physician in Lotus City. Among his patients he attended particularly diligently, were Lord and Lady So and So; transplanted to Lotus City in the early days. Dr X was not only prominent, but an excellent and knowledgeable internist whose opinion was sought after by many of his colleagues. Despite the fact that he was always busy, Dr X nevertheless took the extra time the lord believed he required and in turn was received royally by the lord's wife and himself. The lord had an old Rolls Royce that Dr X always expressed great admiration for and he rarely failed to complement the greatness as to his considerable fortune to have such a vehicle. Despite the rigorous and intelligent care of Dr X, the patient eventually succumbed to old age and died. Shortly after the funeral the lady phoned Dr X to make an appointment with him in her home. She told him the lord had included Dr X in his will and wished him to have an item, which he knew Dr X had greatly admired. She added that this legacy was something he and his patient had often spoken about during their engagements. Dr X attended the appointment with the lady with a great sense of anticipation. Surely the lord would supply his fondest dream! She showed him the will. He had left Dr X his club tie; she said, a prized possession that Dr X had apparently admired! He couldn't recall the event, but conceded in his mind that it was probable. Expect little; receive much! Expect much; receive little!

Oz and the Wizard

The story of The Wonderful Wizard of Oz is, in my opinion, an exciting children's story with beautiful allusions of psychoanalytic nature. Most deconstuctions that have been written about the story have been centered on the political rather than the psychological or mystical. Frank Baum's characters are a reflection of aspects of himself. Dorothy is the psychologically integrated self and therefore the least interesting! Oz the Wizard, is a chameleon and the dis-integrated self. The trio of Dorothy's co-adventurers are the most easily identifiable and have the more interesting pathology from my standpoint. Even though the characters eventually recognized the Wizard was a humbug, they clung to the crutch he offered! Or was he a humbug? The analyst returns a bit of your own juices to you and calls it treatment. He can't give you what you already have. He just puts a knob on your door to yourself. Did the lion recognize his courage other than through a magical process of being given a placebo, a daught of courage? He didn't know that he always had courage! He found it had always been there when it was apparent that the Wizard wasn't a whiz! Did the Scarecrow get his brains from some external magical source? He didn't twig to the fact that he was always smart 'til the magic brain transplant when Oz took off his head and inserted bran, and pins and needles. When we realize that what we seek is already inside us, latent and waiting discovery; then the sharp, bran-new brain becomes a reality. Did the Tinman get a heart other than a silk valentine transplant from the Cardio-wizard using a can opener to the chest? Nonsense! The Tinman always had a heart, but his heart was in the right place; his head! His attitude throughout the journey told us that. He just didn't recognize it. None of this trio realized their gifts 'til they combined their brains, courage and love with helping Dorothy to get home. You can take the story of the Wonderful Wizard of Oz at face value, or the politics of the time, but it seems to me that there is an exploration of the human condition. Who knows what is behind Frank Baum's masterpiece? Some may say it is wrong to dissect this story, or attempt to deconstruct any literature, since we will never know entirely what went on in the author's head. There are two bookends to any story, the author and the intent, the reader and the understanding. What he said and what I heard! They may not be the same! It may not be important that they are the same!

Gumbo Soil

Life on Lotus Island does not include living with gumbo! The thin, stony, acidic loam, with high drainage capacity, needs work of a different kind than the sticky gumbo of our storied past on the bald prairie. In the early spring before planting season in Kindersley your best shoes had 2 pounds of gumbo on the soles that wouldn't shake off when you came home from school. You had to use the mud scraper to get anywhere with gumbo removal. There certainly was a reason we had wooden sidewalks in those days, except you wouldn't expect a kid to always walk on the sidewalk. Here, on Lotus Island, a mud scraper would be a foreign object of an unknown nature to anyone other than a stubble-jumping refugee. The nature of the soil meant of course that a later planting season occurred on the prairies, particularly if the snow load was heavy and the ditches and dugouts were full. That was OK for us since the soil had a better tilth when it dried a bit. Curiously enough when we planted here on the wet coast in April and on the prairies one planted on May 24th, by mid-July the vegetable gardens in the prairie towns were ahead of ours. Hot nights will do it! We didn't have running water in some of the towns we lived in but with gumbo soil you could get away without watering as a general rule. Not always, but the soil was remarkable for water retention. There was no contest from the wet coast for vine -ripened tomatoes, sweet corn, peonies and lilacs. Gumbo soil and hot nights produced!

Golden Bantam Corn

My brother Phil challenged my recollection about the sweet corn of our youth! He maintained that Saskatchewan had too short a growing season to produce a sweet corn superior to that of the wet coast. The pianist, who spent each summer as a child, in the Qu'appelle Valley, Saskatchewan, swears that they lived on beefsteak tomatoes and Golden Bantam corn in the fall, grown in their valley cottage garden. Her memory is as "sound as a dollar". Golden Bantam was the "piece de resistance" of the sweet corn family in those days of yore. It had a large stock with small irregularly rowed ears. It was no match in appearance for the modern hybrids, but so what! It was sweet, matured early and you could save the seed. It's now a Heritage Variety. Phil is probably right that my memory is a bit tricky. I am allowed however, to be extravagant and embellish my anecdotes as part of a poetic license. Everyone must know that sweet corn always tasted better when you were ten than when you were seventy. No ten year old worried that his cob had irregular rows and was unusually small, since there was always more where that came from. One of the great joys of reverie is the pleasure one gets from revisiting history through rose colored glasses. "Precious Memories, how they Linger"! Probably sung by more artists than most any other elegiac song. The past just seems like yesterday!

Bee keeping

Over the years, kindly bee-keeping friends have lent us hives for the apple orchard during pollen season. Honeybees are more reluctant than bumblebees to come out in cool weather, so conditions have to be right for them. My friend, an experienced beekeeper, has been supplying us latterly with two hives, which suffices. We get the pollination and he takes the honey. Our bloom is a little early this year. We usually figure May 5th for maximum bloom of the Gravensteins. I am always in awe of the way bee experts such as my friend handle their job with such ease. I have had to call him for a seething and shimmering swarm hanging on the apple tree like a football, a bee colony in the crawl space of the house, and a bee colony in the hollow of the trunk of an old Transparent. Each time, he responded with skill and dispatch. The only time I was in danger of getting stung was in weeding the strawberry patch when the bloom was good. We had a young family of friends visit us for tea and cookies last summer. The young mother cautioned her children to stay away from the hives. We have a swing and a climbing tree in the orchard away from the hives, however the little boy couldn't overcome his curiosity about the bees and got too close. Then he gave the hive a little kick since there wasn't enough action that he could see. At six or seven you can't outrun bees. Of course he ran right by his sister who was obediently on the swing. Her mother came barreling into the orchard in response to the screams. It was chaos! The bees were in their clothes and hair. The children were hustled into the kitchen and stripped, where we picked out and squashed bees from the hair, bodies and clothing. The kitchen floor was littered with dead bees. The pianist ran upstairs to get the bee sting kit. She applied the sting stick to the spots. The children were fine and so was their mother. After the initial shock there was relief and even a sense of having come through an event. The children were remarkable and suddenly became excitedly good humored. Adrenaline rush! I couldn't get over how resilient they were. It bodes well for their future. Their mother experienced the "Whew Factor". Our forgettable afternoon tea transformed to an unforgettable afternoon. There was no reaction to the stings, thank goodness. Maybe the adrenaline rush! I asked the bee man to remove the hives! The pianist and I are not going through this again! I'll rely on the wild bees.

Powerless in Paradise

The first major storm of November with wet, heavy, sticking snow and high winds has culled the rotten, the weak and leaning Maple and Alder. At the edge of the forest they overhang the power lines. Peripheral trees and ditch- side trees crush the power lines from the awesome might of Mother Nature. She is dealing with the trees as the Grim Reaper deals with the old and the feeble. We were 41 hours on Lotus Island without power, landline, face book, or all the other accoutrements we have come to take for granted. Mother Nature is no doubt going to repeat this a further three or four times this winter but the first big one is the major cull, much like the flu' season. It was always thus! Global pruning! Wolf pack at the edge of the herd! Our anxiety extended primarily to the two freezers in which we park our frozen, value added, fruit creations and the frozen dinners. Valued for the summer and fall work effort, rather than monetary value! Our frozen preserves survived the 41 hours since we scrupulously avoided peeking! Black November, source of SAD for many! Cause of Snow Birding for others! At 76 years, rapid dark adaptation with the older eye and heat transfer from the body core to periphery is not what it used to be, so dark and cold, is dark and cold! We had lots of wood, rock salt, and both the fireplace and the Vermont Casting were going full blast! As long as one rotated the backside and front side it was bearable, but reading by candlelight is tough, by flashlight hard on the arm. We don't have miner's lamps. Hibernating under two duvets and a blanket, nostril to toes, was the real ticket! What was good about all this however was the incredible silence and the sense of power in self sufficiency that one gets from knowing that we are all in the same boat and "making do". Unlike our forebears we knew it would all end. I am ashamed to admit the vicarious pleasure that was obtained by knowing that our children were worried about us! Still ducking the widow makers in Paradise! Still salting the slippery slopes!

Husband

A husband is an archaic noun amongst other definitions, meaning a soft cushion with arms that enfolds or supports the occupant. I hope it is not misnamed given the decades of role change for husbands! Too traditional? Too uxorious? The pianist has a yellow corduroy bed cushion with back and arms that you can sit and lean into, elbow onto, and read in bed to your heart's content without sliding down. It's a good husband, though one of the arms has a tear in it and the padding shows. An old husband! Needs repairs! It may be a bit worn but it's been around a long time and it is comfortable. And what's more it never talks back to anyone. Actually I like the husband too! "To husband" is a verb from yesteryear meaning "to care for". Both the cushion and the elderly eclectic gentleman have that role. We both provide a certain comfort and possibly induce sleep more readily than the past! I am not sure which husband is going to succumb to Father Time first. We both need some patching around the edges. We are both amply appreciated for our contributions. Neither of us is going to end up on a bench at the annual church bazaar. Long life and service to us both and at the last, a fiery end!

Mold

Mold season is here on Lotus Island. Mold always seems to get a bad rap, but it aint necessarily so! It's also the season for spiders and mold's fungal cousin the mushroom, both also subject to bad raps. The only reason fungi grow on anything is because they can. Get rid of the substrate and you'll get rid of the fungi! In the meantime beware of badmouthing the molds. If it weren't for Penicillium notatum we wouldn't have developed the range of subsequent generations of antibiotics, and many more World War Two survivors would have succumbed to overwhelming infections without the first generation antibiotic. We wouldn't have Stilton cheese to go with our Port! We wouldn't have Truffles to lighten our wallets. The Chrysanthemums in our foundation boxes are on the way out with mold. The grey mold may not be beautiful but it is doing its job of assisting in biodegradation. That is where it's at with Mother Nature! Certainly mold does not have the beauty of the mushrooms my Face Book friends are posting today. If the mold on your tea rose, or your wall, or the green fuzz science experiments in the back corner of the fridge, or your basement, or on uncovered tomato plants is a problem, it's not Mother Nature's problem; you're the problem by providing a substrate they will thrive on. If the mold you wish to grow thrives on what you provide for it, you will also thrive. It's a curious paradox that the Genus that can kill you can also cure you. The Genus that can tear you down, can also build you up. Here's to the mold family, beautiful and homely!

Rubber Ice

The first year I was away from home in the 50's two little boys in our hamlet went through the ice on a pond next to the railroad station. One died. My brother Ken, there at the time, raced to the station and called my dad who ran out with a rake and walked into the icy pond and remained for many minutes, trying to probe and find the body in time. He never succeeded. In a small town like ours there were no ambulance, rescue or police personnel. People did what they could. It was a tragedy! The pond was covered with rubber ice at the time of the drowning. Children, despite warnings are impatient to play pond hockey and in many small towns pond hockey is a necessity, not a choice! Rubber ice announces its presence when you step on it. It groans and moans and squeaks and undulates as it speaks to you! Being impatient and failing to heed the warning sounds were drummed into us over and over again but the tendency for the adventuresome is to "try it out". It's a bit like life in general isn't it? There are always those who think they may get away with skating on thin ice and there are those who always wear both a belt and suspenders so they will never get caught with their pants down. Standing on rubber ice can be fatal. At the first sound, getting down on your hands and knees or better still, lying prone will distribute the weight over a much larger ice area and save your life, as people can put a plank or a ladder out to you. It's almost always a little boy that ends up in the water. When trapped on rubber ice, never jump: kneel, crawl, and slither!

Homegrown vegetables.

Growing home vegetables is usually a bust! The cost-benefit ratio in the hands of the home vegetable gardener is a disaster. I like to say, "I spend 10 dollars to grow a dollars worth of vegetables!" I am aware that this point of view will spur fury amongst the committed, the seed catalogue producers presently mailing their colored pictures, and their devotees. They will accuse me of egregious incompetence but I have to come clean. I have tried my best off and on for forty years. I have read, studied and inwardly digested the books of the great vegetable gardeners and tried their techniques. Arthur Willis, Bill Vander Zalm, W. G. Smith, Dr. D.G Hessayon, Jill Severn, Bernard Moore, and Marjorie Hunt. I have subscribed to Rodale's publication, Organic Gardening and various Ortho publications. All to no avail! I have grown everything from salsify to stevia, from peas to potatoes. The occasional success is not worth the effort for me. There is a solution to get the great taste of home grown organic vegetables that will cost less in the end. My daughter has organically farmed vegetables for 20 years but it is hard work. She is exceptionally knowledgeable and can make a living but it's a tenuous thing. She does it because she loves it and sees safe food production as an essential in the "food world" that is spinning out of control! Lotus Island has a salubrious climate that allows both winter and summer vegetable growing, but it is also kind to many of the pests. Carrot fly, leaf miner, cabbage butterfly, cut worm, a myriad of fungi, rabbits, slugs, sow bugs and earwigs. Water logging, tomato blight, unexpected frost, and a sorry lot of other enemies combat you. If you love it anyway, then bring your Remay, your fibrecloth, your little collars for the Cole crops, and your lumber for the raised beds. Bring your compost, and your slug bait, and Rotenone. Not me! I'm sticking to Rhubarb and Globe Artichokes in the vegetable category and growing ornamentals. We'll buy our vegetables from the organic marketers. It's easier on the budget and we won't need Hope Springs Eternal.

Father of the bride

My daughter and her husband told us they are celebrating their 25th wedding anniversary this year, escaping to Hawaii for a three week period in September.

When my daughter was married in the mid 80's I gave a toast at the reception. The reception was in our home at Lotus City and the house was "chockablock" with family of the bride and groom and many friends! It was a joyous occasion! I had not prepared a toast since it was only at the last moment that I was informed to do so! I quickly searched my memory and came up with the idea to describe the day David asked me for her hand in marriage. Of course I said yes! They were a good match and brought different strengths to a marriage. He came from a principled and rich Mennonite tradition and his quiet strong faith was true to his roots. They had met at the summer programme for L'Arche where they worked with handicapped adults and recognized in one another a common good. I described the scene to the guests as follows--- "My son-in-law came up to me out of the blue a year ago and said that he'd like to speak to me about something. It didn't take much intuition to know what was coming! I looked up the long hallway as we spoke and could see my daughter peeking out of a bedroom door and then pulling back quickly when spied. It was a telling, classical scene. David said, "I would like your permission to marry your daughter." I was actually at the time pleased to be asked! I said, " Do you love her?" "Oh, yes", he said," I really love her; she is such a happy, joyful person to be with!" He spoke with such vehemence! I paused to fully take in this response. I then said to him, " I would be really pleased if the two of you married! You both have a lot to give to a marriage!" " That was my toast and it was what I remembered of our conversation. What I apparently said next at the reception was, "I thought at the time, holy shit, he really does love her!" A guest said to me later at the reception, "Do you know you said shit?" Hmm--- I didn't know. My sister-in -law, standing with us said, "Of course he said shit!" She understood. It is a word of passion, in a moment of insight!

Credibility

When I was newly arrived for practice in Lotus City one of the first cases I treated was an operator of a front-end loader working on an industrial site. The bucket of his machine contacted high tension Hydro wires. An electrical charge ran from the bucket to both his hands, which were on the levers, and through his body, and out the left foot, which was on the pedal. An attending plastic surgeon looked after the severe electrical burns of the hands and I dealt with the left leg burns. The operator went on over time to develop quite severe cicatrix of both hands and gangrene of the lower leg requiring a below knee amputation. Several years later I went to court as a witness in this case. Who was liable and how much were the main issues; the parties were the employer, the then WCB and the Hydro! The judge was a senior man of long experience in personal injury cases and a reputation for well-honed asperity! As I was still relatively new to Lotus City, I had never appeared before him. In cross –examination when I was asked to describe the appearance of the leg by the defense lawyer, the plaintiff's council rose and told the judge that "we" had a series of pictures of the hands and leg. I did not know there were pictures since the plastic surgeon had been taking photographs regularly for his teaching portfolio and they did not appear on the hospital chart! The plaintiff's lawyer had obtained these pictures. I must have appeared evasive or confounded by this information because the judge gave me a withering glare! I could see a cartoonist's balloon over his head, thinking, "This greenhorn orthopedic surgeon has taken pictures to somehow justify his actions!" The judge however actually said, imperiously, "What pictures! Orthopedic surgeons never take pictures!"

He glared again! The plaintiff's lawyer said, "Oh, no my lord, the plastic surgeon took the pictures." "That's alright then", said the judge, "plastic surgeons always take pictures." He smiled at me. Exonerated! Credible after all! He was right. We never take pictures!

A Little Helper

When my son was five years old we received a letter from the Sunday school discharging him from the Little Helpers group at the church. The ignominy of the event didn't seem to faze him, but for the pianist and me it was disturbing! I cannot recall exactly what he had done, or not done, but it had to do with the Lenten Box. The Little Helpers were engaged in collecting for the African poor. At least as I remember, the box, a triangular cardboard tent, purple, with an African on the side, had a coin slot for the Little Helpers' donations. He may have lost his box, spent the money, or we may have failed to maintain his attendance, or encourage a good attitude toward his charity. Whatever the cause, the failure was ours, the dismay was ours, but the price paid was his. Being fired from Little Helpers is an enormous blot on your copybook. Whether this unfortunate interface with the Anglican Church in Winnipeg was a signal event in his spiritual journey I do not know. It is certain that an earlier experience in the Anglican Cathedral church in Plymouth was also a watershed moment when he was four years of age. He admired greatly, the garb of the Dean, a very fine fellow of whom he remarked, "When I grow up I want to be dressed up like God." We never know the inklings that proceed to one's chosen priestly vocation! Clearly enough impetus was gained to overcome the firing from the Little Helpers. Up from the mustard seed!

The Archive Committee

I went to the Medical Archive Committee the other day. We meet a couple of times a year. The committee is comprised of the old and the very old; ourselves a form of archival interest. We had a nice lunch supplied by the Lotus City Medical Association and discussed historical matters. Interest in history seems confined at the moment to those of us who are history. Our main man, the Chairman, has devoted much of his time to what is now, finally, a National Historic Site. This is the first freestanding operating room in the Pacific Northwest, built in 1896. That area comprises all of the Pacific Region north of San Francisco. This newly built little 24 foot octagonal building was heartily approved by Lord Lister when he visited Lotus City. Lister supplied the operating room with a carbolic acid gas spray machine of his own design. The significance of "freestanding" was the recognition of the importance of separation from the hospital wards, which fitted with the newly developed concept of germs, and the need to avoid cross infection. Despite the significance of such a site, it is difficult to generate much interest in younger physicians who are dealing with today's realities and impossible to interest the hospital bureaucrats for whom the bottom line is king. This small building now sits in a site surrounded by a massively reconstructed hospital and is a little treasure that needs further restoration and preservation. What we require are dynamic younger physicians, or individuals with an interest in preservation of our history. Whether it is medicine or any other endeavor, it helps us to see ourselves as part of a long chronological line of participants in a Way of Life, linked in continuity with our past and our future.

Pee on your compost

My friend Earl told me years ago that his prospective in-laws, who had never met his parents, came to visit them unexpectedly. The old boy was out, said to be turning the compost pile at the time, and the enthusiastic visiting mother-in-law to be volunteered to get him and rounded the house only to catch him taking a pee on his compost pile. Since he was an Englishman he raised his hat to her. What else could he do? I was relating this story to my family as I thought it was funny and the pianist said to me, "You've never done that have you?" She looked at me through querulous eyes. "No", I said. My daughter said, "Yes he does. I've seen him stand and pee on the compost." You can rarely get away with anything in a family! I told this whole story to my friend Ez'. I excused our behavior based on the fact that both Earl's father and I lived in an area of Lotus City that was private and secluded. Ez' lived in a wealthy enclave of Lotus City that was less secluded. I said, "You, on the other hand couldn't get away with it because your properties are more open. Your neighbors would see you." "Yes", he said, "that may be true but my neighbors have too much, 'je ne sais quoi', to say so." Touché!

Crum jelly

We have a forty-foot plum tree (Prunus cerasifera), that is an "escape" from somewhere. It is a red leaf plum that produces an abundance of small, one inch, somewhat sour red plums in such an abundance that the birds cannot keep up to them. I probably collect fifty pounds of plums and boil them down for the rich red juice of superior color. There is however little or no pectin in these plums. We, the pianist and I, also have a mature Dolgo crabapple (Malus domestica), from which we also collect a great many crimson crabs and boil them down as well for juice of a similar rich color. I have been doing this for decades. The crabs have lots of pectin and when the two juices are combined for jelly making a very superior, piquant jelly emerges. This is Crum jelly and the family favorite for bread and for meat. I hang the boiled fruit in the basement from the rafters in big cheesecloth bags that I make from bolts of muslin. The boiled mash drips overnight. The scene may appear grotesque to some in the semi dark. Years ago, my little daughter came screaming upstairs when she looked in the semi dark basement. Her elder brother had told her we had butchered and hung our white Samoyed and it was dripping blood. Forgiveness sometimes needs a long reach!

The Church Bazaar

This morning the pianist and I are taking our culinary efforts to our church bazaar. The putative purchasers are certainly of a highly discerning nature when it comes to the culinary arts. I have tasted a sample of the pianist's products! They are brown sugar meringues with walnuts and pecans, and a flat cake loaded with flaked pecans. Delicious! My product is Dolgo crabapple jelly that has great color. My jelly is in jars that I haven't sampled recently. It usually is just for the family so it doesn't matter if it is hard jelled or lightly jelled but now that I'm into the quasi-commercial racket the pressure is on me; it has to be just right! I suppose it is pride but I hope it doesn't "goeth before a fall ". Since it's been stored for a short while and was just intended for our use I had given short shrift to cosmetics. Now that I was going public I needed a cosmetic upgrade. I washed any sticky bits off the lip sides of the jars and polished the brassy lids for presentation purposes. I removed bits of ancient label that I had previously ignored. I carefully labeled the jars with new stickers in my best printing, which does not measure up to the pianist's hand. I've done my best. I appear to be the only male providing a product in the food division! I seem to be the only member of the food division with primitive printing on my labels! So what! Grandma Moses did well with primitive! They'll probably say, "It's OK, he's just a man!" I hope whoever buys my jelly is more interested in what's inside, than what's outside. Comfort food!

Balance or Focus

I was privileged several years ago to be part of an interview team for applicants to medical school in a major Canadian university. These were applicants that had already succeeded from the long list, where marks were the consideration, and our job was to interview short-listed candidates, assessing character. The interviews were searching. The candidates were outstanding scholars. Most had higher degrees and long resumes with focused science backgrounds, and a history of community, national and international service activity. All interviewees were on an equal footing since we did not know the marks they had obtained in their previous life. All we knew is that they all had exceeded the high threshold marks agreed upon. The information we were provided by the applicants, oral and written, described personal accomplishment and vision. What was intriguing to me was the singular focus on science, and social contributions. There was not one applicant I met that talked about or responded to, questions concerning a wider avocation of literature, history and culture, for it's own sake. I think we have made it so competitive and forced such a requisite focus on utility that somewhere along the line, balance is sacrificed. I really have no solution given the edge necessary to succeed today, but I hope there develops awareness at some point in the career of not only the value, but the need, of broadening those magnificent brains.

The Wet Coast

This is monsoon season on the wet coast in the Salish Sea. We have had a solid week of heavy rain and wind and another week to come of the same. Lotus Island is soaked through and through and the water can merely traverse the surface of the full sponge. The tides are high during the day so with a southeast wind and a flood tide, the waves are at least brisk against the rock wall. All decked out in rubber rain gear I look like Captain Ahab on a bad storm day. Living on the seashore is a weather experience. One is always aware of its presence. Luckily when we had our builder construct the house he made sure the underground drainage piping was placed in critical lies to carry the water away from the foundations. They need to be checked and cleared from time to time to prevent silting up. Water does not flow up hill. This wet weather is a boon for the Rhododendrons and the Western Red Cedars. They had been stressed by the long hot and dry summer, particularly the Cedars which showed a lot of leaf death. We are experiencing El Nino (the Boy), arriving with the warm, wet, windy weather of the early Christmas season. Some call it by its secular name, the Pineapple Express. A wet is a wet, by any other name, a wet. In a world that is frequently suffering for lack of water, most if not all of the time, we should be thankful for large mercies and minor inconvenience.

Au Revoir ain't Goodbye

The pianist and I are selling our home we have lived in for 32 years since it is now too much for us to look after! We want to turn the page and start afresh in our mid 70's. Still, one's decisions in these matters are always conflicted with the losses that we will experience despite what is ostensibly the pragmatic and sensible approach. It is always a difficult matter when one ages, to choose to march to the tune of sense, or sensibility! Once the page is turned we cannot go back. Reluctance to part with your "stuff" makes one hesitant to sell but losses are inevitable! Cherish it though you may, a house is not a home. Whoever sells it for you of course will see it as a "product". Those who purchase the property are buying a product and will need to change something to feel ownership. New insoles for different feet to fit in old shoes! Lotus Island isn't going to get rid of us. Change your house but keep your home, because home is where the people are! I understand how hard any change is. It comes down to doing the right thing at the right time and the only matter of real importance in life is relationships, not "stuff". Memories will continue; after all, they are memories!

Failed Handyman

I changed three light bulbs in our spotlights yesterday. Since retirement I have convinced myself that I have become a bit of a handyman. Now that is truly pathetic that a man who can change a light bulb considers himself to have become handy! I have had many colleagues that have been handymen of note. They built cottages, repaired plumbing and electrical faults, fitted windows and built furniture. I lacked all these interests and during my working career when presented with a handyman problem, I would suggest we call "a man" to fix it. The pianist, early in our marriage, gave me an encyclopedia of home repairs that I confess I never read and conveniently lost. My eldest daughter is handy in spades. She can build and repair anything from buildings to tractors to barns. I asked her where she learned all this and she said she just read a book if she needed to. These skills are acquired by doing them. I never ventured forth in the handyman world. " Better do nothing than display my feeble handyman talents", I said to myself. It was an excuse. Though I was competent at work, and could grow a good garden, my skill at handyman matters wanted for lack of trying. I confess I rarely bothered. I confess I just wasn't that interested! I excused myself by the feeblest contention that "the shoemaker should stick to his last! "

Alchemy

When I was five years old and living a life of crime, alchemy occurred, and I went from sounding brass to gold. C. G. Jung, the psychoanalyst and alchemist would have fully understood. I have some early memories of this period but my mother filled in the gaps over the many years we traded stories! I sojourned briefly in Davidson, Saskatchewan with my mother and infant brother in 1939. My little friend and I stole beer bottles, eggs and a chicken from a man who accosted my mother about this. I vaguely remember enjoying our naughty activities with my friend. My mother was on her own at that time and was horrified because the man had suggested reform school as a cure. She told me that up until then I had been a good little boy. Now Borstal bound at five! She told me that when I was sent to the attic room, she came up and spanked me every time she thought about my crimes. Her fear was rampant and she was alone and newly in town. I remember standing in that attic room at sundown by myself. I can still see the sepia like color of the room at sundown; the quiet atmosphere of the room; the blind pulled; and feel the complete sense of abandonment. The spankings were nothing; the sense that my mother would be lost to me was everything. I truly believed her admonition that the man would bind me over. That must have led to the alchemy, an epiphany of childhood. Things only change when they get bad enough! My behavior became exemplary. I can't say I didn't lapse back into brass from time to time in my life but I never forgot the sense of abandonment that straightened me around. I wonder if they still remember me in Davidson?

Apocalypse

The spate of popular apocalyptic writing, movies and articles these days would amuse that sage of yesteryear, Alfred E. Neuman. I do not claim to be free of worries but hopefully most of them are rational. Certainly the seriousness with which the students of pessimism order their life and advise everyone else to do the same is perpetuated by this overburden of fear. It is the "spirit of the age". Of the apocalyptic movies my preference is Waterworld and the Mad Max series, all of which clearly defined themselves as outrageous entertainment rather than prophetic. What a serious bunch otherwise! How a secular world, without admitting it, could steal from Revelations, the most cognitively strained part of the Bible, yet reject almost all of the sensible bits of the rest is a reflection of the unreasonable fear that surrounds us. No one I know would advocate literalism in interpreting scripture, but it does give some good general advice. As Alfred E. Neuman says "What, me worry? " In the darkest days of the world the most hardy of the survivalists, retained a sense of humor along with tenuous hope and some energy. They had no guarantees! Think of Viktor Frankl! Think of Corrie ten Boom! Think of Nelson Mandela! Guido Orefice! Then think of Alfred E. Neuman and relax. The world is unfolding as it shall; governments notwithstanding! When I think of someone saying, "I'm from the government and I'm here to help you", I think of "The Ministry of Silly Walking". No one can change the big picture! Change the little picture! Experience tells us that change first comes from within, not without. Change what you can and adapt to the rest.

Pecking order

In my late adolescent and early teenage years we moved frequently from small town to small town since my father bid in a succession of railway jobs to gradually increase his income. Each time we moved, after a few weeks of settling in, it was customary for a boy of roughly my age to wrestle with me to establish where I fitted in the pecking order of local boys. It had something of a ritual and was an invariable consequence of each move. The wrestling match was never angry and once over was not repeated. I accepted where I was slotted in the hierarchical structure and as a result, adapted relatively easily. This establishment of hierarchical placement, though primitive in adolescent boys, is widely applicable in societal structure generally. If I join the golf club or the faculty club in Lotus City, there is a "hydrant sniffing activity" that both precedes and follows admission. Some free spirits may have a problem with being sniffed out, but in fact the "Free Spirit Club" will also perform it's own due diligence and classify its newly arrived members as it will. Much of this is surreptitious in the adult world. If however you have never seen the enactment of the "wounded chicken syndrome" in the chicken coop, you will be thunderstruck at the barbarity of the attack on the vulnerable. This is pecking order in spades. Disembowelment is the usual outcome. Civilization for what it's worth has softened the pecking order somewhat. The "wounded chicken syndrome" is still around in society but usually not so overtly violent. Let's not kid ourselves! Pecking order still happens!

Give and Take

Convention usually says we may adopt much of our behavior from our parents, but the reverse is also true. We may struggle to avoid copying the characteristics of a parent, often with less success that we might have hoped. Alternatively I have learned much in my adult life from my mature children as they encountered the template we provided when they struggled against and succeeded or failed to separate from it. I have learned as much observing the arrows as they have from the bow. As I have watched our grandchildren move from under the shadow of their parents I see the sequence repeated again. What goes around comes around! When the pianist and I, years ago went to the wedding of my son in Montreal, his friends, who I had never previously met, expressed how astounded they were at the mannerisms and dialect that I had ostensibly copied from my son! I told them I was equally astounded at how dumb they must be! The blessing of children is, in time both give and take, but always a blessing! As the sadness of Remembrance Day approaches; we sang Psalm 127 today.

"Children are a heritage from the Holy One
the fruit of the womb, a gift from God.
Children born in one's youth
are like arrows in a warrior's hands

Happy are those
who fill their quivers with them;
they shall not be shamed
when they talk to enemies in the gate"

Oh! Give them softness and strength!

Bologna

When the pianist and I were first married in 1957 we made our nest near the hospital in Olympic City where I interned. The pianist was developing a culinary style that has served her for many years. Food was a major interest for her family since my father-in-law was a wholesale grocer and his wife a discriminating cook. Shortly after settling in I asked my newly wed if she would fry bologna slices for supper. She had never experienced such a request or even considered it before but she gave it a try. It made her nauseated. My request arose because I recalled that when I was a youngster I had seen a picture in a magazine of the King brothers. They were Hollywood B movie producers and the photo showed them eating chunks of what I remembered as tube of bologna and swallowed down with ginger ale. That image captured my attention as a child, mentally labeled as, "what famous people eat!" I must have retained that critical piece of trivial knowledge in my subconscious soft wear and stored it up to my early marriage period where it emerged unbidden. After that dinner fiasco my newlywed never took any representation of mine to pose as a gourmet seriously. My suggestions "cut no ice" for some time. I have never, since that culinary embarrassment, lusted after bologna. The pianist would ignore me if I did! Subsequent to the bologna meal, I researched the photograph to assuage my shame. The picture I saw was in Life Magazine, Nov 22, 1948, and lo and behold, it was salami, not bologna! Another life long illusion shattered! A gourmand yes, a gourmet never!

Surf riders

My mentor was reading from "Gargantua" yesterday in our little literature group on Lotus Island. Rabelais (b.1483 d.1553) was an Eminent Elderly Eclectic Gentleman; lawyer, cleric, physician and author. Rabelais asserted that populations began political movements at a critical time for change and that the leadership arises opportunistically as a result of the movement rather than initiating it. I expressed the metaphor to the group that such a role reminds me of a surf rider, waiting on his board, sensing the right wave developing out at sea, anticipating and catching it at the perfect time, standing and steering the board through the violence of the wave, avoiding getting ahead of the wave and then taking a tumble. All waves eventually come to an end on the shore. When all wave movements end, as they must, they add to the changes on the shore; some more than others. Tidal waves of history will often swamp the would-be leaders and certainly change the shore. Those leaders who manage to ride throughout the wave will often end with it. When we think of leaders in the past and present, both the good and the bad, they caught a populist wave at a critical time of change. Some managed to stay afloat for extended periods for better or for worse. Whether Devil or Messiah, we probably, as Rabelais suggested, attribute too much to the individual and not enough to the movement for change, however subtle. Rabelais was not always "rabelaisian" in his writing! Moreover he speaks for today as well as yesterday! Nothing changes! Everything changes! Good literature always presses a contemporary imprint!

Toilet reading material

The criterion for useful material in this arena is short, interesting and light reading! As we age, the material can be of somewhat more length, though care should be taken that your leg doesn't go to sleep. Usually on a visit to the washroom I snatch whatever I spy en route for perusal. I was somewhat taken with my random selection encountered today. First, "Collapse" by Jared Diamond, "How Societies Choose to Fail or Succeed", and then next, the Aeroplan magazine, fall winter, 09. What a contrast! Aeroplan promises a life of exotic travel, fine dining and bauble-mania if you spend, spend, spend, and use your points to advantage. "Collapse" promises disaster after disaster with societies living a life of waste and wanton disregard of the consequences of overuse by individuals. What an edgy world we live in! Clearly I did not have time to do justice to the reading material in my stay in the washroom, but I got the idea. Picking our way through a pockmarked world littered with minefields of our own making, or striding briskly through a world of enchanting fantasia with not a shred of misgiving. Certainly in a free society such as ours we are free to choose our own poison, within limits. I wonder sometimes whether greed and voluptuary activity, or paranoia and envirophobia are taking hold, or are the ordinary people still in charge. I hope so! The truth about most issues exists somewhere in the middle. It's just less interesting and harder to sell. The washroom remains a good place to think things through.

Winter moon

The full moon is small and silver tonight! It looks like a winter moon and appears to be moving rapidly through the grey drifting cloud in the blackness. It seems early for a winter moon. The tide has been out at night here on Lotus Island for the past month but it has not been my inclination to dig clams then. I like to make clam chowder with tomato sauce and lots of chunky vegetables. We have abundant little neck and butter clams. The pianist is not keen on clams so I do it for me. I'm waiting for daytime low tides, as it is difficult digging under a torch. The moon is too small to cast a good light and it's cold out on the beach in the dark. November really kicks in with dark nights, wind, low tide, clam chowder, fireplace, and pale silver winter moon riding the dark clouds. You have to take November by the neck and shake it to get rid of the doldrums. Probably the brisk winter winds will drive out the doldrums by allowing one to spread one's sails! There is nothing like energy to get your wind up to banish them. The winds push you forward, flush out the lethargy, give new oxygen, and tingle and burn your skin. Beautiful summer days are easier. Lovely fall weather is exhilarating. I need to work at November to make it palatable.

The crack in everything

Leonard Cohen says, "That's how the light gets in." He also says, "Only drowning men can see Him." I can't say exactly why, but I never gained any spiritual insight myself when things were going swimmingly for me. Drowning is something that may threaten when you and your ideas are all wet, but it is also a wakeup knock. My exterior at one time was as smooth as a snooker ball. I learned how to slide smoothly by and get to the pocket. Adversity caromed off me. It sure was comfortable! Not! Inside I did have a growing unease that things weren't perfectly right and one's life began to get progressively more and more uncomfortable. There was a crack in the wall and it was my wall! Then you find out there is a crack in everything! Then you find out slowly and haltingly that's how the light gets in. The light may show you what you don't want to see. The difficulty with insight is, it always precedes action! The minute one changes in response to the insight by action, further insight appears and one is in a domino effect that cannot be fully controlled. Let go! The flashlight shines only as far as the next step. When the light gets in we see with the heart as well as the head. Thank God for the crack in the armour! That's how the love gets in. That's how the insight gets in. Flow downstream like the fingerling you are. The current carries the fingerling along! You can't control the river once it starts to run to the Great Water. Leonard's, Book of Mercy, is truly for him creative stations of the Star of David. The pianist pointed out to me it was copyright in 1984. He has done a lot of living since then. May he continue to do so!

Peony Leaves

It's curious how often a visible sign is a reminder of an invisible presence! Now that fall is here, the peony leaves are turning to a russet red and beige that melds with the still vivid dahlias! They remind me of our friend, now departed, who first suggested this combination to produce the spectacular flower arrangements she routinely produced for the Altar Guild. The peony leaves are of such a color in the fall that the entire spectrum of dahlia colors read with them. They belong together! Our friend was an elder of our church and had sung for almost fifty years in choirs. The pianist acted as her church ward when she became significantly confused over the latter few years before her death. She never lost her discerning eye however for an incompetent flower arrangement. Moreover she was always able to the last, to read music and sing the complicated choir arrangements with considerable skill. As long as the pianist ensured the hymns were prepared for her in sequence, the pages turned for her, and a guiding finger identified the line from time to time, she sang like a lark. What an interesting software we have for a brain that allows a savant area, retaining our favorite and valued aspects despite the failure of the rest. I never walk by the turning peony leaves without a moment of thought that like them, she will sprout again to grace a new altar and sing a new song!

Kee Heep

My dad was a farm boy and the phrase "kee heep" was used to call the cows! It was a peculiar throat sound! The shrieking and shrill "e" sound of kee heep carries a distance and was invariably pleasing to the recipients since it meant food and drink. If one of us was at a distance and dad wanted to get our attention he also hollered "kee heep." My dad was not a soft-spoken man. If dad wanted to make himself available he always said, "Holler if you need me." He was not hard of hearing. Holler was a figure of speech, but for him it was literal as well. It was particularly useful in hockey and ball games, then generally ornamented with colorful phrasing. My dad always whistled while he worked as a young man and particularly when he rode his bicycle to and from work. As he became older he stopped whistling as he worked, but could still whistle a little if he sat and caught his breath. He stopped hollering and stopped calling "kee heep". You need breath to holler "kee heep" and to whistle. The cigarettes had finally caught up with him and he became progressively disabled with Chronic Obstructive Pulmonary Disease or COPD! He was still cheerful but quieter when he was confined largely to his chair and the oxygen tank. The day before he fell and cracked his hip and two days before he died, the oxygen man who visited him to replace his tank wrote, "Mr. W. is cheerful and doing well, in his slippers, washing the breakfast dishes." Wellness is relative! He has been dead some 20 years but I still think back to the hollering "kee heep" and whistling merrily the same monotonous tune. You could always tell he was coming on his bicycle from a long way off.

The Watchbird

When I was a little boy in the forties, the cartoon, The Watchbird, appeared in The Ladies Home Journal; a magazine my mother subscribed to! The cartoon always featured a bad boy being observed by the Watchbird. The cartoonist would draw and describe the naughty, whiney or stingy bad boy being surveilled by the Watchbird. The boy was caught in the sinful act and then the clincher would come! " This is the Watchbird watching a Sneaky"! Named and shamed by his sin! A second view of the bird would be drawn facing the young reader. The heading read, "This is the Watchbird watching YOU!" Pediatric ethics 101 from the lips of The Ladies Home Journal! What was always most interesting was that naughty activity, which provided the young reader a certain vicarious pleasure. The Watchbird was a simple line drawn fat little cartoon bird peering at the offender and then at me. The assumption that we all bore close scrutiny at six or eight for our dirty little secrets was never really challenged in those days. My mother told me she occasionally spanked me with the hairbrush for no definable reason other than the gut feeling that I deserved it. She was probably right. She was a stay-at-home mum and probably knew far more than the Watchbird. I don't think the cartoon had any lasting ethical benefit because even then, naughty was more interesting to watch than goody-two shoes. I guess it wasn't the enlightened child raising that we see today but there was never a feeling that I was short changed in the love game. We are still under scrutiny today by Watchbirds of a different name!

Garden Party

My oldest and some of our dearest friends came over to Lotus Island from Lotus City to put my garden to bed one weekend in October of 2001. That year I had broken my tibia in July and it had not healed by September. The plates and screws had broken and the screws extruded. The fracture was freely mobile and progressively angulating. It was re-operated on in September, bone grafted, re-plated and re-screwed. I was six months non-weight bearing in a three-wheeled electric scooter from July until Christmas. I was able to do some gardening from the scooter but it was pretty limited. One of my friends planned and organized a work party of a dozen old friends with whom we had had many adventures. They were a group that we had hitherto often celebrated Halloween weekend at her country home. The party came with tools and zest and worked like Trojans, cutting down the spent perennials, cutting down the Gunnera, raking, blowing and hauling an enormous leaf fall from the big leaf maples. They buried a deer discovered under the leaf fall during the rake up period. Work included covering the Gunnera with 3 feet of leaves for the winter and filling the compost bins. It was like the old time barn raising. I was on the scooter and raced from pillar to post giving free advice and exhilarated by the help. I needed to do something without getting in the way of good work. The pianist capped things off with a big turkey dinner and liberal libation. I can't remember a time when I was more touched than by this good natured and spontaneous act of generosity from my friends. It may seem strange that in the midst of my limb disaster I would be so happy, but I was. At the end of it all I graduated to crutches, partial weight bearing and became "right as rain" by the spring. That was the best garden party I have ever been to!

Sensory Adaptation

My parents, my brothers and I lived in the railway station for years. It was our home. We lived on the mainline of the Canadian National Railway. In the fifties there was a train every hour or so on the main line, day and night. In our little town the trains went through at close to full speed and they whistled twice at the level crossings, 400 yards and 200 yards from the railway station. The track was about 25 feet from the station and our bedrooms shook when the train whistled through. Many were very long freight trains and the shaking was minutes long. The station shook because the platform attached to the station was like the leg bone connected to the hipbone. Though most of the train traffic were long freights, two transcontinental passenger trains also came thundering through at at night and we never woke up with the shaking and the noise. My mother, who was a light sleeper under certain circumstances, rarely awoke! The station caretaker, came into the station at 4 am, lit the fire in the pot-belled stove in the waiting room right beneath us, met the way-freight that stopped, unloaded mail and manhandled jangling cream cans. We never woke up! Sensory adaptation! However, when the running employees went on strike and the trains stopped for a few days the silence was eerie! We all woke up repeatedly during the night, alert because of the silence. We adapt to the familiar however unusual, but change, however seemingly innocuous, brings sensory adaptation to a halt. Unconsciously alert to danger!

Relish and onions

As I witness the engagement of those I love in the throes of planning life's work, I think of the aspect of jobs that one relishes and the portion of the same job that is onions. No job always provides the piquancy of relish or is free from the shedding of tears from onions! We are privileged to soar on the high moments, and given to drudge through the low moments. I was a man under orders! They may have been my own orders due to an Oath of Hippocrates; formal in my case; but frequently an informal oath exists for those who pursue their own muse! The jobs may be under orders from others, where both relish and duty bound onions are also the expected. Give me the person each time who works diligently through the duty bound process, rather than depends on the piquant flavor provided by the high spots. We all want to be useful and to be thought of as useful! There are few jobs in life that are not useful in the hands of motivated people. Usefulness does not have a pecking order! Usefulness is created within the job. The changing nature of jobs or the seeking of new horizons will not avoid relish and onions! There is no escape! Thank goodness for that! Walking uphill is healthier for you than going downhill! Retirement may mean continuing to try to walk a gentle uphill slope. The hall-mark of the successful is the staying power that knows a job includes embracing the role of slicing the onions! The beginning of exposing yourself to all the elements starts with rolling up your sleeves!

Atom and Leave

Some might say, "From atom you became and to atom you shall return!" Certainly some have said, "From compost to atom in an expanding universe until you disappear down or up the black hole." These are systems of belief. It's a mechanistic view of the world fitted for today's need for certainty, from science. It smacks of a Tinker Toy world. Some say, "Though from dust you came and to dust you shall return, there is more!" Elysian fields, happy hunting grounds, a mansion over the hillside with streets of purest gold! It smacks of a Fuzzy Wuzzy world, fitted for a need for immortality! What is it about people who really know? Not even St. Paul, with all his bombast, had the temerity to really know. He said so; but he had an inkling that sustained him, though he saw through a glass darkly. For the elderly eclectic gentleman the glass is certainly darkling. It is enough for me to believe that I will eventually find out and it's intriguing! In the meantime I'll live my life with uncertainty. It's a lot more interesting and authentic than fanciful theories! What I can't control I had best let go! I do suppose that I can prepare a Whereafter Kit! Certainly Tutankhamun took heavy baggage on his trip just in case! Things he prized! Useful accessories! My Whereafter Kit might include a small vial of tears that the pianist and I have shed over the years, a can of laughter and endearments that we exchanged with one another, and photos of everything we loved. I'm going to travel light! I won't need shoes, but I don't think I'm going to be an atom and leave! If one waits and listens closely, there is something going on! It's soft and nuanced, but when you think back it's always been there. That too is a system of belief! It's harmless! I might get to see my dear ones! I can hardly wait!

Harrow my Roadway

I have a small gravel driveway on my bucolic property and it has compacted over time and become pack-ugly! The fine material comes to the top and the 3/4 inch stones descend to the nether! The fluffiness is lost, as well as that wonderful crepitus we hear as the wheels move over the loosened gravel, greeting our return. The characteristic of a gravel driveway lends itself to better traction as there is less slipperiness than a smooth driveway surface of any material. However, the structure of the pack-ugly roadway is lost in a picture of homogenized banality and adopts the physical characteristics of the smooth surfaced applications. My neighbor has a garden tractor and a coilspring-loaded harrow he purchased from the catalogue. He harrowed my driveway and parking area with considerable assiduity to a Zen-like creation! The theory is that the 3/4-inch stones will, with repeated harrowing, rise to the surface after the loosening of the packed powder and small stones. The first rains that arrive will drive the powder below the larger particulate matter and give rise to a renewed, bold, formed structure of gravel. Physics 101! My neighbor is a master of tractor control and wove his way like an artist as I watched with admiration. His price to do this work was some earthworms for trout fishing from my rhubarb patch. I was anxious to retain the center grass down the driveway that adds to the gumboot essence of our hidden treasure, which he skillfully preserved. I look forward to seeing the end result following the monsoons to come on the wet coast. Petroleum free Zen roadway!

a parentis loci

In the movie Scent of a Woman, when Al Pacino became 'a parentis loci' to the student, Chris O'Donnell, he simply returned the parental love he had been given the previous few days by Chris. Parenting may be a role but 'a parentis loci' is a choice and therefore often a gift of Grace! When one gives that gift to an old parent, a failing friend, the stranger on the corner, you have returned favor you have been given. We all have been given a spoon to take from the bowl what we need. To use your spoon to feed another when you have been fed, is to take the step of faith that the bowl will be filled again! It's always a risk! The cynic in Al Pacino's role smacked to me of, "Life is a series of missed opportunities and then you die!" He was fed from the bowl and then found his own spoon! He fed someone else. Then he could feed himself!

Socks

The top drawer of my dresser is the lowly sock drawer. The socks have to share the drawer with old matchbooks, small change, single cufflinks and other untoward paraphernalia. Socks are one of the more underrated items of apparel. In most cases they are only glimpsed, unless you are in a kilt or plus fours and then they are part of your statement. My father had a fetish about socks that drooped around the ankle and throughout his life he eventually became the only man in the world who wore calf garters. My mother said to me years ago that, "It's getting harder and harder to find garters for dad. I went to Eaton's the other day and they only had two left in the warehouse. I bought them both!" Setting aside statement socks and calf garters, the run of the mill socks could be described as foot underwear. They have no status with the average male though they may with the occasional fetishist! In the process of examining feet for many years in the office I found people are often reluctant to remove their socks. In fact if they came with a single foot problem, it was always necessary to examine the other foot for comparison. I always asked them to remove the other sock and compared the feet. This provided some discomfiture to the occasional patient who took the precaution to wash only the problematic foot. I don't ever remember seeing memorable socks on any male patient that I examined. Socks were always under the radar! I guess it's the fate of the unseen and the unappreciated that they are neglected. Covered up by the shoe from below and the trouser from above, coping with sweaty feet, long toenails, stones in the shoe, protecting heel callus and corns, hammer toe, fascitis, steeped in athlete's foot fungus and constantly rubbed by old shoe leather! What a life of duress for the unloved. Damned by life shortening toe and heel holes! They are never darned in this day and age as I observe, though my mother used to darn socks in the olden days. When I was a student

I tried to darn, but I ended up simply sewing the edges of the hole together and the sock became progressively smaller. The alternative I learned was to cut the toenails. At least my mother and I tried to care for what we can truly say are the "downtrodden".

Video your mum

I made a video of my mum in conversation with me about ten years ago. She was ninety, but she did not have senile dementia at that stage. I did not make it for her or me, but for the two or three generations to follow my children. It was just a conversation of the things we had in common. The salient events of one's life are obtainable without a video deposition, but the character of the person, how they looked, spoke, gestured, laughed and pondered are not available in print or a static photo. I envision today that my great grandchildren, who will never meet her, will get an inkling of not just who they are, but a sense of how they are, what they are. It's all very well to say, "I am an individual and I am what I am because of my own efforts", but we are also a link in the great chain of continuity. An old grandmother says," Little Mary has my mother's nose. She is her spitting image!" What spit has to do with it I do not know; but I do know that though physical characteristics are handed down, much more is handed down in terms of manner of communication, body language, thinking and expression that is not available over time without recording it. It only really becomes important to the succeeding generations as they age, because life is like that. The time to do this record becomes urgent before one realizes it. I missed the opportunity with my dad. He had the prescience to write his life story in old age but a recitation of the facts is not a holistic expression of the person.

Pruneophobia

This dreadful disease can render the aging Homo sapiens inhabitants confined to a jungle cage of green that requires stooping at frequent intervals to avoid hitting their head. One sees them sweeping their arms constantly in front of them to advance through the tangled branches! The light gradually dims and the view disappears. The wet becomes wetter! Animal droppings increase and if you don't step on them from below, they drop on you from above. The house windows eventually seal over and the vines penetrate your siding and enjoy the interior warmth. The plants no longer have to fruit or flower since reproduction is low on the agenda for the vegetatively unrestrained. They don't need to be fruitful. I confess pruneophobia has always afflicted me. The pianist and I have a continuing issue over this matter. I never promised her a rose garden. I have avidly read self -help books on pruning to cure my condition but I still debride plants in a surgical manner. Pruning and debridement are not the same. Gardening on the wet coast consists of controlling things from growing. Gardening on the bald prairie consisted of encouraging things to grow. Surgical debridement of plants would consist of, removing broken branches, diseased branches, crowded ingrowing branches, dead wood wounds, and drainage of pockets of debris. That comes naturally to me. Shortening something to fit, or cutting to encourage fruiting, flowering or branching is not part of my surgical lexicon. It seems anathema to me and yet I know, down deep, it's necessary. I still get anxiety if I have to cut for non -debridement reasons. If the saw or clippers cut through normal tissue I hear a small still voice that says, " Are you doing this for me, or you?" Cognitive dissonance!

Roots

A Canadian friend of mine of Egyptian origin began, after retirement, to read in Arabic again, something he had set aside for many years. The pianist I live with has plunged into her Celtic roots, genealogy, music and literature. She and my daughter are off to the amateur music camp for a week for piano, fiddling and bodhran! It's in their collagen. I have embarked on rooting up old truffles of prairie life. It may be trite but it seems to me that the more you have become history, the more you appreciate history, including your own! My brothers I suspect have better and more replete memories of past events than I do, but they are younger and are not yet pursued by the specter of dementia and the need to get it down before it is lost. The biggest thing one has going for oneself at this stage is available time. The more one remembers the past, the more one's doomed to report it! The pianist and I spent 5 days in Argyll and the Islands. We spent some pilgrimage time at Iona. In 1822 her family left for the new world from Tobermory on the sailing ship, Pilgrim. I can appreciate her embrace of her roots and the feeling it invokes, but I reserve the right to tease. These Celtic roots for instance! I can't think of another word where "e" follows "c" that is pronounced with a hard "c" (k). Think Boston Celtics. Think celebrate, certainty, etc. All are soft "c ". I kid her that there are no rules for English language up there in the Argyll. Gaelic I guess!

Father's day

I don't ever remember celebrating Father's day very much in the past. Lately it seems to be happening more. On Sunday the available wives and offspring treated my son-in law and me to a celebration. It was nice! My present from my daughter was a scroll that had an outline of her hands, and she wrote, "For you, helping hands!" She is going to help me paint the decks on Monday and Tuesday next. I have had to get cracking this week, since on the wet coast there is a coating of algae and loose paint with a bit of rot here and there on the deck plus abundant crow guano despite periodic power washing. Preparation for painting is necessary. I power washed yesterday and today I sanded and scraped, treated, replaced and filled. I have my own power washer but I rented a large, upright oscillating sander. The rental guy looked at me and said "Are you sure you want this one, it's kind of heavy. "Oh sure", I said, " I prefer to stand rather than work on my hands and knees." Well, I got home and I could hardly lift it. It's 80 pounds. The pianist said to me, "You shouldn't be lifting that. You'll hurt your back!" I didn't want to admit I couldn't manage it, but it was apparent that I couldn't. The pianist is too gracious to say, "You're a damned old fool to try to lug around a machine that is heavier in pounds, than your age in years!" I knew however what she was think-ing! I went for a small belt sander and worked on my hands and knees. I ate crow at the rental shop. I guess it's not true that "father knows best". I'm looking forward to Monday and Tuesday and reaping the benefit of my daughter's Father's day present. She's a treasure!

The car

Our family never had a car when I was growing up. In the forties and fifties in small towns there was no need, and no other families that I recall had a car. You could walk everywhere in no time flat in Lestock, Saskatchewan, where we lived in the early fifties. The breadth and length of the town would have been about six stone throws by a husky boy with a good right arm. My mother and I went to Regina with a friend in his truck to buy our family their first car. It was a year old, 1949 Meteor. I was amazed! I never thought of us up to then as "car people". I had never seen my mother drive and that was amazing too. I remember thinking she wouldn't be able to do it. I felt as proud as punch about her that day. She was nervous about being alone on the country roads so she took me along for company. I was 16, and in her mind, capable of protecting her. We never ever felt the lack of having a car prior to that. The farmers all had trucks, and in big towns some people had cars but we always had the train to travel on and since my dad was a railroader, we had passes. Walking was our principal means of locomotion, which is why most of us are still healthy. After we got the car our life didn't really change much, though we could go to the Touchwood Hills to swim in the lakes and pick wild strawberries. We could drive ourselves to Regina to watch the Saskatchewan Roughriders. That was about all of the car's usefulness for us and nothing changed. The next year I left for University and was car-less for most of the next decade but it didn't seem to matter since the buses were good in Winnipeg! They are always good when cars are scarce. The car has destroyed public transport. I am not afflicted with car love!

First Nation's Spirit

It has become increasingly apparent that the First Nations in this country often have deeply felt spirituality and equally deep appreciation of their roots. Despite troubles and frustration, they have remained deeply rooted. Such is hardship that it gives birth to the expressions of continuity with the Earth and the Spirit! This continuity they retain provides a leadership in matters that a fragmented and increasingly secular world has lost. They have a new strength and the Spirit is moving amongst them. They are unabashedly celebrating the Spirit and the Roots they have taken ownership of. It is uniquely their own. There is a resurrected willingness to proclaim a heritage that was undermined for centuries. There is not always blame in my mind for the past injustice that was perpetrated on the First Nations since it was often out of ignorance rather than malice on the part of our "white culture". We can really never walk in ancient shoes! Cultural genocide, ignorant or evil, is "a darkness" by any other name, "a darkness". The current move to forgiveness the First Nations are providing us is a blessing, but we should never forget! The strong sense of a coming together of First Nations seems to have gained a momentum that will hopefully grow like the snowball down the hill. What a turn about! The former, that we proselytized in the old days have now provided a new, strong and needed example of spirit and unity to the rest of us. Would that we would listen!

Clods and furrows

The ground we walk on; the field that we traverse; may not be disked or harrowed. If so, the field is rough and one can trip on the clods and sink into the furrows! In the past, I may have thought in an idle moment that a finer tilth might have been laid for me. If it had been, I wondered if I might have run a little faster and got a little further over the field than I did. At least I said that to myself. The pianist and I began by trying to make sure we used a harrow for our kids to smooth their way, but the plan disappeared with the busyness of our life before it was used, and so the kids had their own clods and furrows to traverse. I realize now, thank God for that! To have it otherwise is an insult to the connective tissue your children naturally bring into the world. We can't raise our children in a greenhouse. The growth becomes rank and sappy. There's always unseasonable weather outside the greenhouse and some of these sweet plants may eventually either toughen or fail. "It's the way of the world", some say, or, "It's dog eat dog!" or, "When the going gets tough, the tough get going!" There is another way. One doesn't have to toughen or fail. Though entitlement is still available in our affluent world, it is a blessing to know finally, that one is not entitled. In fact the more entitled you feel you are, the more impervious to the truth you become. Someone says," I have come to the end of my rope. I can do no more!" I say," Hallelujah, now you have the chance to give up and grow!" Thank God for humility! Thank God for clods and furrows that brought you to that point!

Goal or Process?

My friend liked to cut his lawn in two directions in order to give diamond shaped surface images within the cut lawn. Most of my other friends just wanted to get the lawn cut; process be damned. I often, at some early point, read the end of a book so as to avoid reading it quickly just to find out how it ended. I enjoy the leisurely process of reading good writing. Getting to the end then, seems less important. The quilters in our church hope they will not complete the quilt too soon as they have a lot of fun from the process. If one enjoys what one is doing, and can savour every moment, why want the process to end? When I engage the process, I am living in the present. In fact, in reality, there is only the present. If I am focused only on the goal, I am living for the future, and if dissatisfied, I may be reliving the past. Neither of these entities, the past or the future, is real. I don't mean to say there should be no goals, or to minimize the importance of goals, but it may be a barrier to engaging the process fully. I don't mean to say one can't learn from the past, but it is different than reliving the past. Moreover if the process is fully embraced, and it is rational, the goal may change or useful surprises may be discovered. Goals achieved means I have to start on something new toward a further goal. Someone may say of me then, "That person is a go-getter!" If I extend my process because I enjoy doing it, the risk is someone will say," Are you still working on that?" Fortunate is the person that embraces both the process and the goal. Doubly fortunate is the person that the process enlarges or multiplies or changes the goals that can be achieved! Some of mankind's greatest discoveries arose unexpectedly, as a result of a process originally directed at something entirely different. It is possible to overlook that serendipity if the focus is not on the process and only on the assumed goal. What this approach to process requires is time and patience, in short supply for the young, brilliant, and impatient!

The Humanities

My friend and also my teacher will become 80 this month. He guides a group of acolytes, including me, in Middle English literature. He is a young 80, and his style of teaching is Socratic. When I blurt out a throwaway statement, he looks at me and says, "Speak to me of that!" One had better have one's shit together! We gather once a week for the morning and our curriculum is chosen with care to provide a broad understanding of the world as it is, not just as it was. All good literature of any age is contemporary. Some of us have finally come to experience the right brain as well! The burden of largely left-brain functioning over the years has now been put to rest for me. The new world of technology has overshadowed the humanities. I suppose that happened more out of necessity due to the competitive edge needed to uber-succeed in one's vocation. Sadly the time, cost and stress of obtaining a higher education has led to this. We say facetiously, "The specialist knows more and more about less and less until he knows almost everything about nothing much! The generalist knows less and less about more and more until he knows almost nothing about everything! " This mentor has opened a new world for some of us, especially me. I spent a lifetime in the rat race and though I was, I profess useful, I didn't look after the whole man. Now is my chance though I'm not so blind as to think I can ever achieve wholeness! The teacher I am sure has mellowed since his active professorial years, but his Socratic style allows the initiates to develop critical thinking with wonder and discovery, rather than burdened with didactic instruction. Good literature leads to self-discovery, and good company leads to respect for diversity! May we continue to grow!

Organic slug bait.

As I sit here pounding my keys in the computer room I see the Northwestern Crow is busy eating my so-called organic slug bait just after I scattered it. It's an iron compound and when spread it looks like short little rice grains scattered on the ground. The crows I guess suppose it is a somewhat bland, but interesting carbohydrate meal. So much for my feeble efforts with this material to control the slugs eating my dahlias to the ground. Crows move faster than slugs. I am about to commit to poison warfare instead and reject this fruitless, politically correct organic stand. Let the chips fall! I'm tired of always being good. I'm tired of being a fall guy. It's for the birds! That's the trouble; it seems it is for the birds! All it gets me is continuing stubs for dahlia sprouts and poor little tubers, trying to thrive without protection from predators. They do not tell you on the box about potentially enticing crow food. I have long suspected I was providing a mineral meal for my feathered enemies but was never sure until I observed first hand this blatant act of gorging on my futile efforts. I'm not going to complain to the manufacturer since they may say it's probably my fault that I have crows. They may say. "Get a life fella', or move." I don't want to be a whiny crank. I'm just quietly moving to a toxic alternative that the crows will ignore. Forewarned is forearmed!

One-A figure of speech

I worked for a man for a period of time, fortunately brief, who referred to himself as, "One"! Not I or Me or the Royal "We", but solely and deliberately "One". As in, " One thinks this", or "One does this", or "One has no patience with--". At least it would be a recognition that he was saying more about himself than the subject he thought he was talking about if he started with "I", or alternately, "For me". The pronouns we use may be a marker, revealing our inner self. It occurred to me at that time that we could classify people, in one form of measure, as those wanting to please, and those wanting to be pleased! It's not that he was difficult to work with because he wasn't; he just saw himself as not one of the "little people". I am occasionally astounded at the boundless self-confidence of those in command. " What is good for General Bullmoose is good for the country!" The wanting to please may be seen as a "toadying" by some, or reflective of a wish to get ahead by any means, or at all cost, by others. Undoubtedly this may be so, but that view fails to account for the dictum that, he who would lead must first be a servant to all. If I follow that dictum it doesn't mean I should discard my boundaries. It just means hard work! The lofty outlook of "One", who saw himself as exercising faux "noblesse oblige" at every opportunity, revealed in fact that he was a social innocent. Needing to be pleased may be a precarious and fragile walk of life. The hounds will be at your heels. "Uneasy lies the head that wears a crown."

The Three Sisters

This morning the Three Sisters islands in our harbour are backed by dense fog and so look like floating islands, discreet and resplendent in brown and green. They are unimaginatively named, 1st, 2nd, and 3rd Sister and are mostly uninhabited since they have no potable water. They are not parks, but we all treat them as such for excursions to what is called Chocolate Beach, which is on the middle Sister. The beach is a favorite spot for novice tourist kayakers. For the pianist and me, it used to be 700 pulls of the rowboat oars to cross the harbour to the Chocolate beach. The composition of the beach consists of fine, tide deposited ground seashell, as the islands were used as a Salish aboriginal gathering place for shellfish processing in the long distant past. Chocolate beach is not named for the chocolate candy, but for the Chocolate Lily, (Frittillaria camschatsensis) that grows there. The Salish First Nations used the bulbs as a food source. Woe betide anyone who picks this protected species now… Our kids in the past, explored the islands, since there were several, haunted squatter's shacks at one time. Now we have no kids, there are no shacks, and we only watch. Since we have moved toward renaming the Gulf of Georgia—"The Salish Sea", we could give the Sisters more romantic Salish names in keeping with their centuries of use. George the third lost some of the gulf islands to the Americans in settlement after the Revolutionary war. Given that fact and his miscalculation, I think it reasonable that we change the name of the Gulf of Georgia along with these islands to names reflective of the original inhabitants. John Ralston Saul, in his most recent book, A Fair Country, makes the point that Canadian identity is greatly influenced by the aboriginal healing circles, justice and mediation. Maybe we need to acknowledge the importance of that by having the Three Sisters renamed by our First Nations, since they were significant to them as a home and food resource and have little significance for anyone else!

Apple Surplus

When we have surplus apples, so does everyone else on Lotus Island. What to do? The Community Services have a glut of donated apples. The deer are still available for handouts! There is a shortage of their preferred food in the fall and I am not about to plant things that they enjoy. It's a perfect use for the apples as long as the deer balance their diet. I used to spread apples on their customary pathways but feeding troughs keep the place a little neater. The troughs are under cover so the apples don't drown. After a while they contain lots of deer slobber and grotty bits. The deer don't seem to mind. I have just cleaned up and blow dried the area and will pull the troughs back under cover. In the past I have composted old apples and they add a lot of speed to the rotting process. We also make cider in the summer in volume, so there is lots of apple and pear mash for compost as well. I am still troubled by "waste not, want not " so I avoid being agitated as a result of these useful alternatives for surplus fruit. We never fully outlive our backgrounds. Growing up on the bald prairie, apples were in short supply in the grocery store, particularly during the war. My brother, age five, stole an apple from the grocery store in Kindersley. My mother sent him right back with the apple to apologize. That was a mistake! The grocer said to her, " I told him, if he was going to steal an apple, he should steal a good one." I don't think that my mother was satisfied with the grocer's admonition. She resorted to the hairbrush.

The Need for Certainty

A psychiatrist friend of mine said that the measure of maturity of a person was their ability to deal with uncertainty. I think there is some truth in this assertion. If as a physician I promise certainty to a patient it may be consoling but I am probably stretching the truth! Some physicians provide patients with such a long and exhaustive list of possible complications that they frighten them to death. This has less utility for the patient than for the physician! Some offer treatment alternatives to patients who aren't really equipped to make such a decision. An abrogation of responsibility, I believe. Hippocrates, the Father of Medicine said in his book of Aphorisms, "cure occasionally, comfort always." We have a lot more tools to cure now than we had in 400 B.C. but it still applies. One can comfort a patient without lying, and outline risks without frightening them to death. One can admit that they aren't always certain about outcome, but are prepared to proceed with the course of action recommended. Many people are attracted to the dogmatic because of the strong certainty that they appear to provide. Down deep everybody knows we take one step at the time in the dark and despite someone holding your hand, they are also taking one step in the dark. Life has no guarantees. I have had colleagues who were very careful in many ways to avoid trouble at all cost. If we cherry-pick our way through surgical decision-making, or for that matter through life, never taking a chance and avoiding risk at all cost, one will probably miss opportunities. There needs to be an ability to handle some tension and anxiety and have a clear alternative exit strategy. There needs to be intelligent risk assessment and transparent communication. Once those criteria are met, "go for it ". Dealing with uncertainty is not for control freaks!

Surgeon's lounge

There was always a certain amount of ribald humour in the surgical lounge and in the surgical change room. When one does a job that has a certain amount of tension and stress, humor is a useful relief valve and probably helps one to keep on their feet. Dr. B was an old time, busy, general surgeon in the 60's when I first started. He was famous for his surgical skills but even more famous for his long penis. It was a source of admiration and considerable conjecture amongst us as to its measurement. The more envious among us suggested it might be an optical illusion from short femurs. When he operated in those years he wore a very identifiable pair of white surgical rubber boots. They were unmistakable. Someone, no one knows who, put his boots neatly together in front of one of the toilets behind the swinging door. If, in the process of changing for a case, two colleagues were to gossip about another, it was customary to look at the floor space under the swinging door to ensure privacy and avoid offending. Dr. B's boots sat neatly in front of the toilet for several hours, casually checked by successive surgeons 'til one, who had observed the boots earlier, panicked and hollered, "Call the arrest team" just before he swung the door open to find nothing but a pair of empty boots. That was not such a misapprehension as one might think since many abrupt and sudden deaths occur while sitting and straining on the throne! The cardiac arrest team mobilized for naught! It added to the legend of Dr. B who had been long gone from the operating room, his presence in the john another optical illusion!

The past is not a foreign country

David Lowenthal wrote a book in 1985 called The Past is a Foreign Country. It's a wonderful book describing history, memory and reliquary amongst other things; plus the desire to relive or collect the past. One of our daughters, two of our granddaughters, the pianist and I, made apple cider yesterday from some of the Gravenstein windfalls. We made 30 quarts of juice heated to 200 degrees to pasteurize. Our press is a sturdy 30 year old, hand crank, and our routine is long established. The design of the press is probably hundreds of years older. The mash is great compost. We have a country kitchen and we press on the grass just outside the kitchen door. This link from the past is lived by us today in a real sense. The software we call a brain, somewhere has a face book page that records part of my father's farm and my grandfather's orchard. It is indelible and structural. My granddaughters, as sure as the sun rises tomorrow will one day press their own apples in their own orchard. Yesterday as well we went after church to an old folks home. Some are blind or have short-term memory problems but they respond to the singing of the old chestnuts that we sang in church yesteryear. Old chestnuts such as, "Jesus loves me", but now modified for the oldsters as, "Jesus loves me this I know, though my hair is white as snow"... and so on. They also love "In the Garden". I love the song too, primarily since the funerals of both my mother and my dad had this hymn at their request! The old folks have intact long-term memory. So do I! These linkages to the past are for me, evocative of the connection with my grandparents and my parents. I do not long for the two-holer, or the town pump, or the kerosene lamp, nor do I wish to see one. But I don't believe the past is entirely a foreign country.

Fall Season

Fall is my favorite season. Gravenstein and Cox's Orange apples are ready to harvest and press for juice and pies. Pears-- Anjou, Bartlett, Clapp's Favorite and Conference! Transparent apples are put away in pies in early August, and Northern Spy and Red Delicious for keepers come later. The summer heathers are still hanging on and the split leaf maples are changing into riotous colors. The Big Leaf Maples, indigenous to the west coast, provide great compost material, and, the leaves cover the Gunnera to prevent frost kill. The Dahlias are in slow decline but the Chrysanthemums have taken over, and what muted but beautiful colors they are. We don't spray so we have some scabby fruit that composts beautifully as well and reacts with all the shredded branch prunings that provide cellulose to the compost mix. The Hawthorns are turning leaf yellow with reddening haws and look like a gorgeous shawl. The Dolgo crab has been picked for juice and will be mixed half and half with the wild cherry plum to make what we call Crum jelly. The pile of the summer's compost is out of the bin, which is empty now and ready for this fall's new compostables. When I was young and strong I used to haul seaweed up for compost; sea lettuce shed in June, and eelgrass in October; but I am too feeble to do this now. The quince doesn't ripen 'til November here and often cracks. I haven't been able to solve that. The Rhodo's have made it through the very hot summer with frequent watering so there is no further need to do anything 'til the spring. I have more than enough to do, to bother heading them. I suppose I should if there were enough hours in the day. Stone fruits don't do well in my hands. The peaches and prune plums produced well for fifteen years and then have rapidly declined. The Japanese plums bloom here in March, which is too early for the bees except for a few bumblebees. We have a lot to think about here in the fall. It's easy to get fragmented. I guess as our parish priest once said in a sermon," the mind of God for you is to always do the next necessary thing." The pianist and I assemble ourselves early in the morning with several cups of coffee, to decide on our day and reckon whether we are doing the next necessary thing!

Babe and the secret of life

"Baa-Ram-Ewe, Baa-Ram-Ewe, to your breed and fleece be true, Baa-Ram-Ewe!" In the movie, this was roughly the password Babe learned to communicate and gain the trust of the sheep, and he never let them down in the end, nor did they him. Remember, these are sheep. Babe knew this. They as sheep, follow a creed and the flock leader. Babe became an individual, but it was hard for him to be a pig and learn to be an individual. He had no parenting that prepared him to pighood, but when a Border Collie with the right stuff began to mother him, he began to realize an apotheosis; pigness with the mantle of dogness! He developed the right stuff because of the kind Border Collie's "parentis loci"! Babe was never pigheaded but always open to suggestions. He suffered derision through the pilgrimage of his life, but despite his parlous state he remained loyal, saw things with optimism and ultimately he prevailed. The farmer that believed in him was not let down! The farmer saw the greatness in his pig. Babe's individuality, his courage, but his willingness to open his heart led the farmer to the same willingness to risk as Babe did. To be an individual in this world and to be true to oneself takes courage. I don't want to be like a sheep, running with the crowd. No matter how consoling it may be to run with the fleece, if one has a muse, there is need to follow it. The need to belong may not be one's karma. The need for a creed by which to live will limit one's horizon. It's safer to belong! In the end, Babe and the farmer overcame. This is a fairy story and real life does not always come with a win. That's the risk! Better alone, and have followed our star, than compromised for the comfortable second best. In the end we have only to answer to ourself, and our Maker!

Eating styles

Having lived with the pianist for 54 years, our clearly apparent difference in eating style has remained largely unchanged throughout the years. She eats a bit of the four portions on her plate in rotation. I eat all of one portion and then proceed to the next. Both she and I are fork stabbers but I stab where the food lies, and she moves the food around on her plate, gathering it into the center and then stabbing. Neither of us do that ergonomically unsound American way of pinning down the meat with the fork so it will not run away, cutting and then, changing fork hands and scooping. We're Canadians eh! When we eat soup or cereal, the pianist spoons away from herself and I spoon toward myself. I often end up with a spot of soup on my front and more cereal crumbs on the tablecloth on my side. I'm not sure whether speed, direction or portliness is the main factor. Probably all three! She cuts her apple fully into quarters and removes the core on each. She likes to dip them in melted chocolate. I cut slices of apple with a sharp knife and work toward the center, eating as I go, knife and thumb. She says my style reminds her of a medieval barbarian. We both chew and swallow at the same rate, but she takes much longer intervals between bites, so I finish much faster. I have learned to wait between courses. In my family, once we began to eat, we didn't talk, we ate. After the plate was finished, we talked. In the pianist's family they ate and talked. I fancy this can be risky for choking so the Heimlich maneuver should be at the ready. I have now adapted to eating, drinking and talking, but with precaution. She puts sugar on her tomato slices and salt on her corn on the cob. I put pepper and salt on them both. She always insists on a serviette, with which I am always provided but rarely seem to use; I can't say why. If these observations are boring you, then you are under 50. At 75, food and mealtimes assume an importance of major degree. The eating styles that people display are an accurate reflection of their persona. Before you marry someone, watch the way they eat!

The Worried Well

The bane of a surgical practice over the years was the frequent referral of the worried well by general practitioners. They knew they were referring the neurotic who needed an opinion to confirm what they had already told them. I understand the need, but it was tiresome in a busy surgical practice to repeat what everyone knew. Occasionally however there is a surprise which leads the prudent surgeon never to say," No"! One has to be careful and cautious with the repeatedly symptomatic patient without objective findings. Longitudinal observation and masterly inactivity will eventually sort things out. A decision to operate on a patient based on symptoms, or sympathy, or speculation is a recipe for disaster. It is not dangerous to send someone for unscientific treatments that carry little or no risk, but there is considerable risk to ill-advised surgical treatment. Harm can be done! Surgery is never however, the last resort. It is best done at an optimum time and it has to be based on the objective (that is the measurable) findings rather than based on the symptoms (the subjective findings), or the patient's desire. That may seem an unsympathetic approach to some, but it is a reflection of the science rather than the so-called art of medicine. Hippocrates may have said in his aphorisms, "Cure occasionally, comfort always", but it is cold comfort if you do an operation for reasons other than on a scientific basis. It is incumbent on the surgeon to be selective, which may offend some patients. A surgeon may get away with doing the wrong operation well, and may get away with doing the right operation poorly, but they never get away with doing the wrong operation badly. A little vignette from the distant past I remember is; someone asked the professor why did he do that non-indicated operation. He said it was a mistake. "They came to see me once too often!"

Innocents abroad

In 1961 the pianist and I along with our one and three year old children, moved to Plymouth, Devon to complete my training. The Consultant that I worked for was an elderly (fiftyish!) bachelor; a transplant Australian who was both an avuncular boss and a friend. Plymouth was still rebuilding after having been substantially destroyed during the wartime bombing. Consultant jobs were scarce, so non-Englishmen such as me were a boon since they knew we were transient and therefore not competition for consultancies. We lived in the upstairs flat of a decrepit council house owned by the hospital. Budgets for hospitals were tight in a Britain that was regaining her feet. The first thing I was told was that a Registrar should have a dinner jacket. I went out dutifully with money I didn't have and bought a "shark skin" dinner jacket, cummerbund, starch-fronted shirt, silk black socks, patent leather shoes and a clip-on black bow tie .My first foray was to the Plymouth Medical Society annual banquet. Wives were never invited. The Consultant prepared me for the customs. Stand to toast the Queen, do not smoke until the toast is over, speak to the persons on both sides of you, preferably one with the meal and the other with dessert and don't drink too much. I dressed for show that night. I was elegant. I left my bride, the pianist, to wrestle with children, trying to stay warm with the kerosene heaters, and went to my dinner. Things went well initially. I avoided smoking until the toast to Queen. I took tailor made Woodbines rather than my "roll your own". When we toasted the Queen however, as I stood with the company, glass aloft, the tail of my dinner jacket was caught between the back of the chair and the seat. The chair rose with me, hugging my backside. I wasn't sure what to do so I shook a little and it landed with a clatter up side down coinciding with the declaration "The

Queen". The company was faintly amused and forgiving, after all I was a new Colonial needing a bit of polish. I returned to my council house needing a hug. As I now consider it, it was the pianist that deserved all the hugs. I did need the polish!

The exhibitor

My dad was a good gardener and loved to exhibit the results of his efforts. The garden club's motto in Lotus City was " Share what you know and show what you grow." He gardened there in his retirement and was an avid member of the Lotus City Garden Club, but he had mellowed by then. He and I often gardened together when I was a boy in the olden days living on the bald prairie. He grew up on a farm and had no training in horticulture, but he had the knack, in spades! His exhibiting on the prairies started with sweet peas and vegetables; growing sweetpeas on a single stalk for the longest stem, the most florets and blemish free. Growing the cucumber that is perfectly straight, sweet, evenly green without a flaw and big, but not too big! Exhibiting and competition were everything to him. We exhibited gladiolus and dahlias in specialty shows in Regina, Calgary and Winnipeg. His whole energy went into getting the biggest and best of specimens for the show and it started in the early spring. In our little town, the farmer, whose field we used, ploughed the gumbo soil with added cow manure. The freight-shed floor in the railway station was covered with gladiola corms and dahlia bulbs: corms that we had peeled, disbudded, dusted for thrip, and positioned for straight sprout growth. There was hardly any room left for the freight. I remember once driving to Regina all through the night in a truck with a load of glads, all staked, sitting in washtubs, stabilized through chicken wire. Regina was 120 miles away and I was not allowed to drive more than twenty-five miles an hour or the glads would shake too much on the gravel road. He drove the car in tandem, with all the paraphernalia needed for display. My mother went with me and kept nudging me to keep me awake. Going to Calgary or Winnipeg he could take his flowers in the baggage car because he had a railroad pass. He went to no end to compete! I, and most of my brothers and my children inherited his knack. It is no surprise to me however, that I am totally averse to exhibiting. My garden is personal. We take what we will from our parents and leave the rest behind.

Fortunate bullet wound

Some years ago a male patient in his forties came to the office with a hard swelling in the left buttock. He stated that it had been present for several years but had become larger over the latter few months and it was becoming more and more painful to sit. My examination revealed a hard, tender, localized swelling over the ischial tuberosity; the boney prominence that bears the seated weight in the normal buttock. It was much more prominent than the tuberosity on the right side. The history the man provided initially was vague and seemed evasive, or at least uncertain. He had never seen a doctor about the complaint until his general practitioner referred him to me. I obtained an x-ray of the pelvis, which showed a 22 bullet situated within the ischial tuberosity and surrounded by an expanding intraosseous cyst in a reactive shell of bone. Having established the diagnosis without any doubt, it was apparent that the history needed better disclosure if a surgical cure was to be undertaken. The patient confided that he had been surreptitiously visiting the wife of a man who suspected her of a sexual liaison. The irate husband waited for proof and received it when in a rage he opened the bedroom door, with his loaded 22 rifle in hand. My patient was frantically clearing out of the bedroom window when he received the gunshot wound in his buttock. This patient was fortunate on several counts. The offended male never saw his face and couldn't describe any identifying features on his buttocks. He was shot with merely a 22, and so was able to still run on the fuel of adrenaline and avoided a hospital or clinic. The bullet remained intraosseous because of its low velocity and the high resistance of bone. It did not stray into the bowel and bladder area where much damage could have ensued. We booked his surgery with the generic description of, "Removal of foreign body".

A Prairie Harness Racer

My great grandfather owned a livery barn in Miniota, Manitoba in the first and second decades of the 20th century. He raced in various harness racing events throughout the province into his fifties and sixties. He was Irish-Canadian and had the love of trotting and pacing horses that enchanted many of the northern Irish, along with horse racing. His earlier family immigrated to Canada from Belfast in 1830 and my great grandfather was Irish Presbyterian to the core. My great grandfather had his own colors and sulky and as a liverybarn owner had ready access to Standard bred horses. The pianist and I visited Miniota a few years back. Like most small prairie towns it is now a hamlet with a few old pioneers! They have a museum from the heyday of Miniota when it was a bustling town with a weekly paper; the Miniota Herald. We drove in on a Sunday in the summer and we were peered at as all the windows, one after the other opened up. Then a woman came out and asked us what we were there for! A visitor was clearly an event! She offered to open the museum for us if we were interested, which we were. We browsed for a while at the artifacts of a time now gone, when the pianist came across a 1912 edition of the Miniota Herald with the headline, " James Wellington Warren has 18 good driving horses for sale". What a find and no Hobson's choice in that notice! In 1950 I traveled with my father to visit my great grandfather who was in his 90's. Mary MacDonald, his wife, was long gone. He was lying in a bed by himself in an old care home in Miniota. His leg had been amputated, a long-term urinary catheter in place and he was alone in a dingy room with a bare light bulb. The room was ten by ten feet. He told my father and me that he prayed every day that he would be " taken away, but his heart was too strong". The early photo's I have of him show a vibrant, engaging and dapper man! At fifteen, I came to realize that sometimes we could live too long!

Self Deception

How often we eventually come to believe what we have told ourselves so often, in the face of the bald facts? Mea culpa! This is not really news. Shakespeare covered it pretty clearly in Prospero's observation about his brother, to Miranda! "--like one, who having, into truth, by telling it, made such a sinner of his memory, to credit his own lie, he did believe---". You could paraphrase this by saying, " Who is kidding who?" or "Don't kid yourself!" I often am impressed with the capacity of the mind that eventually comes to believe it's own PR. The standard we hold for others, we must hold ourselves to, and that may take some digging deep. I watched Part Five of the series, "The Civil War" on PBS the other day. It included the Gettysburg Address of President Lincoln. He stated "--the world will little note nor long remember what we say here--". How wrong he was! One of the world's great speeches in a paragraph! There was no confabulation, no over-weening pride, no self-serving adulation and no certainty. There was vision and humility and generosity without a carapace of false opti-mism. The issue was too important for Lincoln to come to believe in any lies about himself. He knew he was simply a player in an uncertain world. He knew what he was, and more importantly, he knew what he wasn't! Would that candor towards one another and towards oneself, delivered with kindness, succeed belief in our own mythology.

Tree Crop Failure

This spring on the wet coast has been unusually moist for prolonged periods and the tree fruit crop on Lotus Island is almost nonexistent. I see a pitiful apple crop on the Gravensteins, Transparent and Red Delicious. Cox's Orange has nothing. The Italian prune plums are completely free of any fruit. Same with the Damson and Victoria plum though they don't perform well for me in any year. In their case I suppose I should follow the Biblical suggestion; dung the plums for three years and give them the heave-ho if they don't produce. The early pears have a some fruit as they seem to tolerate the wet a little better. Clapp's Favorite is early; it caught the warm weather in the two weeks of April and has some fruit, but Bartlett, Anjou, and Conference have less. They bloom later. A few Montmorency cherries are present. We never get the sweet cherries because of the birds. I'm not whining about all of this since the processing of that much fruit is a lot of work and now I don't need to feel guilty about wasting the product. All the small fruits are doing OK and that will keep us busy. There is no shortage of bees at the moment since the weather has now turned, but too late! I don't blame them for not working in the rain. I understand they don't really care about my apple appetite. It is just that I need them because apple pollen is somewhat heavy for the wind, and the bees lug it from the pollinator trees to the Gravensteins since they are not self pollinating.. Just give it a rest! Hope springs eternal!

Eggs

My daughter- in -law in Scotland has ducks that produce lots of eggs. I had not had the pleasure of eating duck eggs before our trip in May. They were good, smooth and large, but the curious thing about her duck eggs is that when they were poached they retained the original ellipsoidal shape like a rugby ball. Now, if you poach a chicken egg it becomes round. I assume it is a function of the viscosity of the duck egg versus the chicken egg. Speaking further of eggs generally, I love eggs. In the forties my father always got the egg at breakfast and we boys usually settled for toast and cereal. He was the workingman and needed his protein. My brother Phil reminded me dad called eggs, "hen fruit". I remember the pleasure of receiving an occasional egg in those days. Now, the pianist frequently has eggs. We get free-range eggs from the farmer. They are orange from the bugs the chickens eat. Some say that the orange yolk is produced in the factory chickens by feeding them with a dye in the food. I can't say whether this is true or not. The pianist says our eggs that we obtain from the farm are of superior quality. I accept she must know. For me, yellow or orange, I don't care. Round or ellipsoid, I don't care! What is of significance to me is, that one who is an egg eater at breakfast, has arrived! I am now, Protein Man! Eggs as a breakfast staple give me a sense of affluence! I am not just a cereal and toast man any more. I am an egg and bacon man! Voila!

The Dream

I have a recurrent dream that I have had for much of my adult life. I think there are significant dreams and there are idle dreams that one can simply enjoy and then ignore. The recurrent dream of mine is that I am in an urban crowd of people and am in my underwear shorts, trying to find my clothing. The people observe me but make no comment. I do not recognize any of the people in my dream. They are generic. I feel exposed and embarrassed and have a sense of urgency to get dressed. The dream is accompanied by some anxiety that I will not find my clothes. In the dream of course, there is no resolution because the resolution to the awkward dream comes from the outside, not within the dream. As a result, I never find my clothes and the dream fades. Clothing can be both a cloak and a statement. How much of each, the individual will come to decide! One's inner man and one's outer man are hand in hand. Leonard's song about "My Secret Life" is a touchstone. One can fool most of the people most of the time, but one cannot fool the inner man. I don't pretend to be much of an expert of Jungian ideas, but he was always clear that aside from the principles of interpretation, the ultimate testing comes from the individual whose dream experience it was. I think, in my case, I could take the boy out of the country, but I can't take the country out of the boy!

Weeding and squatting

Weeding for prolonged periods in a fully flexed knee position, particularly with strapped kneelers, is dangerous. Popliteal artery occlusion, peroneal nerve compression and thrombophlebitis are all reported, particularly in Asian literature. I thought of this yesterday as I was weeding my permanent strawberry patch. It is a flat patch in the grassy orchard and Mother Nature's plants, designated as weeds only because of their location, are a tough little bunch. They consist of various grasses, as well as plantain, dandelion, daisy, knotweed, speedwell and clover, along with the worst, bindweed and quack grass. I'm sure it is easier weeding to have an elevated strawberry bed or strawberry rows, but one needs space for this. There is always urgency to weed early enough to interrupt the seeding of these weeds. I will probably, after this patch crops in the summer, dig the whole works up and select and replant the best plants. In the meantime I avoid a prolonged deep knee bend by going to another job every half hour or so but it is darned hard to get up from the deep knee squat. I carry a burden of rectitude by using elbow grease rather than herbicides to deal with the unwanted. Some of the unwanted make good compost and the grasses can be used here and there to stamp into bald spots on the so-called lawn. The so-called lawn is mixed grasses so it doesn't mind added variety. So, I vary my workload; don't stay too long in this squat position, and know that kneeling for short intense periods is good for the soul as well as the strawberries.

The lady and the gardener

Dr Y. was an old-time doctor who was a member of the establishment in Lotus City when I first arrived in the 60's. In a moment of utter madness he had purchased a large, old Tudor mansion on acreage in the high-end district of the city. It was a beautifully landscaped property and he did the gardening work himself rather than hiring help, as the rest of his neighbors were wont to do. He gardened in baggy, cast off trousers and an old slouch hat. Pruning, spraying, weeding, applying mountains of fertilizer and mulch; he toiled in the soil with his customary efficiency. A newcomer to the district and a neighbor seemed to take a particular interest in his work habits and eventually she came to Dr Y's fence and hailed him. She said, " I've noticed how you work and wondered if you might consider working for me as well. I'm close by. What do you charge? " He thought for a moment and said, "The standard amount, but the lady here feeds me lunch." "Oh ", said the newcomer, "I can feed you lunch!" "But", he said, " The lady here lets me sleep with her!" I don't know whether it was the slouch hat or the dirty baggy pants, but that seemed to bring cessation to the negotiations. It was said that despite the perhaps infelicity at the time, they became good friends and enjoyed a laugh. It is however likely that she was hesitant to become his patient.

Random width siding

A longstanding technique of cladding houses on the wet coast is board and batten. Houses built 100 years ago have this application of vertical siding using cedar boards with the joins overlapped with vertical battens. The use of random width boards is achieved by cutting the boards from the diminishing widths of the entire log. As a result there is less wastage of the log. The appearance provided by the randomized widths is pleasing and the randomness is not obvious at first glance. It gave me a sense , in building, of having provided a green contribution in respect to utilization of materials to the maximum. When we built our house in 1995, the architect and the builder had the use of 30 large Douglas fir and Western red cedar trees taken from our property, felled and skidded off to the sawmill for eight months. The logs were custom cut, for the timber frame, the 2x6's, plus the randomized siding and battens. We had the length of the siding and battens custom cut on demand as well. I was an innocent in building matters but loved the idea of using our own wood. They like to say, in houses with large picture windows, "The design of this house brings the beautiful outside INTO this house!" In this case you could say in addition, "The design of this house brings the beautiful outside ONTO this house!" Probably there was no real cost saving, but the idea of recycling your trees from the little plot onto the house imparted an aura of romance. The trees never left home! That this matter of cladding, used a time-honored tradition, and British Columbia's unique wood resource, was for me an authentic expression of my roots. There is no place like home!

Rat race

In November 1963 I went to Montreal to do the oral examinations for the degree of Fellow of the Royal College of Surgeons of Canada. This was a follow-up to having passed the written examinations in the fall of '63. These exams were the culmination of five years of post-graduate specialist training for the hundred odd aspirants to the higher degree. The pianist was home with two children and overdue with the third. The risk of failure was high and meant another year of training and impecunity. At the end of the two days the results were provided in a large auditorium in the Montreal General Hospital. Adjacent to the auditorium was a large room used for catering. We all gathered in the auditorium awaiting our name to be called in alphabetic order. The wait seemed interminable! It was then that I might have envied mythical Aaron Aardvark and felt sorry for despairing Zoltan Zolotony. When the name was called, the candidate walked down the auditorium stairs to receive a sealed envelope. The candidates were initially, either greeted with a handshake to congratulate them and directed to the catering room to the right, or greeted with a nod and an envelope and directed left, out of the auditorium. Later, as those of us who were successful drank sherry in the room to the right, through the window in the darkling gloom we watched the unsuccessful trudging along on the snowy path! "Man's inhumanity to man!" They should have never served sherry to the so-called "select" and left the others some dignity to bear their grief privately! I hope they don't do that now!

Puberty, Jim has hair.

As a very young teenager I was shy about my incipient physical changes. Though I slept in the same room as my brothers, I was careful. One of my young brothers however caught me unawares one day and ran down stairs with the loud announcement to all that "Jim has hair!" My father raced up the stairs in great anticipation and pulled down my pajamas greeting my wisps of hair with satisfaction. It's amazing that I was able to avoid detection up to that time as we, in those days, were still using the galvanized tub in the kitchen for Saturday night bathing. I was the oldest boy and probably the dirtiest, so tended to bath last in the recycled water when everyone else was clean and in pajamas. I must have been stealthy as we had only a kitchen and a living room in the railway station living quarters on the main floor. The close quarters and the intense exposure of all of our habits to one another was such a departure from today's separation and the demands of privacy as a way of life. Everyone in the family knew everyone's business because of the physical nature of the living quarters. The only one who was able to achieve a modicum of privacy was my mother, but even that was marginal. It gives new meaning to, "they were a very close family."

Crow world revisited

Three Ravens visited our plot this morning prompting a collective pursuit by the Crows who really own the place! The Ravens (Corvus corax) appear to produce extraordinary rage on the part of the Crows (Corvus Caurinus). The Crows do not seem to mind the Eagles, Heron or Seagulls, though they do maintain distance. However there is something about the Raven that always produces a noisy pursuit. The Crows have a congregational life and the teamwork they display is remarkable. They always have a watch bird and a distant early warning system to alert the pianist and me to the presence of their enemy. The Crows play frequently; diving and wheeling and rotating with one another at regular intervals. Life for them is not always serious. The Raven tends to be a more solitary bird and seems more of an outsider; largely unwelcome by our birds. Unlike the Raven, rhe range of vocalization of the Crow is rather outstanding though I cannot tell precisely what they are saying. Certain phrasing seems consistent in certain identifiable situations. They have learned from the Seagulls how to crack clams by dropping them from a height onto the rocks and they have no trouble competing with the gulls for shore side delicacies. I think the Seagulls are too stupid to learn anything from the Crows. The Gulls appear to have no time for one another and though they congregate together they are always competing, unlike the teamwork displayed by the Crows. The Crows know precisely when the smaller tree fruits ripen and they preemptively eat them completely two weeks before ripening, thwarting the now empty handed orchardist. I wonder at the choice of the Stellar's Jay (Cyanacitta stelleri) as the provincial bird of BC. They do not have any skill or "savoir faire" to compare with the Northwestern Crow. They may be beautiful, but they are noisy, obnoxious, and have attention deficit disorder. I frankly cannot think of any bird that could compete with the brains of the Crow. It seems "Beauty before Brains" was the operative phrase when a B.C. Committee made the unfortunate choice.

Dinosaur Rhubarb

The Gunnera, since it is winter is, resting. In the summer, it is "arresting". At mid-summer time the plant is ten feet tall with four feet wide leaves and the patch has a spread of forty feet and growing. Now it lies covered and dormant in a bed of mixed leaves; its own plus maple and plum leaves. It takes me and my helper a whole day to rake, blow and haul leaves to cover it in the fall. Three feet of leaf covering is needed as Gunnera is tender and damaged by a sharp frost. The leaf covering will compost down over the winter and the wonderful shoots will push the rotted leaves aside and emerge in the early spring. The growth of this plant is phenomenal if given the ample moisture it requires. It has been in its current spot twenty or so years and will take over our garden if I let it. I had it in another spot in the garden for about eight years and when we transplanted it to this spot, I needed a front-end loader to move the monster root balls. I have not investigated the underground stems of this plant but Brian Minter on his radio show described the need for a chain saw to cut them. My variety is Gunnera manicata. They say it may be eaten and is used for food in Brazil, but I am dubious. The deer in rutting season in the fall see it as a challenge and will savage some of the leaves. I don't mind, as it is starting to decline by then and it diverts the bucks from attacking the dahlias. I never bother to fertilize the Gunnera as it is buried in rotting leaf mold. The plant is large, coarse, spectacular, tropical, and in your face. It is probably a man's plant.

Baseball

I was 14 yrs old and we were playing baseball at Porcupine Plain, Saskatchewan. Our team was from Prairie River. It was a practice before the game. As we were shagging fly balls, I was at home plate hitting out. My attention was diverted for a moment by something or other and when the fielder threw the ball in from left field, it conked me on the head. I fell to the ground and had a momentary lapse in consciousness. My dad ran over to me as I was groggily awakening. "Always keep your eye on the ball" he said. Good advice, if a trifle cavalier given my state of recovery. "Eye on the ball "is called focus. It's the same advice as "keep your stick on the ice". It's maintaining a state of readiness. Life is so fragmented these days that we have a hard time to achieve this effective state. You can only do one thing really well at a time if you are anything like me. It's easy to be distracted. If one is easily distracted on the ball diamond, you are known as "rabbit ears". The catcalls will be relentless. If you are not easily distracted you may be provoking those who want your attention now! Fuggedaboudit! I'm not about to get conked on the head again. I'm following my dad's good advice!

A point of view

Like Trollope's Mr. Arabin said, "I can become equally convinced of the logic of completely opposite points of view." This is tantamount to the assertion that, "He always believes the last thing he read or was told." I have envied those who have strong and lasting points of view, though possibly they fall in the category of "frequently wrong but never in doubt". Nevertheless, they have a thing to be grasped! I suppose the ability to see all points of view gives one the capacity to mediate; a utility always in short supply. The great danger to this state of mind is the tendency to become easily persuaded. Argument that is marshaled in a facile way by which the dogmatic or manipulative can beguile, is a fault commonly seen. I remember when my period of Chief of Medical Staff at the hospital began, my predecessor saying to me, "You're going to have trouble with this job unless you get rid of your naivety!" There is a difference between being open-minded and having "holes in your head". If one hears, or reads reasoned arguments for polarized points of view and does not have the time or inclination to search the logic of the opposing views, then I put the matter on the shelf 'til I do. There is nothing like time to resolve issues, and the urgency is rarely ours. Eleanor Bold's retort to Mr. Arabin was, that she believed he had strong points of view he was unwilling to reveal. She had to give him a nudge, but he loved her and she knew it! Those who care for you always tell you the truth about yourself!

Beach Walk

Some magazine has said Kitsilano beach in Olympic City is the third sexiest beach in the world. Yo! Not to take anything away from Kitsilano, I went for a walk on our beach today. I hadn't walked the entire mile of beach for at least six months, but the tide was out and it was a dull and somewhat blowzy day with a little west coast drizzle. My walk was sexy. There were three river otters playing and cuddling and watching me about fifty feet from the shore. They stick their little heads way out of the water because they are curious. I think two of them were pups. There were over a hundred Canada geese eating eelgrass that had shed. Some of it may have had remnants of the herring spawn from March still glued on. Mm, mm, good! There is a sand bank of geoducks and if I touch the siphon gently with my foot to tease them, they give one a big squirt! One lone eagle flew across the harbour and two turkey vultures cruised the shore. The wind was pretty brisk so they had updrafts. The sand banks have periodic congregations of sand dollars in the millions, but so far they remain very localized. The oyster beds seem diminished to me, but there is still a large oyster collection on the rock outcroppings of shale that dot the beach. They are Japanese oysters since we no longer have indigenous oysters here. I see someone has built a large and attractive house on the beach down the way. I hadn't seen it before. There was no one on the beach throughout my walk until I arrived back at our beach stairs. A young woman and a dog on a leash walked by, but she averted her eyes. Training I guess.

Courtroom Antics

I was testifying in the Supreme Court as an expert witness on on behalf of an insurance company in an accident claim. The previous day, my honest and esteemed colleague had testified for the plaintiff. This was a jury trial. The plaintiff's lawyer was challenging my report that had been submitted earlier to the court. My opinion differed from my colleague's opinion, rendered the previous day. I was sitting in the witness box, under cross-examination, when the judge made an observation to the jury. He said, as nearly as I can remember, "You, the jury, have heard two distinguished physicians arrive at different conclusions based on consideration of the same set of facts. This reminds me of old Judge So and So, QC who defined an expert witness as 'a sonofabitch with a briefcase." I was speechless. So were the lawyers. There was a long pause as the jury looked at one another and inwardly digested the lord's remark. After the fact, I thought of many clever things I could have said, but the judge is Master of the Court and contempt is not easily undone. We often place a jury in a difficult situation when the evidence of both witnesses may be persuasive. Medicine in many instances is not an exact science. That thought led me to feel less insulted since the judge probably wanted to sideline my possibly cogent evidence. He seemed to be singling me out. As you may expect, a large settlement was awarded to the plaintiff. The defense had a basis to appeal on the grounds of possible judicial bias, but did not do so. In retrospect he may have been expressing a frustration many judges and juries do have and that is the tendency to have to choose between evidence that they may believe is conditioned by "who pays the piper calls the tune". In fact, after examining expert medical testimony, it is more usually, "The payer shops for those pipers whose tune he knows he can dance to!" Judges should know this since lawyers judge shop as well. It's a question of shopping, not collusion!

Wallace Stegner and Wolf Willow

Wallace Stegner was a professor of literature at Stanford, and lived some of his early life in the dry land of the Palliser Triangle in Saskatchewan. His book Wolf Willow is a Canadian classic. In his book he describes his experience providing the dinner meat for his family by going to the ice house and chopping off a piece of frozen meat from the side of beef. It took me back to the identical act that I often provided for our family. I was frequently sent out to the icehouse by my mother to saw a piece off the side of our frozen beef carcase. I had no idea whether it was steak or roast or whatever. It was a meat chunk. It seems to me that I removed about the right amount that we could eat without identifying any features. It seemed my mother never objected to my offering. I assume it was because I was strong enough to deal with the rock hard meat and she wasn't. I think, as I entered manhood and refined my tastes a bit, the recollection was somewhat embarrassing. I admitted this pre-culinary maneuver later because I thought that if it was OK for Stegner, then it was OK for me. The reason I had been constrained was that the pianist's father was a dollar a year man for the rationing board of Canada during World War Two. He was a wholesale grocer on loan to the rationing board and to Donald Gordon in Ottawa. He was responsible for the implementation of rationing by way of the meat charts and ensured a strict adherence to the requisite cutting and distribution by meat sellers. It was the Holy Grail of meat for him! Imagine the scorn he would have applied to the aspirant for his daughter's hand and heart, had he known of my butchery.

Bee Cradle

Some of the honeybees,"overnight", on selected flowers. Some flower's anatomy provides a quality petal cradle adjacent to the pantry. The bees are choosy where they sleep! Jomanda is a ball dahlia that has smallish, upturned edges to the petals that are form -fitting for a demanding bee body and suitable for an overnight retreat. It also keeps them close to the pollen larder. They are worker bees so they don't have to go home at night to a wife, but just have to bring food home in the daylight. If they don't bother going home, they can start working in the early morning which is admirable in the eyes of the workaholic, though I have found them a bit sluggish at 6.30 this morning. I roused them but they only showed modest enthusiasm. They left a few minutes ago and the cradles are empty now except for a messy dropping or two. We've always had hives until recently and I think these are escape variants that Mother Nature now harbours in some sort of tree hollow or wild dry refuge. Whatever! They are welcome here and perhaps have escaped the possible mite vectored disease, Colony Collapse Disorder, that has assailed so many of their colleagues! While we celebrate their hard work bringing home the bacon, we know fresh air, sunshine, and freedom from crowding is the answer for them, and for all of us! We are also less likely to succumb to colony collapse in that environment.

Organic Food

There is no doubt that food grown naturally is good for your organs. The organic movement has, by common usage now, co-opted the word that I think in the olden days would have been a misnomer. Organ is either a musical instrument or a part of one's anatomy. When I grew up in a small village in Saskatchewan, everyone had a vegetable garden. The only amendment as I remember was manure, and because it was prairie gumbo, the dirt was always deep and never required watering other than initially after seeding. There were no chemical fertilizers or pesticides I can think of, other than Paris Green. What we grew we ate and canned, or at least my mother canned, in glass sealers. There was no plastic. There were no snap lids. There were no freezers. In a sense the organic movement is archaic; a throwback to my time and earlier. The pianist and I went to the farmer's market yesterday and bought the most beautiful vegetables, full of sweetness, naturally grown, by slim, healthy, bronzed people. What a pleasure! My daughter is an organic farmer and I understand the work entailed to grow that sort of food in the scrupulous fashion that requires a diligence we never had to provide in the olden days. Certainly there were pests and diseases of plants but they were far less numerous as I recall. When one is largely confined to eating what one can grow, the palate becomes limited. When you have been through all the eating styles and limitless choices over 75 years, your palate may eventually return to foods limited by choice to those locally grown. Though organic food grown locally may, of necessity cost more than the supermarket, we are so lucky to be able to return to food that is good for our organs.

YOU AT THE WATER'S EDGE
PSALM 1

"Hey! You at the Water's edge! You can skip stones only if the Water surface is calm. If the Water is rough your stone will sink. If you wish to skip a flat stone you will have to stoop down so you are parallel with the surface. If you want to skip the stone well you will have to be one with the Water and choose a stone that is round and flat and reads with the Water's surface."

Thank you for letting me touch and skip the surface of the Water and return again and again. I know I can't go on forever and my stone will finally sink into the Waters. Thank You for the stone that gave me time and distance to touch You! Thank You for teaching me to stoop to your beauty!

SUBJECT INDEX

C

D

E

F

G

H

U

V

W